THE HISTORICAL JESUS
OF THE SYNOPTICS

JESUS OF NAZARETH YESTERDAY AND TODAY

Volume I   Faith and Ideologies
Volume II   The Historical Jesus of the Synoptics

THE HISTORICAL JESUS OF THE SYNOPTICS

JUAN LUIS SEGUNDO

Translated from the Spanish
by John Drury

ORBIS BOOKS
Maryknoll, New York

DOVE COMMUNICATIONS
Melbourne, Australia

SHEED AND WARD
London, England

Originally published as the first part (pp. 1–284) of *El hombre de hoy ante Jesus de Nazareth*, Volume II/1, *Historia y actualidad: Sinópticos y Pablo*, copyright © 1982 by Ediciones Cristiandad, S.L., Huesca, 30–32, Madrid, Spain

English translation copyright © 1985 by Orbis Books
Published in the United States of America by Orbis Books, Maryknoll, NY 10545
Published in Australia by Dove Communications, Box 316, Blackburn, Victoria 3130, Australia
Published in Great Britain by Sheed and Ward, Ltd., 2 Creechurch Lane, London, England

Manufactured in the United States of America

Library of Congress Cataloging in Publication Data
Segundo, Juan Luis.
  The historical Jesus of the synoptics.

  (Jesus of Nazareth, yesterday and today; v. 2)
  Translation of: Historia y actualidad—Sinópticos
y Pablo
  Includes index.
  1. Jesus Christ—Historicity. 2. Jesus Christ—
Person and offices. 3. Kingdom of God. I. Title.
II. Series: Segundo, Juan Luis. Hombre de hoy ante
Jesus de Nazaret. English; v. 2.
BT303.2.S4413 1985   232.9'08   85-7146
ISBN 0-88344-220-5 (pbk.)

DOVE/ISBN 0-85924-387-7
SHEED AND WARD/ISBN 7220-4123-3

Somewhere in this world there exists a group, a community of persons, with whom I discussed the themes of this volume one night a week for almost twenty years. We, the members of that group, became more than friends. We became brothers and sisters. By now it is almost impossible for me to say which thoughts are my own and which I owe to others in the group.

Participating in that group were people who became Christians only in adulthood, who were not yet Christians when we were talking over the topics that fill this volume. But all of us were equally captivated by Jesus of Nazareth, and the quest for him made us even more brotherly and sisterly.

Some members of that community are now far removed in space, though not in affection. Others became part of that reflection and affection at a later date. To all of them I dedicate this volume, not as a personal gift from me but as a duty honored: a work returned to those who brought it to life.

Contents

Abbreviations

DS   Denzinger, Schönmetzer. *Enchiridion Symbolorum.*

GS   *Gaudium et spes.* Pastoral Constitution on the Church in the Modern World. Dec. 7, 1965.

JB   Jerusalem Bible

Part One

GENERAL INTRODUCTION

CHAPTER I

The "Gospel of the Cross" and Its Key

Leonardo Boff has written about preaching the cross today. The rest of this section comes from his *Pasión de Cristo*. I have altered his text only in two matters. Direct references to the New Testament writings are italicized, and explicitly religious expressions are placed in brackets. I want my readers to note the difference in idioms or languages for later reflection and interpretation.

Preaching the cross of Jesus Christ today means all of the following things.

1. It means committing oneself to building a world in which it will be less difficult to exercise love, peace, fraternity, openness, and self-surrender [to God]. This entails the denunciation of situations that engender hatred, division, and [atheism] in the realms of structures, values, practices, and ideologies. It entails proclaiming and realizing—through committed behavior—love, solidarity, and justice in the family, the school, the economic system, and political relationships. Such commitment has as its consequence crises, confrontations, sufferings, crosses. To accept the cross inherent in that struggle is to shoulder the cross as the Lord did: enduring and suffering for the sake of the cause and the life that we have chosen.

2. The suffering resulting from this commitment, the cross to be borne along this road, is a suffering and martyrdom [for God and God's cause in the world]. The martyr is a martyr for [God's] cause, not for the system, martyred by the system but for [God]. Hence those who suffer and are crucified for the cause of justice in this world are witnesses to [God]. They break up the closed system which is considered just, fraternal, and good. Those who suffer are martyrs for the sake of justice. Like Jesus and all those who follow him, they disclose the future and leave history open so that it may nurture and produce more justice than exists at present and more love than is now to be found in society. The system seeks to conceal and close off the future. It is fatal-

istic, believing that no reforms or alterations are needed. Those who endure the cross and suffer in the struggle against the fatalism of the system shoulder the cross and suffer with Jesus, and as Jesus did. That sort of suffering is worthwhile; that sort of death is meaningful.

3. Shouldering the cross as Jesus did means entering into solidarity with those who are crucified in this world: those who suffer from violence and poverty, who feel dehumanized and stripped of their rights. To defend them, to attack the practices which turn them into nonhumans, to espouse the cause of their liberation and suffer for it, is to carry the cross. The cross and death of Jesus were the result of his commitment to the disinherited of this world.

4. To suffer and die for the sake of the crucified means to put up with the fact that the system defames the values of those who fight against it. The system says that those who espouse the cause of the defenseless nobodies are subversives, traitors, and enemies of the human race, that they are [execrated by religion and abandoned by God] (*"Cursed is the one who dies on a cross"*). They are people seeking to revolutionize the existing order. But the suffering martyr opposes the system and denounces its values and practices because they are nothing but the order of disorder. What the system calls just, fraternal, and good is really unjust, discriminatory, and evil. The martyr unmasks the system; that is why he or she suffers its violence. The martyrs endure suffering for the sake of a greater justice, a different order (*"If your justice is no greater than that of the Pharisees . . ."*). They suffer without hating; they endure the cross without evading it. They shoulder the cross out of love for truth and the crucified, and in so doing endanger their personal security and their lives. That is what Jesus did. That is what should be done by all his followers throughout the course of history. Jesus suffers as one ["accursed"] but is blessed, dies as one ["abandoned"] but is welcomed and taken in by [God]. Thus [the Lord] confounds *the wisdom and justice of this world.*

5. The cross, then, is a symbol of the violation and rejection of the sacred right of [God] and the human being. It is a product of hatred. Those who fight to wipe out the cross of the world must shoulder the cross imposed and inflicted by those who created it. Those who struggle accept the cross, not because they see a value in it, but because they are breaking down the logic of violence with love. To accept the cross means to be greater than the cross. To live like that is to be stronger than death.

6. Preaching the cross can signify an invitation to an extreme act of love, trust, and total self-abnegation. Life has its dramatic side. There we can see those defeated for the sake of a just cause, those who have lost all hope, those condemned to perpetual bondage, those who face an irremediable death. All are somehow suspended from the cross, even though they may not have to carry its weight. We are often obliged to

witness the human drama in impotent silence because a word of conso-
lation would sound empty and a gesture of solidarity would seem like
useless resignation. The words stick in our throat. Perplexity and confusion dry up our tears before they even start to flow. This is especially
true when suffering and death result from an injustice that lacerates the
heart, when the tragedy is irremediable and we see no way out of it.

Even in the face of cynicism, resignation, and desperation, it still
makes sense to speak of the cross. The drama need not necessarily turn
into a tragedy. Jesus Christ, who went through it all, transfigured suffering and condemnation to death. He converted them into an act of
liberty and self-sacrificing love, into a [possible access to God] and a
new approach to those who were rejecting him. He offered pardon and
entrusted himself confidently to a greater Other. Pardon is the afflicted
form of love. To entrust ourselves fully and confidently to someone
who infinitely surpasses us is to entrust ourselves to a mystery as the
ultimate bearer of a meaning that we share but do not create. Here is the
opportunity offered to human liberty. We can seize it and place our
confidence in it, or we can lose it and sink into desperation. Pardon and
confidence are the ways we avoid letting hatred and desperation have
the final word. It is the supreme gesture of humanity's grandeur.

Only by contemplating the Crucified One restored to life can Christians assert that death, as confident self-surrender, has an ultimate
meaning: a meaning pointed up by the resurrection, which is the full
manifestation of life present in life and death.

7. To die that way is to live. In the death of the cross there is a life that
cannot be annihilated. It is hidden in death. It does not come after
death. It exists in a life of love, solidarity, and courage that is willing to
endure and die. In death it is revealed in all its power and glory.

St. John expresses this when he says that the elevation of Jesus on the
cross is glorification, that the "hour" is simultaneously the hour of
passion and glorification. Thus there is a unity between passion and
resurrection, between life and death. To live and be crucified for justice
and for [God] is to live. *The message of the passion is always to go hand
in hand with the message of the resurrection.* Those who died as insur-
rectionists against the system of this age and refused to be *"conformed
to this world"* (Rom. 12:2) are now the "resurrected." Insurrection for
the cause of [God] and others is resurrection. Death may seem to be
meaningless, but in this case it has a future and holds the meaning of
history.

8. To preach the cross today is to proclaim the way of Jesus. It is not
the exaltation of sorrow or the negative. It is the proclamation of something positive: i.e., the struggle to ensure that it will become increasingly impossible for some human beings to crucify other human beings.
That struggle entails embracing the cross, carrying it courageously, and
resolutely letting oneself be crucified on it. Living that way is already

resurrection. It is living a life that the cross cannot sacrifice. The cross merely proves it more victorious still. Preaching the cross means following Jesus: i.e., following his course and his cause and winning his victory.

9. [God] did not remain indifferent to the victims and sufferings of history. Out of love and solidarity (John 3:16) [God] became poor and was condemned, crucified, and killed. [God] shouldered a reality objectively contrary to himself because [God] does not want human beings to impoverish and crucify other human beings. That fact reveals that the privileged mediation [of God] is neither the glory nor the transparency of historical meaningfulness but rather the real-life suffering of the oppressed: *"If God so loved us, we also ought to love one another"* (1 John 4:11). *To draw near to God is to draw closer to the oppressed (Matt. 25:31–46) and vice-versa.* To say that [God] shouldered the cross is not to glorify or eternalize the cross. It is simply to point up how much [God] loves those who suffer. He suffers and dies with them.

Neither is [God] indifferent to the crimes of history. He does not leave its wound open until the manifestation of divine justice at the end of the world. In the risen Jesus, God intervenes and justifies those who have been despoiled and crucified in history. The resurrection seeks to point up the true meaning and guaranteed future of justice and love, of the seemingly fruitless struggles for justice and love in the process of history. In the end they will triumph. In the end sheer goodness will reign [Boff 1981, pp. 437–44].

I

What is the text I have just cited? It is undoubtedly a gospel. Some readers may be surprised by my failure to put quote marks around the last term. At this late date in the twentieth century, they may feel obliged to treat the term metaphorically. It is to such people that I address these first reflections.

I grant that Boff's version is partial because it refers to only the passion and resurrection, but it is no more partial than, say, the Letter to the Hebrews. So what exactly is the problem in giving it the same status as the four canonical Gospels or what Paul called his gospel?

There is certainly one difficulty of a relevant nature. The above text is not, and never will be, a part of the Bible. The latter is also called the "deposit of faith." Not without reason. That brings us to a decisive event in the process whereby God's people are led to the truth, truth about God and the human being (since the two never appear apart from one another). Scripture takes that long educational process and puts it down in writing, *deposits* it. And we say that this deposit culminates in the direct witnesses to Jesus, in whom is concentrated the totality of faith and the human wager.

However, we must ask ourselves two important questions in order to evaluate what comes later and reaches us: for example, Boff's text among many others.

The first question is: Does the process stop when the deposit is closed? *Not at all.* The Bible itself tells us how and why the process goes on. To make sure of this we can look at the Gospel in the New Testament that seems to be most conscious of creating a new formulation of Jesus' message for new listeners: John's Gospel. It records a remark made by Jesus on the eve of his death. From the standpoint of inspiration it does not really matter whether the words are those of Jesus or the evangelist. We are told that Jesus said: "I have yet many things to say to you, but you cannot bear them now. When the Spirit of truth comes, he will guide you into all the truth" (John 16:12–13).

The second question is: Isn't there a certain danger in turning too quickly and automatically to the deposited truth because the Spirit has still so many things to tell us and so much truth to guide us to? Yes, there certainly is. And the proof lies in the fact that there are four Gospels in the New Testament, not one, and that even in the New Testament we already find new interpretations of Jesus demanded by new contexts.

The fact that the deposit is closed, then, does not mean an end to the process whereby God, through the Spirit of Christ, leads us to the whole truth. But if our divine education continues, why is the deposit closed? Undoubtedly for the same reason operative in the educational process of every human being: at some point each must depart from the deposit of paternal or maternal counsels—not to deny them but to confront them with the challenges of life. By trial and error the deposited store will be deepened, turned into life and the possibility of creation. In the face of new circumstances it will acquire new facets.

Jesus himself, and Paul even more explicitly, warned about the danger of resorting to the "dead letter." There is no a priori reason to assume that the same thing will not recur, at least to some extent, with the *letter* of the Gospels. People sometimes resort to it, not to find inspiration in their contact with the inspired word but to find infantile security, just as young people may resort to their parental deposit for the same reason. They shun the healthy risk of interpreting Jesus anew in the face of equally new problems. In the face of those new problems the words of Jesus, if taken literally, betray his Spirit. Viewing them as something magically endowed with truth, people end up offering inhuman solutions in Jesus' name (*GS* 11).

So we must keep going back and writing gospels. That does not take any of the wonder or exclusivity away from the moment when the first canonical Gospels were written. Today, centuries later, the Spirit of Jesus can see to it that the new gospels are spiritually as faithful to Jesus as the first ones were.

II

The previous section offered one of the main reasons I began with a text by Leonardo Boff and did not hesitate to call it a gospel. Now I would like to offer another reason of equal importance: Boff's text is, strictly speaking, a *gospel,* not a *christology.*

Like any other reasoned discourse, a christology is worked out, studied, and taught. A gospel is *preached*.[1] Notice how Boff's text begins: "Preaching the cross of Jesus Christ today. . . ."

Boff's initial sentence is not unfounded, debatable, or pretentious. As a part of theology, christology is framed within the overall effort to understand the faith (*intellectus fidei*). A gospel, by contrast, is preached or proclaimed. In it the faith is offered to people. They are summoned to let themselves be captured by its allure and to structure their world of meaning and values accordingly. That is what Jesus did, according to Mark, one of the evangelical sources: "Now after John was arrested, Jesus came into Galilee, *preaching* the *gospel* [= good news]' of God, and saying, 'The time is fulfilled, and the kingdom of God is at hand; repent and believe in the gospel [= good news]' " (Mark 1:14–15).

From what I said in Volume I, it should be obvious that this call to *faith* is not, and cannot be at the outset, a call to some *religious* faith. The only way to arrive at the latter is necessarily through the communication of one world of meaning and values to another similar world already existing in some way in the listener. That world of meaning and values is what Jesus designates by the term "kingdom of God." And its affinity with a parallel world of values existing in *some* of his listeners—rudimentary, perhaps, because they still need to undergo conversion or repentance—is what permits him to say logically that the nearness of that kingdom constitutes *good* news. It does not cease to be *news*, however, simply because of the affinity. The similarity in expectations does not mean that his listeners believe the kingdom to be "near" or "at hand." They must convert to that hope. They must accept that datum, which goes beyond empirical possibilities (which is why I call it a "transcendent" datum).

We find the same thing in Boff's gospel of the cross. It proclaims the good news of the Crucified One's real, complete, and victorious solidarity with all the crucified of this world. It is not my purpose here to verify whether Boff's good news is *faithful* to the earlier good news recorded in the Gospel of Mark. The point I want to make here is that through Boff's gospel Jesus allegedly continues to invite those already passionately concerned about the crucified of this world to believe in the good news of his solidarity with them. Boff's project is, in fact, parallel to that of the other Gospels.

Now let us briefly analyze the language in which Boff's gospel is expressed. If we do, we will see that it is the kind of language suited to the interpersonal communication of a meaning-world.

Here is the place for us to recall some of the results of my analysis in Volume I. Real, effective communication of meaning between human beings requires a proper dose of iconic language. Digital language, which is much more closely bound up with ratiocination (with merely pointing out *things*), does have its own proper function, but it is based on *premises* that are self-validating to a large extent. Those premises are acquired through the mechanism of testimonies: that is, repeated, familiar images of the satisfactions inherent in value-worlds, which we see reflected in the way other people act, and which we then use as the model for structuring our own value-world.

We also saw that artistic language in general, and poetic language in particular (a mix of digital and iconic languages with the latter predominating), was the most appropriate for conveying the living image of a satisfaction associated with a particular values-structure. And we saw that when this language reaches its maximum expressiveness, it conforms to the following basic scheme (expressed in abstract, digital terms): given this *fact,* which the limitedness of any human existence prevents me from verifying for myself, *in the end* it will be obvious that it was better to act *thus.*

Readers can readily see that there are three basic elements in this general (empty) scheme: (1) the ontological premise (the structuring of our action in terms of what is worthwhile in reality, of what ought-to-be), reflected in the word "thus"; (2) the epistemological premise (the key transcendent datum enabling us to affirm the possibility of imprinting that ought-to-be on the resistance of the real world), reflected in the "fact" that I take for granted without being able to verify it empirically for myself; and (3) the self-validation of those premises, which is not a fanciful whim but a wager that the future, "the end," will prove the rightness of acting on those premises.[2]

But this, as I said, is nothing more than an empty digital scheme—waiting to be inhabited by the spirit of an iconic message. It is obvious that a value-world cannot be communicated effectively in a linear, expository way. Communication comes from the repetition of the living image of that world in our activity. That is how the *thus* of Jesus' way of acting is turned into a theme with variations in Boff's gospel as well as in the other Gospels. And each variation points up a different facet of the same meaning-structure, one which says: it is worth joining in solidarity with the crucified of this world as Jesus did, even to the point of enduring the same cross, on the proviso that this will put an end to the crucifixion of some human beings by other human beings.

To act thus, however, one must accept the *good news* (and in this case the news is good, at least at the start, only for those who are already deeply concerned about the unnecessary suffering inflicted on humanity). One must accept the *transcendent datum* that the cross of Jesus is not a closed but an open door, through which life, justice, and love are already filtering and beginning to transform historical reality. Only by punctuating events with that epistemological premise can we keep finding signs of that liberation as we move through history. In short, we must end each sequence of events by placing the period, not at the martyr's death but in each step of love, of solidarity, of justice, as provisional, weak, and threatened as each instance may be.

Finally, none of the above would make sense if we, with our world of meaning and values, were not embarked on a wager (necessary in every human life) that the choice we have made will be validated in the end—that is, eschatologically. Here the eschatology is the resurrection of Jesus. It unveils the future and lets us see the victory of life and the human cause already present in the midst of a life apparently subjected to death. But the full scope and reality of that victory will show up only at the end of history.

That does not give us what Hans Küng deprecatingly calls a notably inexact "religious truth" lacking in binding force and hence similar to "poetic truth" (Küng 1976, 87).[3] The inexactness is nothing more than the room all individuals need to create their own way of living out such a meaning-world within their own distinctive coordinates. It is, thanks be to God, the very same poetry and inexactness we find in the canonical Gospels.

But I would like to add two more observations about the language used by Boff.

First, remember that I took the liberty of italicizing those passages in his text that were practically quotations from the New Testament Gospels. And I use the latter term in the broad sense here, to include nonnarrative interpretations such as that of Paul. My question is: Why did Boff change his language in those passages and even add references to biblical passages?

Viewing those passages in terms of the iconic development of his gospel, I would say that they come from a remote context, interrupt his own line of expression, and take it captive. Why, then, were they inserted? The most likely explanation, it seems to me, is connected with the points I just tried to make above, and it is particularly applicable in the case of theologians. Lack of creativity in making our (poetic) translation today tempts us to take the path of least effort: to stick to the letter of the Bible. Those biblical passages, it seems to me, will only arouse the erudite interest of the exegete or the theologian. And even though we are not wont to advert to the fact, their interest is very different from the interest we arouse in the average person when we offer our own development of evangelical images and ideas in contemporary terms.[4]

My second observation concerns the words in Boff's text that I put in brackets. Readers will notice that they make explicit reference to the *religious* realm and, in particular, to God.

As readers of Volume I know, I have no a priori opposition to the use of that kind of language, but I do think there is a danger involved. The danger is particularly evident, and such is the case with Boff's text, when an author does not provide a context sufficiently explicit and meaty so as to correct what his audience might be inclined to include under the term "God."

The canonical Gospels, to be sure, do express the good news in religious terms. But I would like to point out several things here that are especially relevant today and cannot just be overlooked.

The use of a religious terminology in a totally or almost totally religious world cannot be disputed. It is inevitable. And in that use the Gospels themselves possess two important correctives. First, in Israel at least, the words in that religious language were fraught with a specific content. The Old Testament as a whole had decanted the religious realm to no small extent. In addition, as we shall see in greater detail later in this volume, Jesus and the early Christian community gave a privileged place to certain specific traditions in the Old Testament: for instance, Elijah-Elisha, the prophet like Moses, the Suffering Servant of Deutero-Isaiah, and so on, with their corresponding images of the divine. In the Gospels, therefore, the word "God" has a much more precise and profound ring than it does in texts of our own day. Implanted in Western culture, the word "God" has largely lost its reference to those traditions, at least insofar as the average reader is concerned.

The second corrective was provided by Jesus specifically. In the midst of the polytheism prevailing in the Orient of his day, Jesus rejected religious differences as being decisive. What were decisive, he said, were even more fundamental human attitudes. The idolatrous Ninevites, for example, had a sounder conception of the divine than did the orthodox Yahwists of Pharisaism. Jesus would accuse the latter of practical idolatry, using the biblical term "adultery" (Matt. 12:39; 16:4; and par.). The same thing probably occurs on other occasions (Matt. 8:5–13 and par.; 25:31f.). This relativization of the distinctions introduced by religious language (Gal. 3:28; Rom. 10:12; 1 Cor. 12:13; Col. 3:11) seems designed to point up the special danger of language when it is applied to the sacred, and the consequent necessity of using the criterion of human attitudes (meaning-worlds) to find out whether people are talking about the same thing when they use the same words.

But what is the case today with that language? In the West the forced unification of all the divine names into one common, specific noun, "God," only accentuates the ambiguousness of its content. I need only cite, by way of example, the fact that the very same word is used by philosophies conveying totally different or even opposite concepts of the divinity. The same thing could be said of theology and piety within the Christian tradition or even within the Roman Catholic tradition.[5]

A new phenomenon has come along to complicate the matter still further. We have seen the rise of atheism on a massive scale and of the mistaken view that an abyss separates that atheism from anything and everything religious. But as readers of Volume I know, I think there is every reason to believe that Jesus' view of the different religions of his own day holds equally true today for the difference between atheism and religion (Acts 17:23; 1 John 4:20).

This brings me back to Boff's text. Even taking into account the religious context of Brazilian culture, perhaps because of that context, I get the feeling that Boff's explicit references to God somehow represent a challenge not taken up. At one point Boff writes about "a greater Other. . . . Someone who infinitely surpasses us" (see p. 5 above). I think the solution lies in that direction, as well as in allusions to a cause worth more than our lives and similar terms. And I would readily admit that the overall context provided in the cited passage, brief as it is, does get rid of the ambiguity to a large extent.

I bring up Boff's talk about God because it ties in with the basic point I am trying to get across here, not because I would reject religious language a priori. For all the reasons cited above, I think that human beings should communicate and share their respective meaning-worlds slowly, amply, and deeply *before* they begin to discuss whether they do or do not share a "religious" faith. In other words, the religious question about Jesus takes on relevance and precision only when we are already standing on a solidly built bridge of *anthropological* faith. Proving this point will be a chief concern in Volume II.

My introductory remarks in this chapter may well strike readers as odd or alien, so let me spell out the basic point I was trying to make: If there is such a thing as a christology, in no way can it serve as a replacement for the ongoing task of remaking the gospel message in the Christian community. It is in that precise sense that I take Karl Rahner's enlightening comment on christological dogmas and dogmatic formulas: "Yet while this formula is an end, an acquisition and a victory, which allows us to enjoy clarity and security as well as ease in instruction, if this victory is to be a true one the end must also be a *beginning*" (Rahner 1961, 149; my italics).[6]

CHAPTER II

Antichristology?

The aims of this second volume, and of the subsequent three volumes that are closely connected with it, are basically two.

1. On the basis of the two human dimensions (*faith* and *ideology*) discussed in Volume I, we will now try to determine methodically what contribution, if any, Jesus of Nazareth and the tradition stemming from him makes to the process of humanization.

I will not conceal the fact that one idea tempts me. Remember my discussion of Machovec̆'s work in Volume I, his effort to depict a Jesus for atheists? Well, I am sorely tempted to take up that very task again, to carry it through even more methodically and logically, if possible, and to describe a Jesus for potential as well as actual atheists. Volume I demonstrated, I hope, that human beings who are not ready to set up certain human values as criteria prior and superior to any specific religion are incapable of recognizing the significance and importance of Jesus. Thus, even though they may end up calling him Messiah, Son of God, or God, that will not prevent them from turning him into an idol.

Even if we take it for granted that Jesus is truth incarnate, we must realize that there is only one way for that truth to be communicated to us in history. Realizing that fact, we must conclude that a person can believe in Jesus for false or wrong reasons, and stop believing in him for authentically right reasons. As we saw in Volume I, Jesus himself pointed up the danger here, a very serious danger because it offers us a false security under the cover of a sacred label. He demanded that people lay everything on the line where he was concerned, in a world without signs from heaven, that they stop running off to consult God when they came face to face with a human being in need. Hence I am not speaking paradoxical nonsense when I say that even believers must take a gamble in approaching Jesus and that the whole positive or negative future of belief in God is wrapped up in that gamble.

Espousal of such a view would hardly be suspected of a church that historically has manifested such a clear tendency to sacralize itself as the Roman Catholic church has. Well, it is official Roman Catholic teaching that athe-

13

ism is partially due to the fact that many Christians, as referential witnesses to (moral and social) values, present an inauthentic face of God (*GS* 19). Consider the conclusion that rightly and logically follows. If people necessarily dependent on those witnesses say no to that false god, they are basically right in doing so (at least until they meet or find different witnesses); and those who accept a false, inauthentic "God" on the basis of those witnesses are wrong in doing so.[1]

Jesus will never be accessible to people who think that the danger of not believing in God is worse than the danger of believing in a God that isn't. And this book will have been written in vain. That is why I suggested that a potential atheism is an unavoidable hermeneutic prerequisite. In the previous volume, I tried to show that it is a precondition for any hermeneutics of religious elements, but that more general issue is not my concern now. Here I am talking about the acceptance of atheism as a serious possibility vis-à-vis Jesus of Nazareth because it is a concrete, historical demand that he himself makes.

In line with its first objective, then, this volume is addressed to people who take that gamble. I want to dialogue with them about that figure who made a fleeting public appearance in Palestine almost two thousand years ago, who is part of a long tradition that precedes him and of another long tradition that follows him. What significance did he have, can he still have today, for human fulfillment and our understanding of the human being?

2. This aim links up with a second one. Let us assume that *theology* is the effort to comprehend an authentic religious faith along the basic anthropological lines outlined in Volume I. How, then, might we characterize Latin American theology and its efforts in the past fifteen years or so? I would say that its thrust has not been to make new contributions to the specialized branch of knowledge known as theology (with its soundly or shakily established scientific status). Instead Latin American theology has been mainly interested in going back to the primitive circumstances where, in the proximity of Jesus of Nazareth, Christians began to do theology.

Now one of the criticisms made of Latin American theology, insofar as it alleges to be an effort to understand the faith, is that it has not chosen, or perhaps dared, or perhaps been able, to structure its own coherent, systematic way of thinking about Jesus Christ. To put it in more technical terms: Latin American theology, call it liberation theology or not, lacks a christology.

For the sake of argument I will accept that as a fact[2] and then try to explain it by recourse to methodology. In our vernacular languages many sciences and scholarly disciplines get their name from a combination of two things: the subject they deal with, followed by our version of an appropriate Greek suffix. Thus the Greek suffix *grafía* becomes the ending *graphy* in English and has the basic meaning "description." Geography describes the earth's surface, for example. The Greek suffix *logía,* derived from Greek *logos,* becomes the ending *logy* in English. It has the basic meaning of "discourse," which here refers to a systematic, reasoned effort to explain the whys and wherefores of some subject. *Theology,* then, is a reasoned discourse about the "facts" relating to God (Greek *theos*).

Let us set aside any questions we might have about the term "theology" in general, pertinent as those questions might be. The fact to be noted here is that the academic discipline of theology is divided into various tracts or branches (*logies,* pl.) when it is studied. So we have eschato*logy* (study of the last things), ecclesio*logy* (study of the church), soterio*logy* (study of salvation), and so forth. One of the central tracts or branches of theological study is christo*logy,*[3] and that is why its absence in the theological work of Latin Americans surprises people.

There is no need for readers of this volume, whose interest lies in a human problematic, to delve into the themes or procedures of all those subtheologies. One point does deserve to be noted, however, because it may be relevant for what follows in this volume. Every scientific or scholarly subject, every *logy,* entails some objectification or reification. Since every scientific discipline is a reasoned effort (*logos*) to grasp something of universal validity, it studies its object under some aspect, making a category out of it. In that way it can avoid individual or singular facts.

Take the human sciences, for example. In order to rid themselves of the single case, the individual human being, they tend to study a *verbal noun* (reification), one which often ends in *-tion* or *-sion.* That is the category which serves as the basis for one or more scientific disciplines. Thus sociology, animal psychology, and human psychology may study phenomena of adapta*tion* and inhibi*tion,* and various theological disciplines may deal with crea*tion,* redemp*tion,* revela*tion,* or salva*tion.* In short, they deal with categories, not with single things or persons.

What might we mean, then, when we talk about a *christology,* a *logy* about *Christ?* We know that the word "christ" is ambiguous, particularly in view of its etymology. Originally it was not the proper name of anyone. It means "anointed" in Greek, equivalent to "messiah" *(mashah)* in Hebrew. That could give us the category of "anointing" or "unction" for further study by some theological discipline. It could examine the special function or destiny given by God or God's intermediaries to some person. *Christ*ology, then, might study cases in the Bible where God, by anointing or unction, gave a specific function to certain persons, kings, priests, or prophets.

It is here that the problem becomes very complex and ambiguous. First of all, christology limits itself to the study of only one messiah, one christ, one anointed: "These things are written that you may believe that Jesus is *the* Christ [= *the* Messiah]" (John 20:31). Second, and even more importantly, we find that already in the New Testament the word "christ" has been turned into a surname inseparable from Jesus of Nazareth. In other words, it is quickly ceasing to designate a category (the function or mission of Jesus) and turning into a proper name that can be used interchangeably with Jesus. Today we do not give it a second thought when we use the following expressions interchangeably: "Jesus said . . . Jesus Christ said . . . Christ said." And

Paul was already doing the same thing in his Letter to the Romans (50–60)!

So we have a very curious situation. Our christology is a tract, a discourse or *logy,* about one single person! Where in there do we find a specific category that would enable us to get beyond mere description of facts, introduce a reasoning process, and draw conclusions? And even if our only purpose is to look at Jesus in order to *seek out* such categories, that very step means that we are radically falsifying our encounter with the one, single, historical human witness known as Jesus of Nazareth.[4]

In that sense I must say that my effort in this volume would better be defined as an *antichristology,* rather than as one or more christology. Nor would I even describe it as *the* christology that goes with Latin American liberation theology. It is an effort to talk about Jesus in such a way that it may open people up to seeing him as a witness to a more humane and liberated human life.

If history itself had not told us, the previous volume should have made one fact clear: that is precisely how Jesus presented himself.

John the evangelist is accused of having elaborated a theology from above in his Gospel, of having rewritten the life of Jesus on the basis of his assumption that Jesus was God incarnate,[5] rather than on the basis of Jesus' real-life history. Yet that very writer upholds the fully historical nature of Jesus' life ("dwelt [= pitched his tent] among us," John 1:14), offers us the materiality needed to interpret it ("we have beheld his glory," John 1:14; see 1 John 1:1–2), and goes even further. He tells us that Jesus demanded the very sort of faith we have been discussing—basic anthropological faith in human witnesses to values—as the only possible way to see him as the bearer of something transcendent: "If I have told you *earthly things* and you *do not believe,* how can you believe if I tell you heavenly things?" (John 3:12).

The surest thing we know about Jesus is that he positively would not let people *define* him, would not let them say *who or what* he was, before they had grasped the values represented in his words and deeds.[6]

Let us drop the esoteric terminology of academic theology, which has blossomed greatly in recent times, and get back to a few basic facts that can be readily verified.

Sometimes the opening words of a modern christology are highly suggestive. We are told, for example, that a contemporary christology cannot enjoy the false certainty of an earlier day that it is faithfully capturing the historical figure of Jesus.[7] But there is an unspoken assumption beneath these words because the same thing could be said about countless human beings who lived in the past. In their case we have no interest in considering them or talking about them. What, then, is the implied assumption about christology? Why must we or should we do christology today, despite the historical distance that separates us from Jesus of Nazareth?

That brings us to the essential issue. There would never have been any christology at all if the human being named Jesus of Nazareth had not profoundly *interested* some of his contemporaries. Whence that interest, and can it reach down to us?[8]

That interest clearly has two poles, both of which must be taken into account. Jesus *bore witness* to certain human values *in the presence of* certain persons or groups of people.[9] We cannot talk about the *real* Jesus without taking his listeners into account.

Jesus was an ordinary human being. He had no religious title whatsoever. He was just another layman in the religiously structured society of Israel, a common craftsman (to specify his social status). At a certain point in his life his words and deeds began to attract attention, then adherence or rejection. As a result of the adherence or rejection, both his partisans and his detractors reached conclusions about *what* he was. It would be not only anachronistic but terribly wrongheaded, however, to fashion a discourse about *who or what* Jesus is for people today who, in the ordinary course of their existence, would have no interest whatsoever in him. By that I mean people who, if the exact same events were to recur again today, would pass them by as a curious happening that held no interest for them.

The basic, noteworthy fact is that we have nothing *directly* from Jesus of Nazareth. He *always* reaches us already *interpreted* by persons or groups *interested* in him. That means that we have no access to him except through *those interests* in one way or another.[10]

Time and again academic christology assumes that interest in Jesus is aroused when people, in some more or less confused and inchoate way, recognize him to be God or, at least, an envoy close to God. The presupposition of the *antichristology* I propose to offer here is exactly the opposite. If people came face to face with a specific, limited human being, ambiguous as everything involved in history is, and came to see him as God or a divine revelation, it was because that human being was of interest, was humanly significant. And if people today arrive at the same final vision of him today, it will only be because the latter fact is verified again: that is, because he is of interest and humanly significant to them.

I have already mentioned John's Gospel, and the general opinion that it, with its Prologue on the incarnate Word, represents the christological line that is the direct opposite of mine, that dovetails with the christology established centuries later by Christian theology and based largely on the formulas of the Council of Chalcedon. Well, St. Augustine is certainly in the line that leads from John's Gospel to Chalcedon. So I think it would be of interest here to consider some of his comments on John's Gospel *(In Ioannis Evangelium Tractatus)*, and specifically his comments on a particular verse in that Gospel (John 5:25). Jesus is talking about a transition from death to life, resurrection, to those who believe in him: "Truly . . . the hour is coming, and *now is,* when the dead will hear the voice of the Son of God, and those who hear will live."

The present nature of the promise ("now is") suggests to Augustine that Jesus is not talking about the final resurrection (of bodies also) but rather about the passage from death to life signified and effected here and now by faith in Jesus. It is a resurrection of the spirit (or "mind," to use Augustine's word), even before that of the body, that Jesus is talking about. After all, asks Augustine, is there not a recovery of (spiritual) life involved in changing from unjust to just, impious to pious, foolish to wise? Leaving aside the issue of the validity of Augustine's exegesis, I want to focus on one point he makes. Augustine points out that this sort of spiritual resurrection is common. At least it is common for people to promise it. He tells us that every founder of a religion or sect has preached it to his followers: "None of them has denied this spiritual resurrection lest he be asked: If the spirit does not rise *why are you talking to me?* . . . If you don't make me better than I was, why are you talking?" (Augustine, XIX:14).[11]

As my readers and I move through the chapters of this volume, I want that same question to echo repeatedly, to serve as the keynote of everything we discuss about Jesus. The respectful but unavoidable human question we must put to Jesus here is : *Why are you talking to me?*

Unfortunately it will not be easy to answer that question. First of all, the fact is that Jesus never spoke directly to me. I only have the testimony of other human beings about Jesus. In their different ways they believed that the words and deeds of Jesus showed them something of decisive importance, something that made them "better than they were."

But the very fact that increases our difficulty also enriches our quest, or should. From the time of the first witnesses to the testimony of Jesus, his testimony has continued to say something to people who have had the boldness—and the methodological knack—to formulate and pose our key-note question: Why are you talking to me?

Certain methodological indicators, basic to our present task, derive precisely from the fact that Jesus speaks to us through the answers that *others* received from him regarding their own differing problematics. One line of thought, espoused and reiterated by many, maintains that in such a situation we are making an exaggerated claim when we say that we believe *in Jesus* of Nazareth. Actually we believe in successive "interpreters" of Jesus, various witnesses interested in Jesus on the basis of their own different expectations. Hence I cannot ask Jesus of Nazareth why he is talking to me. I must pose the question to Matthew, Paul, Francis of Assisi, and today's Christians.

A second line of thought tries to get to the "historical" Jesus through those interpretive witnesses. Its advocates want to get down to the deeds he really did, the very words he actually spoke. They want their faith to be faith *in him,* not in his intermediaries. And there is no doubt that an adequate historical method can discover a great deal, particularly thanks to variants in the Synoptic Gospels (Matthew, Mark, Luke) and to solid knowledge of Jesus' milieu. It can pinpoint words and deeds that can be attributed historically to Jesus with reasonable certainty.

Thus our dialogue with Jesus might be restricted to that more or less historical data, or at least begin there. But watch out! There is a booby trap on that road! The great danger is that we may forget the key question: Why are you talking to me? Because it is quite obvious that the historical Jesus is not speaking *to me.* Whence my obligation to listen to him or the advantage *to me* in doing so? Does it lie in the fact that his words are the words *of God,* whether or not he is speaking to me, whether or not his words are of interest to me, and whether or not they revive my spirit (to use Augustine's phrase)? If the answer is yes, then we are back at the theology of the Pharisees, at the central misunderstanding of christology that I have been trying to dispel.

The correct solution, it seems to me, lies in the realization that the study of the historical Jesus, far from depriving the *interpretation* of the witnesses (Paul, Matthew, etc.) of importance, gives it its real value and ensures its future relevance. When we establish a certain distance between Jesus and his interpreters, it is easier for us to discover the creative work of the latter, the reasons for their interest in Jesus, their set of problems and how the human being Jesus shed light on it. Instead of being mere screens between Jesus and ourselves, such people as Matthew, Mark, and Paul become witnesses in and of themselves, not just to Jesus. They become real people with their own meaningful content, and the latter makes them interesting to us in turn.[12]

Recapturing this distance that lies between the historical figure and his interpreters opens up space and room for my own dialogue with Jesus of Nazareth two thousand years later, if for no other reason than that it does away with the inhibition imposed by the false but all too common question: *Who*, then, correctly interpreted Jesus?[13]

We cannot hide the fact that John's Gospel runs counter to the Synoptic Gospels to some extent, that Paul runs counter to both, that the Synoptics run counter to the Book of Revelation, the Letter to the Hebrews to Paul's writings, and so forth. Let me give you examples. The *poor* were a central object of Jesus' message as it is presented in the Synoptic Gospels (in different shadings, to be sure); but that central theme disappears completely in the christology (pardon the anachronism!) of the first eight chapters of Paul's Letter to the Romans. In the interpretation of both the Synoptics and Paul, Jesus is apparently quite insensitive to the monstrous evil embodied in the almost absolute political power of the Roman Empire, but in the community from which we get the Book of Revelation (or, the Apocalypse), Jesus becomes the slain Lamb who emerges victorious over the Beast, the very embodiment of that absolute power in its various transfigurations.

Who interpreted Jesus correctly? It is a question that goes unanswered by the historical Jesus, if for no other reason than that a Jesus interpreted by no one does not exist. There is no Jesus-Jesus. Even the things that can be historically attributed to him with reasonable certainty are interpretations: because the documents available to us for that task are interpretations; because we ourselves must interpret in order to distinguish between what comes from Jesus himself and what others attribute to him; and because Jesus of Nazareth engages in a process of self-interpretation, making use of the interpretive traditions of his own people to define his own mission and destiny.

In what sense, then, does the historical Jesus make room for me, so that my own question reaches him and gets a real, meaningful answer rather than a fanciful, imaginary one? The answer is that I am enabled to see that the different interpretations of the same historical Jesus do not show up as contradictory. None of them exhausts the rich significance of the principal witness, but all of them point up the richness of the secondary, successive witnesses. Each witness leaves its own separate record of the historical reality of Jesus, which obviously surpasses the record itself; there is obviously and necessarily a gap between the interpretation and the one interpreted. This enables me to pose questions to him that he did not explicitly deal with, without doing violence to history or manipulating Jesus. I can ask him why he is talking to me even though I know that he never did address me or my problems, historically speaking.

This is due to the necessarily limited nature of a human being's real-life history by comparison with the universality of his or her meaning-world; and it holds even more true for the history of a great human being. In its complexity and implications that world of meaning and values embraces the entire universe and the unforeseeable possibilities that reality may offer. Suppose, for example, I ask what Jesus thought about the Roman Empire in valuational terms. Looking at history, someone could answer: *nothing*. But the series of interpretations made of Jesus enables me to *infer*, on the basis of his decisions and evaluations with respect to other things, how he might have incorporated that issue into his meaning-world if he had been faced historically with that particular question.

Take the case of Paul. We can be reasonably sure that the interest that Jesus of Nazareth aroused in his own people—his answer to the key question ("Why are you speaking to me?")—was closely bound up with the expectation that a new and definitive Davidic kingdom was on its way from God. The expectation itself had been growing since Old Testament times. Paul himself, prompted by rejection, vocation, or whatever reason, turned to meet the pagan world of Greek culture. The Acts of the Apostles informs us that he tried to interest the Athenians on the basis of human perspectives and expectations he assumed might be theirs. But they rejected his presentation of Jesus, some mockingly responding to his appeal and making it clear they were not interested (Acts 17:22–33).

What was Paul to do now? Should he attempt the desperate and really impossible task of introducing pagans to the whole Old Testament process, with all its cultural presuppositions? Should he try to link up their interested question with that of the readers of Matthew, for example? And remember that Matthew's audience was not the same as that of Jesus before the resurrection. Paul decided to approach his task along the same general lines that he had employed before, only this time in greater depth. If we compare his talk to the Athenians with the first eight chapters of the Letter to the Romans, we can see the road he took in his effort to speak of Jesus—or better, to have Jesus speak—to an audience that had not been historically his. Paul immerses the pagans in a *school of questions* parallel but dissimilar to that of the Old Testament. And in this case the basic school might be labelled that of humanism.

The tragic imponderables of human existence, as they might be experienced by any citizen of Rome or Corinth, become questions addressed to Jesus of Nazareth. And Paul's Jesus, quite obviously, does not respond with the historical words of Jesus of Nazareth. Like the authors of the fourth Gospel, the Letter to the Hebrews, and the Book of Revelation, Paul clearly perceives the distance between the historical Jesus and the interpretations of Matthew, Mark, and Luke. So he feels free to create his own gospel (Rom. 2:16; see also Rom. 16:25; 2 Cor. 4:3; 1 Thess. 1:5; 2 Thess. 2:14).

Paul does not invent a nonexistent Jesus. Nor does he feel the need to *partially* adapt the Jesus-events so that they might take on their true significance via-à-vis groups perceiving those events from differing standpoints— which is clearly what happens in John's Gospel. Without anecdote or quote, Paul simply interprets Jesus. Instead of referring to Jesus and what he said to his historical listeners, Paul infers from that what Jesus would have said to those outside Israel who have honestly tried to fathom what it means to be a human being in a universe apparently condemned to uselessness and absurdity.

For that reason Paul has been accused of being the "inventor" of Christianity. What he actually did was to show us, even more clearly than the evangelists, the way in which our anthropological faith could correctly root its fundamental questions in Jesus of Nazareth, in the only way accepted by Jesus himself.

Thus the case of Paul sheds light on my aim here, on the question that I would like to begin to answer in this volume: How are we to do a christology today? Using the method outlined in Volume I, can we find criteria that will guide us in trying to answer the question: What exactly is the anthropological significance of Jesus of Nazareth for us today in our present circumstances?

My attempt at an *antichristology* seeks to open a road between Jesus of Nazareth and our present reality, amid the various christologies. It seeks to connect him with the problems of our anthropological faith. Hence we must undertake three readings of Jesus' significance, each of which will be justified in its proper place. Those three readings are: historical investigation (Volumes II and III), anthropological generalization (Volume IV), and formulation of the issues and problems in present-day terms (Volume V). Although they are intimately connected, readers can begin with any of the three readings since they all must be covered more than once if my aim is to be achieved. One or another reading will interest a given reader more, depending on his or her position on the road leading toward the witness named Jesus. And each of the four volumes has its own Introduction, spelling out the method behind my reading as well as the relationship of that volume to the others.

Let me say a word about Volume IV. It is meant merely to serve as a bridge between the two contemporary readings of Jesus in the Synoptic Gospels and Paul (Volumes II and III) and my own present-day reading in Volume V. Two thousand years lie between the first two readings and mine. During that period important events, both positive and negative, have helped to turn interpretations of Jesus in certain directions. Volume IV offers one sample of a past historical reading, one of the many that lie between the New Testament and our own day.

CHAPTER III

Jesus in the Grip of Theology

It should be made clear from the very start that the author of this volume *believes* in Jesus of Nazareth, in a sense that I tried to explain in Volume I and that I will spell out even more clearly in this volume. I am not trying to deceive my readers into thinking that I am approaching this historical personage for the first time or from a position of systematic neutrality.

To be even more specific, my faith in Jesus is what I defined as *religious faith* in Volume I. I believe that Jesus was the Word of God made human, God's very self. Unfortunately these assertions, prompted by the desire to show good faith with my readers, are usually hedged in by so many stereotypes and misunderstandings in our culture that I fear they may lead my readers astray rather than making my position clear to them.

Consider one consequence that flows from what I have said, for example. Only those who closely read Volume I will appreciate the fact that I, *for the very reasons* just given, feel much closer to many people who say they do not believe in Jesus, but are interested in the values carried by that human figure, than I am to the vast multitude of people who say that Jesus is God and think such a stand puts them in an advantageous position over the rest of humanity.

I do not think that *faith in Jesus,* as I mean it here, can be spelled out clearly before we do the three successive readings of Jesus of Nazareth I mentioned near the end of the previous chapter: historical investigation, anthropological generalization, and formulation of issues and problems in present-day terms. Hence only at the end, and for those who have travelled the same road, will my question take on its full meaning: What does it mean to me that Jesus of Nazareth is God?

That question is properly *theological.* In this chapter, therefore, I am going to address a few introductory remarks to those readers who are starting from the same point and who may be interested in the whole theological debate over *christology.* They may also be of interest to people who are not concerned about that debate, but who would like to go back over my reflections in Volume I and explore them more deeply vis-à-vis a concrete example of religious theorizing.

In Volume I we saw that any faith, be it religious or not, begins by constituting an anthropological dimension made necessary by the limitation of any
and every human life. We must structure a world of meaning and values *as if*
we knew the full possibilities of existence from our own personal experience.
We do so, in fact, thanks to referential witnesses who present us with the most
satisfying, beautiful, and fulfilling ways to live that existence.

Jesus of Nazareth is undoubtedly one of those witnesses, framed in one
tradition that precedes him and enables us to comprehend him, and in
another that follows him and enables us to translate and update him for
circumstances today. Indeed he is one of the most important witnesses that
humanity can point to over the past two thousand years.

Another obvious fact is that this historical testimony was lived out within a
religious framework. And, for good or ill, one of the most widespread religious systems on our planet appropriated his name: *Christianity*. In spite of
himself, perhaps, Jesus of Nazareth is seen as the founder of *one* of the religions around today that lays claim to universality.

All religions that attain that level possess their own theoretical system
through which they relate allegedly historical happenings to the revelation of
divine messages, personages, and cognitive data.

I

I am not going to offer a history of that theoretical system (theology) in the
Christian tradition, insofar as it has tried to draw out from Jesus of Nazareth
the divine revelation contained in him. Here I am simply going to begin with
our own present age and examine its gradually acquired possibilities of arriving at some sure and historically satisfactory knowledge of the person involved in this revelation: Jesus of Nazareth.

What exactly is the principal alternative facing theology when it seeks to
deal with Jesus, to form its christology?

In the past, theology did not possess a polished set of instruments to separate the *history* of Jesus from its *interpretations*. Hence only the latter
counted in theology, though they were not then perceived for what they were:
interpretations. I would stress the plural here because it is obvious that there
is a plurality of versions dealing with Jesus. This fact was perceived very early,
even giving rise to serious deviations considered heresies.

At that point a strong ecclesiastical authority helped to minimize the problem. It set a canonical limit on the books that were to be regarded as (divine)
Scripture, as part of the New Testament. The implication was that at least
those versions are *compatible*. The number of Gospels in the list or canon was
reduced to four; other Gospels were left out as *apocryphal*. This helped to
give the impression that the four Gospels were concordant and to obscure
sight of their different approaches, even in such an obvious case as that of
John's Gospel. Proof can be found in the fact that around A.D. 180 a very
popular work in the Christian world was a "concordance" of the four Gos-

pels: Tatian's *Diatessaron*.[1] In it the four Gospels were reduced or combined into one. And if the Gospels with their obvious differences were seen as compatible, there seemed to be even less of a problem when it came to harmonizing, not stubborn facts, but interpretations that were explicitly declared to be such: for example, the Pauline and Joannine letters.

For many centuries theology followed this more or less difficult but ingenuous course of having *one* unique christology. It was backed up by a church magisterium that authoritatively separated compatible interpretations from heretical ones. Then the discovery of the "historical Jesus," first in Protestant theology and then in Catholic theology, stepped in to cause a crisis. It was felt to be a danger to the extent that its necessity was not appreciated. Before being a solution, true or false, it was seen as a danger to the faith.

For the moment there was a loss of confidence in the historicity of many events mentioned in the Gospels, not minor events either. If the resurrection of Lazarus had really taken place publicly in the immediate vicinity of Jerusalem and had had a decisive impact on the attitude of the Jewish authorities toward Jesus, as John's Gospel indicates, could that event have been ignored by the Synoptic evangelists?

It was also necessary to choose between John's version of Jesus (recognized as the Messiah from the very first chapter of the Gospel) and the Jesus of the Synoptics, who got a messianic profession from the lips of Peter a short time before his passion. Even among the Synoptic Gospels themselves there were discrepancies. How could Mark leave out something as central as the Sermon on the Mount, present even in Luke's brief version? And in that sermon itself, did Jesus declare blessed those who suffer "hunger" (social situation) or those who have a "hunger for justice" (moral virtue)?

The crisis deepened even when exaggerated statements about the impossibility of knowing anything certain about Jesus and his history were put to rest. For now it became clear that even the most reliable witnesses, the Synoptics, were also *preachers of faith* in Jesus, not just narrators of his life.

The historical Jesus now appeared to be composed of a small number of reliable data, something very far from the large quantity of presumed facts on which the classical christology had been built. Doubt arose especially about what was assumed to have been the proofs that Jesus himself gave of his divinity: miracles and prophecies. It was noted that *all* the New Testament writings were interpretations based on faith. Worse still, they were different and to some extent opposed interpretations of the *significance* of Jesus of Nazareth, the resurrected Messiah—notice, for example, the conception of universal resurrection in Paul and John.

Moreover, christological diversity had grown in the Christian communities. The Protestant reformers of the sixteenth century did not depart from the common christological tradition, which allowed for differing approaches and emphasis. But free inquiry and the rapid disappearance of what might be called a church magisterium in the first Reformation churches combined to produce in time a considerable fragmentation of the "preached Christ," of the interpretations of Jesus. The reliable historical data on Jesus seemed to depend more and more on esoteric kinds of knowledge that were not up to the task of unifying and grounding the various "Christs of faith" actually evident in the mosaic of living Christian communities.

Within the Roman Catholic church the diversity is practically the same. One need only think of the Christ of popular piety. But on the theological level the effort is to maintain almost perfect christological unity. For the reasons already cited, however, the unity of this one and only christology seems to be based more and more on a kind of double external miracle: (1) the fixing of the written canon, leaving out of the New Testament those interpretations of Christ that were considered incompatible; and (2) the almost magical capacity of the later magisterium to determine the same compatibility when faced with new and complex lines of thought, apparently by having recourse solely to the formula of Chalcedon, which fixed the correct position about fifteen hundred years ago, though problems did crop up after that.

So, from both the Protestant and the Catholic side we have gradually come to the modern christological alternative. In broad outline it is made clear in the following questions raised by Pannenberg:

> Does Christology have primarily to do with the Jesus of that past time or with the Jesus who is present today? The two are certainly not mutually exclusive. The Jesus proclaimed today is none other than the one who lived at that time in Palestine and was crucified under Pilate—and vice versa. Nevertheless, it does make a fundamental difference whether we seek to understand the present proclamation of who Jesus is and what he means for us in terms of what happened at that time or whether, conversely, we speak of what happened then only secondarily, that is, only in the light of what the proclamation says about it today. The question is: Must Christology begin with Jesus himself or with the kerygma of his community? [Pannenberg 1977, 21-22].[2]

As we shall see, Pannenberg will opt for the first choice of the alternative. And that prompts us to ask ourselves: What is at the bottom of his aversion to the second choice? Speaking in theological terms, he and many others who side with his choice talk about a spurious mixture of christology and soteriology.[3] After all, it should not surprise us that someone who believes in Jesus believes in him as savior (soteriology being a discourse or *logy* about salva*tion*). And it is obvious that the Jesus who appears to me as savior is not the remote Jesus of two thousand years ago reconstructed by historical criticism but the preached Jesus I encounter in the Christian community. The latter is the Jesus to whom I can meaningfully pose the (soteriological) question: *Why are you speaking to me?* It is he who can revive my spirit and make me better than I was.

Where exactly, then, lies the danger in the mixture? At first glance it would seem to be the only sensible response to the discovery that from the very start Jesus of Nazareth shows up already interpreted as a savior from something. The fear is obviously that people may *invent* a savior Christ fitted to suit each individual's desires for salvation. That would be the death of christology, so to speak. We would end up instead with "christographies," an uncritical inventory of all the Christs operative in the communities of faith (Borrat).

To put the question another way: "Do not the desires of men only become projected upon the figure of Jesus, personified in him?" (Pannenberg 1977, 47). The rich—to offer my own example—would look to him for justification of their wealth by appealing to "poverty of spirit," and the poor would focus on the good news that God is going to send the rich away "empty-handed."

The churches, of course, are mainly concerned to transport people on their own boats. They have few objections to widely varying christologies,[4] so long as these agree to peaceful coexistence on the practical level and do not try to introduce their languages, clear as they may be, into academic theology. Their main concern is that no one of those human desires will try to monopolize Christ, thereby forcing the church to opt logically and completely for its version to the exclusion of the rest.

The objections of theologians to that extreme are less pragmatic. They are closely bound up with the *scientific* status of theology, and hence of christology (in the singular). Küng's work *On Being a Christian* is at heart a christology. Here is what he has to say on the issue just brought up:

> What is called for is common sense without illusions, since even in the present century far too many theologians have allowed themselves to be blinded by the spirit of the age and even provided a theological substructure for nationalism and war propaganda and moreover totalitarian party programs in shades of black, brown and finally red [Küng 1976, 37].

Küng's appeal for common sense or soberness, in the light of the historical past, is undoubtedly an appeal for "scientificness." But even more interesting is what Küng has to say about a theology that would fail to heed his appeal and thus fall into the waiting trap:

> In this way theologians too can easily become ideologists or champions of ideologies. *Ideologies* are understood here, not as if they were neutral in value, but critically as systems of "ideas," concepts and beliefs, of standards of interpretation, motifs and norms of action, which— controlled mostly by particular interests—reproduce the reality of the world in a distorted form, cover up the real abuses and replace rational arguments with an appeal to the emotions [ibid.].

Another theological expression of the issue, akin to Küng's appeal for common sense or soberness, comes from Walter Kasper. We must be "receptive" to Jesus as he is, instead of introducing him as an element in our own task. To do the latter would be to subordinate him to our own purposes:

> Liberating reconciliation, as it occurs in and through Jesus Christ, is primarily a divine gift and only secondarily a human task. Here precisely is the border line between Christian theology and ideologies or utopias (which nevertheless retain traces of Christian influence) [Kasper 1976, 16–17].[5]

If my readers recall the terminology used and discussed in Volume I, I think they will realize that any such appeal to common sense or receptivity is fruitless as a means of preventing Jesus' ideology or utopia from being transmitted to us along with his real meaning-world. By his "ideology" I mean the historical concreteness (with all the limitations mentioned by Küng) in which his values were turned into reality. The significance of Jesus of Nazareth was made manifest in a specific historical context of tasks, motivations, and interests. That context is not our context. And I do not see how it could be translated soberly to ours by methodically eradicating our own tasks, motivations, and interests today.

I will get back to that point later. What interests me here is the difficulty that the theologians being analyzed here see in fashioning a relevant *contemporary* discourse about Jesus, one that somehow interprets Jesus in terms of human desires and expectation today. To put it in more technical terms, this points to the difficulty of a relationship between *soteriology* and *christology* that is too tight and too unscientific.

What I find unbelievable is that anyone thinks *ideology* can be avoided at such a low cost. And I mean "ideology" in the sense used and defined by the authors cited above.[6] How can they even suggest that not *desiring* anything (consciously or explicitly) vis-à-vis Jesus is a possible, necessary, or sufficient condition for understanding him, interpreting him, and recognizing his significance two thousand years later! Everyone with a certain level of education, at least, knows that the phenomenon of *ideology* is to be found precisely in vaunted claims to neutrality: that is, when we *do not perceive* how our thinking is being influenced by interests deriving from other sources, such as our place in society and its associated advantages. One certainly does not have to be a Marxist to see how ridiculous soberness or common sense is as a remedy against the disease of ideology!

There were people who took pride in their neutrality, impartiality, and (theological) receptivity to anything revealed by God when they came face to face with the historical Jesus: and they were the very people who passed him by without recognizing his importance. They humbly asked for signs from heaven in order to recognize the Messiah (christology) and did not allow themselves to be moved by human desires. And what was the result, according to Jesus himself? Their hardness of heart prevented them from seeing what was right before their eyes.

So let me pick up the thread of my examination in this chapter. The plurality of the "preached Christs," the "Christs of faith," is attributed to the lack of scientificness in approaching Jesus. It is said that people look to Jesus of Nazareth to find salvific responses to differing and even irreconcilable human expectations.

Once this crisis was noticed, many understandably looked to the other extreme of the alternative for a solution: that is, to the historical Jesus. More or less recent investigations do seem to preserve the objective reality of Jesus from soteriological infiltrations, from the subjective distortions introduced by people who see him through the prism of their own unsatisfied desires. Pannenberg puts it this way:

> Going back behind the apostolic kerygma to the historical Jesus is, therefore, possible. It is also necessary. Wilhelm Herrmann properly criticized Kähler at just this point: precisely because the New Testament witnesses proclaimed Jesus as he appeared to faith at that time, "this proclamation alone, if we leave it up to that, cannot protect us from the doubt that we want to base our faith on something that is perhaps not historical fact at all, but is itself a product of faith" (Ebeling) [Pannenberg 1977, 23].

However, it is not difficult to foresee the difficulties faced by a christology that seriously and consistently adopts this second of the two methodological alternatives. What am I to do to make the few facts known to be *historical* decisive for me, when they have to do with a personage who lived almost two millennia ago? Would not it be far more interesting and relevant to have an intimate knowledge of the meaning-world of the "Christ of faith"? The latter is scarcely historical, to be sure, but, according to his interpreters, he was occupied with problems similar to mine, and he offers more wide-ranging, comprehensible, and multifaceted access to the human problematic.

Readers may well find it difficult to imagine the methodological destruction proposed by the second approach (to the historical Jesus). It would tear down two thousand years of christocentrism as transmitted by Western culture, one that is a mixture of christology and soteriology and that makes Jesus—historical or invented—the decisive point of history. Its Jesus is the one who does nothing less than divide the whole calendar of humanity into two parts; who is indissolubly bound up with complete salvation, God's work *par excellence;* and who therefore stands out from the rest of humanity as the most *divine* and *sacred* thing that history has ever possessed.

That is precisely what is rejected by the christology of the historical Jesus, with its *methodical doubt.* At the very least it rejects the Christ(s) of faith as its presupposition or basic starting point. To approach Jesus of Nazareth realistically, it must leave the "Christian" world and confront a historical figure who apparently never presaged such a future; who argued about problems that were very concrete, and hence irrelevant today; who failed to recognize other problems that have now stepped into the foreground; and who based his proclamation on a proximate irruption of the divine that never took place.

The second extreme of the christological alternative methodically separates soteriology from knowledge of Jesus in order to build a creditable discourse about Jesus on the basis of objective reality rather than our own (ideological) desires. Hence it seems doomed to theological, if not scientific, failure. Because if theology consists in understanding the faith, then the historical Jesus can hardly provide a handle for that faith. His facts and deeds are mere facts, *facta bruta* (ibid.,49).

The basic alternative, then, does not seem to offer us any way out. At one end we find nothing but an ideological plurality of christologies without objective criteria of discernment; at the other end we find historical data devoid of theological or human relevance for today. Unless . . . there is a valid bridge between christology and soteriology, one that does not improperly mix the historical Jesus with the Christ of faith, objective data with human desires, but somehow combines both.

Those who put forth the christological attempts under discussion here believe that, in general, they have found this middle road. They feel the task can be accomplished by maintaining both poles or extremes in action simultaneously, though giving temporal priority to the study of the historical Jesus. Walter Kasper writes:

If we exclude both a unilateral kerygma- and dogma-Christology, and a Christology exclusively orientated to the historical Jesus, the right way of re-establishing Christology can be to take both elements of Christian faith with equal seriousness, and to ask how, why, and with what justice the proclaimed and believed-in Christ developed from the Jesus who proclaimed; and how that historically unique Jesus of Nazareth relates to the universal claim of belief in Christ [Kasper 1976, 19].

Here Kasper is following Pannenberg, who offers an even better explanation of the relationship between the two poles and why it is possible to connect soteriology and christology:

This is possible under the presupposition that a soteriological meaning is inherent in Jesus' history. The past reality of Jesus did not consist of brute facts in the positivistic sense, to which arbitrary interpretations, one as good as another, could be added. Rather, meaning already belongs to the activity and facts and fate of Jesus in the original context in the history of traditions within which it occurred, from the perspective of which all subsequent, explicit interpretations can be judged. Thus, Christological research finds in the historical reality of Jesus the criterion for the critical examination of the Christological tradition and also the various soteriological concerns that have determined Christological presentations [Pannenberg 1977, 49].

This is what Pannenberg calls a christology that starts from below (from the historical Jesus), as opposed to one that starts from above (from the Christ of faith).

But beware, readers! Make no mistake here! What question does Pannenberg pose to the historical Jesus *before anything else*? His relationship to the above: "Thus, while Christology must begin with the man Jesus, its first question has to be that about his unity with God. Every statement about Jesus taken independently from his relationship to God could result only in a crass distortion of his historical reality" (ibid., 36). Further on Pannenberg writes: "Hence, the first part of the Christological discussion presented here will deal with the knowledge of the divinity of Jesus Christ" (ibid., 49).[7]

Let us pause over this for a moment. The routine-bound theologian, alarmed by the problem of the historical Jesus, Jesus the human being, will find peace of mind in the fact that Pannenberg and others, despite the turn to the historical Jesus, are once again heading back down the old beaten pathways. But what about my readers, who have already been through Volume I of this work? Does not Pannenberg's theological stance remind them of something very specific that I brought up in Volume I? Is it not looking for the "sign from heaven," which the theology of the Pharisees and Sadducees demanded? Is it not looking for the historical indication or argument (sign) of Jesus' oneness with God (from heaven), prior to anything that might arise out of any human desires or needs satisfied by the historical Jesus?

A strange paradox indeed! The theology that, according to Jesus, came from a hard and insensitive heart (see Mark 3:5, with 8:12), from hypocrisy (Luke 12:56), from an inhibition about assuming the responsibility of judging for oneself (Luke 12:57), from a fundamental idolatry (= adultery; Matt. 12:39; 16:4) is today apparently the best equipped one to recognize the divinity of Jesus of Nazareth—without the inconveniences of subjective relativism and reductivist positivism!

Some will object that my criticism is too facile, that it remains to be seen how, if at all, we can speak meaningfully today of Jesus of Nazareth in any other way.

I said earlier that my effort here could be described as an *antichristology*. It is, in the sense that the christologies of classical theology put the cart before the horse in one way or another. They formulate questions for Jesus of Nazareth for which he clearly and explicitly said he had no answers to offer. Can we not adopt a different approach? Can we not let our interest be attracted by that ordinary human being—however extraordinary he may have turned out to be—who began to act and teach in Palestine in the first century A.D.?

It is not as easy as it sounds. I think we must start by accepting the fact that absolute relativism would rob Jesus of all significance and relevance, turning him into the plaything of human desires in every sense. That being the case, we must necessarily query Jesus *in terms of the questions* that he historically was willing and able to answer. Going through a kind of time tunnel, we must try to join up with the desires and expectations with which Jesus himself entered into dialogue.

If we do that, will we be disguising ourselves in the desire of others or unwittingly basing ourselves on the Christ of faith? And even more importantly, will we be able to come back through the time tunnel again? Will we be able somehow to link up those earlier expectations with our own, without denying the historical Jesus and with some guarantees and criteria that our linkup is more or less correct?

A basic answer of yes to those questions, particularly the latter two, is virtually implied in countless tasks of all sorts that our culture undertakes every day. Consider, for example, our interest in the history of the past—a scientific history, needless to say. This interest is intimately bound up with the possibility of situating ourselves in the vital *context* of those events, of somehow experiencing, with suspense, the anxieties and expectations of a past day, when the future was obscure and the present was very different from ours. Moreover, history is part of the whole educational process because we accept the dictum that it is the teacher of life. This presupposes the possibility of learning to learn, which readers will recall from Volume I, and hence the possibility of living through alien experiences without succumbing to complete arbitrariness.

Much the same could be said of language[8] and of our ability to understand documents deriving from other epochs and cultures. Just consider various literary genres, myths, primitive accounts, comparisons, metaphors, and other figures of speech closely bound up with contexts that never were and never will be ours. The work of *trans*lating, of getting the human realm to *trans*gress the barriers of space and time, seems to constitute a necessity for human beings. Our translation may be designed to uproot or plant roots, to manipulate what exists or create what does not exist. It has many different, even opposing, facets, but all of them are bound up with the task of being human.

II

This presupposition—the basic intelligible unity of the human species—is an inevitable axiom of all the human sciences, just as the rationality of the universe is the necessary springboard for all physical investigations. And it is essential to our effort to approach Jesus of Nazareth. Readers will recall my discussion in the first volume of faith as a basic anthropological dimension. Thanks to faith, human beings transmit to one another data that are central to the human meaning-world. Thus faith, in this general sense, more or less serves as a species-memory and as the deepest bond of its unity.

That brings us to a crucial point in our present inquiry: How exactly are we to understand this basic unity of humanity through different epochs and problematics? In connection with our subject here, we may now consider the christologies of two other thinkers. I think their efforts may well constitute the best starting points for a present-day discourse about Jesus that would break with the dead-end procedures of the classical christologies.

I am talking about the christologies of Rudolf Bultmann and Karl Rahner. Unlike the works of the aforementioned writers, these two clearly seek to establish a dialogue with Jesus in terms of what Jesus has to say to human existence. Jesus' interest *for the human being* comes prior to the establishment of his relationship with God or of his divinity. In short, both Bultmann and Rahner begin by considering the content and significance of an *anthropological faith* in Jesus.

Here I shall not go into Bultmann's polemics with adversaries and disciples about the possibility and importance of basing oneself on the historical Jesus. In a sense we touched upon that issue indirectly in the earlier pages of this chapter. Most people are familiar with Bultmann's basic view of the relevance of the gospel, of Jesus insofar as we can know him. Through Jesus, says Bultmann, the Absolute continues to appeal to our lives, to place them in crisis, and to oblige us to make radical decisions as to how to be a human being or a better human being. And this appeal from the Absolute to us comes through Jesus despite the time and the various cultures traversed by the message.

I say "despite the time" because the way to overcome the growing hiatus between Jesus and us is of central importance in situating and evaluating Bultmann's christological effort.[9] Summarizing greatly, and at the risk of doing injustice to Bultmann, I would say that he proposes two ways to go about this: one negative, the other positive.

The negative approach is *demythologization*. For Bultmann any intervention of divine transcendence in profane events—not to mention numerous cosmological ideas bound up with the religious world of antiquity—would be *mythical* (or mythological). If we want to open up room for the summons issued to us *today* by the Absolute, through the accounts and interpretations of Jesus of Nazareth, then we must clearly demarcate those mythical affirmations. Thus to make room for the summons issued by Jesus we must ignore such things as the idea of God's incarnation, miracle accounts, and even accounts of Christ's resurrection.[10]

My basic view of this demarcation is clearcut and can be put briefly. Insofar as starting from such elements presupposes a theology from above, I agree that the approach to Jesus must prescind from them, at least as an initial step. But I do not agree with Bultmann's straightforward suppression of the mythical. The mythical structure of language certainly does constitute an obstacle for our modern understanding. We live in a world where the latter is (far too much) limited by a positivistic conception of knowledge (and language). But as I tried to make clear in Volume I, what is conveyed by mythical language is not sheer nonsense of an irrelevant sort; it has to be *translated,* not simply omitted.

Take Jesus' so-called miracles, for example. For a correct understanding of the historical Jesus they are a constitutive and indispensable element. One may deny that they are really miracles, divine interventions changing the course of events in spite of physical laws. Or one may choose to disregard the issue. But the fact that Jesus was regarded as a miracle worker, the identity of those who benefited from his power, the occasions on which he exercised it, and the accompanying explanations constitute a significant historical nucleus of decisive importance in trying to learn why Jesus of Nazareth was of interest in his day—to the point that he became a threat to the Jewish religious authorities and was put to death.

It is very important that the scientificness of theology, of our knowledge about Jesus in this case, should never be sought by eliminating the *iconic* or poetic elements of language,[11] because it is those elements that best introduce us into the meaning-world that we are trying to explore and that speaks to faith. For some people, Bultmann's demythologizing means "existential translation," not elimination; in like manner, we are not only obliged to go by way of the poetry but will actually be enriched rather than impoverished in the process.

Now let us move on to Bultmann's second procedure, his *positive* approach to biblical interpretation in general and hence to the interpretation of Jesus of Nazareth. The basic principle is that all human beings bring some sort of *preunderstanding* to their hearing of the word, be it a divine or human word. That is obvious, however much it may leave the word—or better, our understanding of it—exposed to the onslaughts of "the human."[12]

Readers of Volume I will recall my basic agreement with Bultmann's approach insofar as it *substantiates* a hermeneutic necessity. Any reading of a message will be understood in accordance with the reader's—not to mention the author's—knowledge of the language. Knowledge of a given language, in turn, serves as the vehicle for a certain way of seeing things, of perceiving reality. And what holds true for language holds even truer for the human problematic by which every reader or listener comprehends what is said and what response is given.

The problem starts when we ask ourselves how we are to *improve* this *preunderstanding* in order to grasp the message more fully. It is obvious, for example, that a better knowledge of grammar will help a person to understand any message. So it would seem that we could say the same thing about the human grammar we learn by diving into the deeper reaches of existence. Things are not that clear and simple, however.

My bits of knowledge about human existence, you see, are always acquired on the basis of *certain* values rather than other ones. This being the case, will I not be putting barriers in the way of a summons from the Absolute that seeks to lead me to different values, to a change of direction or conversion?

Now the fact is that Bultmann, in at least one part of his work, sought to improve and deepen this *preunderstanding* by seeking support in Heidegger's analysis of human existence as presented in *Being and Time,* the most famous work of Heidegger's early period. Does that mean that one must interrogate Jesus of Nazareth with questions arising out of Heidegger's work? Many objections were raised about such a specific dependency.[13]

Here is not the place for a prolonged, in-depth study of the hermeneutic possibilities that might be afforded by phenomenology such as that elaborated in *Being and Time*. I only want to say what must be said to make my own position on the matter clear. So I would ask my readers simply to follow the thread of my methodological reflections with regard to christology specifically.

What solid objections can be raised against the use of a kind of existential grammar to better understand what in Jesus of Nazareth is issuing an appeal to me?

One objection, an argument without solidity, was that Bultmann was setting up a specific philosopher (Heidegger) as the arbiter of how we were to understand the divine revelation of Jesus. The incoherence of this argument derives from three false suppositions.

The *first* erroneous supposition is that by renouncing Heidegger we would be breaking down a barrier between Jesus and ourselves. Instead of Heidegger's type of preunderstanding, we would assume another type, and in all likelihood we would be unconscious of it. Now there is no worse kind of preunderstanding, none more in danger of constituting a barrier, than one which goes unnoticed and therefore uncriticized. Ingenuousness is not synonymous with transparency as various critics of Bultmann seem to think—among them, if I am not mistaken, a theologian of the stature of Karl Barth.

The *second* erroneous supposition, as readers of Volume I may have already noticed, is that we are confronted with a very special case. Here we are faced with a divine revelation. Unlike any human message, such a message should be above and beyond any criterion deriving from the human being. When we are dealing with a divine revelation, in other words, the *understanding* should pass judgment on the *preunderstanding* rather than vice versa. The profoundly mistaken character of this supposition lies in its claim to start off by recognizing some event, person, or document as the word of God. How can that be done without some preunderstanding? The most elementary human logic and even the historical testimony of Jesus make clear to us that the opposite course is the only possible one. It is precisely because we understand those events, persons, and documents from one particular stance rather than another (signs of the times) that we come to have (anthropological) faith in them; only on that basis do we come to regard them as an appeal made to us from the Absolute.

The *third* supposition will occupy our attention more. As I indicated above, many of Bultmann's critics are disturbed by the apparent role of *preunderstanding,* which is always bound up with human elements and interests. It seems to be an improper imposition on a word or message that should pass judgment on us. Instead we seem to be approaching it with our self-interested prejudices, to be passing judgment on the word of God. It seems that we pick and choose what we want from it on the basis of our prior position and outlook.

What are we to say to this? Well, to begin with, that hermeneutic circle is inevitable, as I tried to explain in *The Liberation of Theology* (Chap. 1). It is part and parcel of any interpretation that a human being makes of testimony coming from another existence. It is the price that God has chosen to pay for our liberty. God must "knock at the door." The same is also true in any educational process or human relationship. All the means used to reduce this unavoidable dose of relativity turn sour. It is better that the word of God reach prejudiced ears and possibly face suffocation, like the seed in the parable, than that efforts be made to sterilize it beforehand. In the latter case it would have no resonance at all. It would be as if the seed of the parable protected itself from surrounding weeds by not germinating at all.[14]

Jesus always perceived with crystal clarity that reception, rejection, and comprehension of his words depended on the attitudes *already* existing in the hearts of his listeners with regard to the terms in which he expressed himself. That did not prompt him to invent an unheard-of language without resonances in order to communicate his message. He spoke like everyone else and was content to add only the following strain: "He who has *ears to hear* [= favorable preunderstanding], let him hear" (Mark 4:9,23; 7:16; also 4:12; 8:18). And he said that precisely when he was trying to carry through a vivid logic by means of parables, when he was trying to break down prejudices and clichés so that his message might be understood.

There is a second point about the hermeneutic circle that ties in closely with what we have just seen. Contrary to what some people think, the hermeneutic circle does not entail inevitable and total distortion. A specific preunderstanding may be the prerequisite for what is objectively the most thorough understanding of some message. Moreover, however prejudiced may be the approach to a person, text, or message, their meaning-world is not merely a passive victim. It has its own power to exert influence in turn on the preunderstanding that has initially gotten a hold over it, at least when something important is at stake.

It is clear, for example, that people can pose offbase questions to the gospel in such a way as to justify the exploitation of some human beings by others. But it is no less clear that the gospel, even when read from this distorted point of view, has its own solidity and is quite capable of protesting. It is not purely and simply distorted. It fights against that distortion and calls for a conversion, and the latter will become in turn a preunderstanding for a new reading and interpretation.

Thus I see no reason to be upset by the *circular* character of the interpretive method proposed by Bultmann for speaking meaningfully today about Jesus of Nazareth. While I disagree with him on specific points,[15] I think it is the one which best integrates, in principle, the present-day interest of the human being with the summons issued to us by the Absolute in Jesus.

To bring this methodological introduction to a close, I want to examine one particular objection raised about Bultmann in his effort to find some means to improve our christological understanding. He is criticized for having chosen *one* specific analysis among other possible ones: that of Heidegger in *Being and Time*.

Whether those who make it realize it or not, this objection is based on the supposition that Heidegger analyzes *one* type of human being and proposes *certain* approaches toward an authentic understanding of existence, that *his results* would then have to be compared with the parallel (?) existential analyses of such people as Sartre, Jaspers, and so forth. Bultmann himself may have laid himself open to this objection by practically ignoring the later Heidegger with his ontological problems.

I do not want to force my readers down the intricate and perhaps dead-end byways of Heidegger's thought. But the fact is that Bultmann minimized the universality that Heidegger was claiming for his analysis of existence, even as early as *Being and Time.*

Now Heidegger did not talk or write about christology. So I think it might be interesting to present the problem as it is presented by another theologian who also felt the influence of Heidegger: Karl Rahner. The latter significantly refers to his christological effort as "transcendental christology."[16]

My readers will not confuse *transcendental* with *transcendent,* I am sure. Since Kant it has become customary to give the label "transcendental" to any investigation of the *prerequisite conditions* that make possible a science, a given set of phenomena or problems, and so on. Logically then, the most salient characteristic of any transcendental thought or investigation is its *emptiness* vis-à-vis the concrete phenomena whose prerequisite conditions it is investigating.

As an example, let us consider Kant's *transcendental* esthetics (understood in its etymological sense as the faculty of sense knowledge). In it Kant studies the prerequisite conditions enabling me to say, for example: "It rained yesterday." For Kant, one of these prerequisite conditions is that my sense apparatus possesses *time* as an a priori form of all that it perceives. This has given rise to the mistake among beginners of calling Kant an idealist.[17] It is important to realize that for Kant the *datum*—it did or did not rain—does not proceed from the form *time.* I take it from my experience (a posteriori) or I find out from the weather service. In the same way the concrete measurements of my workbench do not proceed from the a priori form *space.* The forms that make sense cognitions possible are *empty* as such. The various data fit into them and thus are perceived.

In that sense I think that Rahner's use of the term "transcendental" for his christology is not wholly appropriate. Studying the conditions that make talk about Christ possible tells us nothing about Christ. That would be a *pre*christology at most. As we shall see, Rahner is really calling his christology "transcendental" in a different sense or for a different reason. It is his conviction that the bridge between the historical Jesus of the past and my present-day human interest in him is possible (prerequisite condition) "when humanity has reached the historical stage of a *transcendental anthropology* (don't forget this datum)."[18]

Rahner also states explicity that his aim is to bridge the gap between a human interest that claims to be correct and the historical concreteness of

Jesus: "A 'transcendental christology' presupposes a *mutual* understanding of conditioning and mediation that is given in human existence *as such* between the *necessary* on the transcendental level and the *concrete,* contingent historical."[19]

The concrete lies on the historical side, whereas human existence enters the encounter only "as such": with its necessary elements rather than its free and contingent elements. Here we see the emptiness—not to be equated with uselessness—of transcendental anthropology. Rahner again brings it out when he writes about this human being who enters into a relationship with the historical Jesus:

> The decisions of the practical reason and the relationship with a concrete human being, in their concreteness, can never be the object of a transcendental deduction, even though the understanding of these data is one of the functions of the transcendental reason.[20]

To grasp the point of these fairly esoteric remarks, we might recall some examples I gave in Volume I of data obtained by an anthropological "transcendental deduction." When I talked about the limitations on any human life and how it forced us to resort to referential witnesses to values in order to structure a meaning-world, I was talking about some of the prerequisite conditions underlying human existence. And the emptiness lies in the fact that this transcendental deduction does not tell us which witnesses are preferable, which faith we should hold. It only points up the necessity of faith as an anthropological dimension.[21]

Rahner is speaking in the same sense when he says that "a transcendental christology always starts off from the experiences that a human being has *in a constant and inevitable way.*"[22] In my opinion, Rahner here understands Heidegger, *Being and Time* in particular, better than does Bultmann. The latter searches *Being and Time* for a method that will concretely improve our existential preunderstanding and thus enable the summons of Jesus to penetrate us more deeply. That, to say the least, is a distortion of Heidegger's intention.

By this time my readers are probably itching to know whether a transcendental anthropology can or cannot provide the solid bridge we seek between the historical Jesus of Nazareth who summons us and the interests and problems that confront us acutely today. On the surface it seems that we are close to what we are after. But once again it turns out that our answer must be: no, it cannot.

Why? I have already indicated how worthwhile transcendental analysis of deduction can be. In setting forth the prerequisite conditions for our cognition to be possible on many fronts, it helps us to do away with misunderstandings and naive clichés. But it does not thereby lose the emptiness of its abstractness. We may say, for example, that *faith* is an anthropological dimension, that we encounter it in a transcendental analysis of human existence. But that does not tell us what sort of faith exactly we are dealing with. Indeed the very formulation of the issue tells us that we are dealing with *any* faith *whatsoever:* that of the criminal, the martyr, the rich, the poor, and so on.

Here we confront a trap that must be avoided at all cost and that Bultmann may have fallen into. A transcendental anthropology *seems* to be replete with concreteness and life in what it has to say about human existence. In reality, however, it is dealing in abstract existentialist *categories* (for which Heidegger uses the term *existenzial,* as opposed to *existenziell*).[23] We may think we are dealing with vivid, concrete terms when we hear Heidegger talk about "being towards death"[24] or Rahner talk about "the hope of an absolute savior."[25] But those terms are merely abstractions, open to concrete human attitudes that are not only different but often opposed to one another. Insofar as our present subject is concerned, those attitudes may close off access to Jesus as well as opening up access to him.

Those categories, as *transcendental* ones, were applicable and the same for both those who adhered to Jesus and those who rejected him. Rahner tells us that the hope of an absolute savior is unavoidable for the human being because it is a part of transcendental anthropology, a prerequisite condition for being human. In that case it would have to be present in the questions about Jesus raised by the Pharisees just as truly as in the questions raised by his disciples. But Jesus did not respond to the concrete hope of the former and did respond to the concrete hope of the latter. I am not suggesting that the hope of the latter is superior *because it ended up in faith.* What I am suggesting is that the example proves that transcendental anthropology offers *no* criterion to guide us in determining the correct approach to any personage of the past.[26] Rahner, however, would have us believe it does. The absence of a transcendental anthropology, he writes, entails a twofold risk. We may either view

the affirmations of traditional christology as mythological exaltations (in the worst sense) of certain historical happenings, or completely lack any criterion for distinguishing, in that christology, between that which is a genuine reality of faith and that which is an interpretation no longer capable of communicating to us today what faith seeks to express.[27]

So where does that leave us? Are we right back where we started? Let us get back to our methodology. What exactly have we been looking for? We have been looking for the bases of a *science:* christo*logy.* We have been looking for a scientific method, free of subjectivisms and ideologies, that would enable us to approach Jesus of Nazareth with sure and universal criteria. Is it really so strange that we have found every road blocked?

Perhaps my readers will now understand why I chose to call my effort here an antichristology. I am not proposing to offer a *logy* about the Anti-christ. Instead I am trying to offer an anti-logy about Christ. I am trying to free him from all the false pretensions of human beings, of Christians certainly, to grab hold of him, box him in universal categories, and thus strip him and his cross of their bite and scandal.

That does not mean, however, that I am trying to replace a scientific approach to Jesus with a *naive,* fundamentalist one.

I think that the only valid approach to Jesus of Nazareth is that of the New Testament. It entails a process of successive readings that start out from the concrete, historical interest he aroused in his own time and place and move on to the human problems of later times and our own present day. Those problems are bound up with *meaning-worlds that are radically akin to his* (by virtue of the values sought, not by virtue of confessional labels) and that are open, by existential logic, to the transcendent data brought by Jesus within his own historical coordinates.

Some readers might still prefer to use the term"christology," even for my effort here. In that case I would insist that only one kind of christology is valid and dovetails with the way Jesus himself posed issues. It is a christology that starts off from the historical data about Jesus and *multiplies* the readings of his message, each time *modifying* the *preunderstanding* that is brought to the next reading. A complete and finished christology, consisting of one single reading of all the (biblical and/or dogmatic) material having to do with Jesus of Nazareth, is a dead-end street, in my opinion. Indeed it is not Christian.

CHAPTER IV

Creating Gospels

Liberating Jesus from christologies that imprison him entails the ongoing task of creating gospels that are truly good news for our contemporaries, while still continuing to verify their *coherence* with the gospel that was preached in history by Jesus of Nazareth.

We do not want to talk to today's human beings about things that *should* matter to them; nor do we want to invent an important Jesus who never existed.

By its very nature, then, our effort to speak about Jesus of Nazareth in a meaningful, faithful, and relevant way is open-ended. The work of creating gospels that can be considered his word today is a multiple task that will continue to multiply our assignments. It ever remains partial, incomplete, and perishable, but it is not a hostage to chance or devoid of governing criteria. It means that we leave a parallel task for others to carry out today and tomorrow in different coordinates of time and space. That task will be carried out by people in the living church, the community that shoulders the responsibility of re-presenting Jesus today. And—why not?—by people outside the institutionalized church.

Now I thought it advisable to begin Volume II with a gospel or minigospel excerpted from Chapter IX of Leonardo Boff's *Pasión de Cristo*. Then I went back to methodology to see if it is coherent with the Jesus we know from history on the one hand, and our problems today on the other hand. This approach might surprise some readers in the light of my other remarks in this General Introduction. After all, I have insisted that we must begin with the interest that Jesus of Nazareth aroused in his own day, before people knew anything about his messianic or divine status, before the cross seemed even vaguely possible, and before the resurrection was even thinkable. Yet I myself began this volume with a present-day gospel in which all those interpretive keys were obviously present! Why?

Well, I have already indicated that we are indulging in sheer illusion if we pretend that we can go to the canonical Gospels and find an uninterpreted Jesus there. As if the Jesus of Mark or John had not already been put in some key to solve human problems. Those problems may have been closer in time to Jesus, but the fact remains that they were the takeoff point from which the evangelists sought to explore what Jesus was, said, and did. Even in the history they contain, the canonical Gospels utilize a procedure that no meaningful history can avoid. They project an interpretive hypothesis from our own world, from that which interests us, even though it is clear that the historical figure in question did not live through our set of problems—not in the same way, at least.

In starting off with a present-day *gospel*, then, I was trying to alert my readers, to call them to attention. I wanted them to start asking themselves questions, questions that tend to be covered up by the clichés of our culture, call it Christian or not.

To begin with, does that curious, present-day gospel have any meaning for them? Does it say anything of interest about the meaning of their lives, even though they may not believe it? Does it at least raise a question mark or a glimmer of hope in what seemed to be a barren desert?

Assuming that some readers may answer yes to those questions, I will say here that this and the remaining volumes in this series explore whether Boff's gospel has anything to do with the historical figure we can extract from the gospel narratives and other interpretations of Jesus. Using the available instruments of scholarly science, we will try to explore that historical figure in the Synoptic Gospels (Volume II). In the next volume we shall examine another interpretation of Jesus, that of Paul in his Letter to the Romans (Volume III), which bears witness to the multiple efforts of the New Testament writers to show why the person, message, and activity of Jesus of Nazareth has interest for human existence. That will pave the way for my effort to take a new look at Jesus of Nazareth in modern, evolutionary terms (Volume V), after we have examined one example of Christian spirituality from past history (Volume IV).

If I have been successful in my effort, readers may begin wherever they wish, wherever they feel drawn by their own interests. If an antichristology performs its function properly, Jesus of Nazareth should be able to speak very different languages. The manifold meaningfulness of his life and message for humanity should be clear and free to operate.

Part Two

THE HISTORICAL JESUS
OF THE SYNOPTICS

Introduction: A "History" of Jesus?

Readers interested in methodically recapturing the significance of Jesus need not try to grasp the whole panoply of scientific tools used by the professional historian for this task. Indeed if they wanted to verify for themselves everything connected with what is called the "historical Jesus," no introduction of this sort could provide them with the means to do it. To write a history based on the existing documents that would present Jesus as he was, or at least offer a faithful picture of his life and message, would require scholarly preparation akin to that provided by any university discipline.

Understanding the process followed by historiography in this matter is another question, however. There are certain general lines that can and should be comprehended in order to appreciate the bases for any history seeking to approach the figure of Jesus of Nazareth. Knowing these general lines will help one to understand the process of interpreting Jesus that takes place in every New Testament work and every historical realization of the community that assumes his tradition.

To begin with, consider the so-called *Synoptic* Gospels: Mark, Matthew, and Luke. Even though all the New Testament writings are already *interpretations* of Jesus deriving from faith in him, and even though we possess no neutral or "historical" document in our modern sense of the word, it is obvious that these three Gospels come closest to historical documents in our sense. At the same time, however, modern historical science (or historiography) must preserve the distance that separates the three Synoptics from Jesus himself, and that is not easy.

While Matthew's Gospel may be a possible exception, in all likelihood neither Mark nor Luke were direct witnesses of the events. They did not belong to the group of Twelve who accompanied Jesus during his public life in a more intimate way (as opposed to other disciples whose contact with Jesus was more superficial or intermittent). That public life is what the three Synoptics relate, the period extending from Jesus' baptism to his passion. In the more profuse accounts (Luke and Matthew) we also find something like an appendix dealing with his infancy, and in all of them we also find another one dealing with the events that go from the death of Jesus to his ascension (Acts 1:22).[1] As far as proximity to Jesus' public life is concerned, Luke presents himself as a person who has undertaken a serious investigation among the eyewitnesses (Luke 1:1–2). Matthew is another story. Even if we take it as the name of one of the Twelve, it does not seem that that Matthew is the author of the first Gospel as it has come down to us in its final form.

Now the fact that the three Synoptic Gospels may not be directly or entirely the work of eyewitnesses does not mean that they are unreliable witnesses. But it does underline the need for caution, even if those narratives were the work of authors who directly accompanied Jesus. The fact is that even our witnesses interpret what they remember in the light of the final, decisive events.

That is only human, and it has happened with all the heroes of history. When we know the trajectory of a meaningful life and its final outcome, our memory unwittingly makes a selection of the data dealing with the person's past. We recall, or recall more vividly, the things which seemed to point towards the final outcome and thus give greater coherence to the whole life of the person: in other words, the things that fit in with the interpretation based on the final outcome. Words or deeds of ambiguous or casual significance are unwittingly accommodated to this line of force. They become part of the general orientation, which operates backwards in terms of time. One discovers it at the end and then projects it back to the beginning, retrojects it.

Luke informs us that Jesus gave this warning to the Twelve:

> Behold, we are going up to Jerusalem, and everything that is written of the Son of man by the prophets will be accomplished. For he will be delivered to the Gentiles, and will be mocked and shamefully treated and spit upon; they will scourge him and kill him, and on the third day he will rise [Luke 18:31–33].

Then the evangelist adds this confession: "But they understood none of these things; this saying was hid from them, and they did not grasp what was said" (Luke 18:34).[2] Logically enough, this obscurity was dispelled by the passion and resurrection of Jesus. But here is where our problem comes in. The historian has every right to think that such a precise, detailed prediction of future events must not have taken place in that manner. Remember *from the standpoint* of the passion and resurrection, some remark of Jesus about the danger he would face in Jerusalem could have been selected by the memory as a sign of the coherence of his life and then expressed in terms suggested by the later events themselves, when there was no longer any recollection of Jesus' exact words at the time.

Quite aside from the fact that the evangelists do not claim to be writing history books, it would also be anachronistic to demand the same sort of historical fidelity in Jesus' time that scholarship expects today. The *historians* of antiquity did not think they were sinning against historical truth when they put discourses in the mouths of the protagonists of important events: discourses that were never uttered but that were capable of explaining the import of what was going on. It is obviously a literary procedure or device. Matthew, for example, clearly interrupts the logic of a discourse by Jesus on the sign that Jonah's preaching constituted for the inhabitants of

Nineveh. He attributes to Jesus the intention of offering his own resurrection as a sign to his contemporaries (see Matt. 12:40, cf. Luke 11:30–32 and John 1 and 3).

I

Here we have the *first* criterion of the three that we must now examine. We see that the *postpaschal* is introduced into the *prepaschal* in the gospel narratives. The postpaschal interpretation unconsciously tinges the events that preceded the paschal events (passion, death, resurrection of Jesus). So it should not surprise us that modern historiography, placed in the service of exegesis and theology, attempts as best it can to recover and preserve the prepaschal as it was, without those inroads of meaning based on the already known outcome and projected back into the past by memory.

Now this criterion does not permit us to reject a part of the Synoptics as devoid of importance or veracity. The interpretation, too, is a historical fact. It is a matter of finding a criterion of trustworthiness or reliability, or better, of priority in the reliability of the *facts* narrated. The historical portrait of Jesus—and future christologies as well—must be based on those facts or events which are more certain and then must proceed from that nucleus. And logically what seems more certain, on the basis of the evangelical testimony itself, is what was attributed to Jesus *without reference* to his passion, death, and resurrection.

Perhaps the most obvious use of this criterion has to do with Jesus' alleged predictions.[3] They could be *ex eventu*, to use the jargon of exegesis: that is, placed in his mouth *after* the events in question had occurred and become known to the evangelists. Note once again that it is not a matter of deliberately trying to falsify history. Some vague pronouncement of Jesus could have been illuminated by future events and thus consigned to memory. In later chapters I will deal with two classes of predictions made by Jesus that are central to understanding his historical destiny: those relating to his passion and those relating to the irruption, the breaking in, of the kingdom of God.[4] A more important task here in this introductory section is to apply the criterion, by way of example, to a point that is crucial for understanding the real start of Jesus' ministry.

I have already indicated that one fact is extraordinary and calls for explanation: that is, that an ordinary person, without any authority, should stir the interest and passions of his contemporaries with his message. It is true, of course, as I shall try to show in later chapters, that Jesus' preaching touched upon very concrete aspects of the economic, social, and political situation in the Israel of his day. But that would not be enough to unleash a movement of such (dangerous) breadth and scope as the movement unleashed by Jesus. It should also be added that there were latent expectations in Israel that somehow converged with Jesus' preaching and helped to set it in relief. I refer to the varied and vague *messianic* expectations existing at the time of Jesus.

After the paschal events the interpretation of Jesus offered by the evangelists—speaking in general here—is that he is the *Messiah* of Israel, the one who fulfills the long hopes of that people in accordance with the promises of the ancient prophets. Everything leads us to believe that this identification was made not only by the Twelve and Jesus' other "disciples" but also, in however superficial and dubious a manner, by the multitude itself before Jesus' death.

Among those who followed Jesus to the end, then, we find a faith that they had "found the Messiah" (John 1:41). It is expressed in equivalent terms in other parts of John's first chapter: "him of whom Moses in the law and also the prophets wrote" (1:45); "the Son of God . . . the King of Israel" (1:49); "the Son of man" (1:51). This faith, which probably coincides with the end of Jesus' ministry in Galilee, enters a crisis with the death of Jesus on the cross (see Luke 24:21, "We had hoped that he was the one to redeem Israel [the Messiah]"), then recovers and is clinched definitively with his followers' experiences of his resurrection (see Rom. 1:4, "designated Son of God [Messiah] in power . . . by his resurrection from the dead").

In other words, we have sufficient data, even outside of the New Testament, to think that the messiahship of Jesus was already a prepaschal interpretation. Indeed the reliability of that datum is bolstered by the fact that we are told that belief in this messiahship was eclipsed by the events surrounding Jesus' passion. We know, you see, that the idea of a Messiah was then current in the milieu of Israel. And we also know that it was not associated with the idea of death and resurrection, but rather with the arrival of the kingdom ("reign," to be more exact) of God that would bring about the liberation of Israel.

Now, speaking in general, we find in the Synoptic Gospels *four lines of interpretation* regarding the messianic expectations of Israel. The evangelists have them converge in Jesus, at least after the paschal events. But the fact that Jesus was recognized by his disciples and even the multitude as the Messiah does not necessarily mean that he was so recognized in terms of the four lines of interpretation. Some of them might have been prepaschal, others might have formed part of a postpaschal interpretation.

For the sake of clarity we might describe these four lines of interpretation as follows: (1) the prophet of the last days, or, eschatological prophet: a new Moses or Elijah come back to earth; (2) the Son of David, or king of Israel; (3) the Suffering Servant of Yahweh; and (4) the Son of Man.

The Synoptic Gospels, John's Gospel (very reliable on geographical, historical, and cultural data), and the Jewish literature of the day offer us abundant testimony on the existence of these expectations. Moreover, all of them have a more or less vague biblical foundation even though they may be intertwined with imaginative, legendary, and at times contradictory elements, particularly in their popular forms.[5]

Before we examine them one by one, let us note one important point. The Gospels make clear to us not only that Jesus was interpreted in terms of those four strands of messianic hope. They also claim that Jesus applied those terms to himself more or less cryptically, or that he allowed people to apply those categories to him.

In Matthew (17:12-13), for example, Jesus is the *eschatological prophet*, who is preceded by Elijah: " 'I tell you that Elijah has already come, and they did not know him, but did to him whatever they pleased. So also the Son of man will suffer at their hands.' Then the disciples understood that he was speaking to them of John the Baptist." In Luke, which omits the cited text of Matthew, Jesus himself is the new Elijah, as it were. That is how he explains his refusal to work miracles in Nazareth, his home area: "But in truth, I tell you, there were many widows in Israel in the days of Elijah. . .and Elijah was sent to none of them but only to Zarephath, in the land of Sidon, to a woman who was a widow" (Luke 4:25-26).

Jesus implicitly assumes the *Son of David* interpretation in dealing with the blind beggar. The latter cries out: "Jesus, Son of David, have mercy on me!" Jesus heals him and says: "Go your way; your faith has made you well" (Mark 10:47-48, 52). Something similar takes place with Jesus' triumphant entry into Jerusalem.

Insofar as the *Servant of Yahweh* is concerned, Luke narrates what happened when Jesus went to the synagogue in Nazareth and was given the Book of Isaiah to read:

He opened the book and found the place where it was written: "The Spirit of the Lord is upon me, because he has anointed me to preach good news to the poor. He has sent me to proclaim release to the captives and recovering of sight to the blind, to set at liberty those who are oppressed, to proclaim the acceptable year of the Lord." And he closed the book, and gave it back to the attendant, and sat down; and the eyes of all in the synagogue were fixed on him. And he began to say to them: "Today this scripture has been fulfilled in your hearing" [Luke 4:17-21].

This passage from the Book of Isaiah (61:1-2) is commonly added to the classic passages that describe the messianic function of the Suffering Servant of Yahweh (such as Isa. 42:1-3, reproduced in Matt. 12:18-21).

Finally, both the Synoptics and John tell us that Jesus continually referred to himself as the *Son of Man*. That would be equivalent to assuming the hopes recorded in the prophecy of Daniel (7:13-14) about a figure, "like a son of man," coming with the clouds of heaven to be given eternal dominion.

Now it seems perfectly obvious that Jesus must have gradually developed some coherent awareness of his mission, if he did not possess it from the very start. And for that he most probably made use of the categories in which his contemporaries expressed the messianic and eschatological hopes of Israel, even though he may have corrected them in various ways.

Our first criterion, which distinguishes between the prepaschal and the postpaschal in the redaction of the Gospels, seeks to establish three things: (1) Did Jesus' contemporaries use any of those messianic categories to interpret his words and deeds? (2) Could Jesus himself have used one or more of those categories to comprehend his own mission? And, in any case, (3) In what way did the paschal events retroject those categories on the prepaschal Jesus?

From this viewpoint we can see a difference between the first two lines of messianic expectation (the eschatological prophet and the Son of David) on the one hand, and the latter two (the Servant of Yahweh and the Son of Man) on the other hand. The first two do not point out the personal destiny of the messianic figure; the latter two indicate respectively a glorious destiny and a sorrow-laden one. Hence, speaking in general terms and in principle, we can classify the first two lines of interpretation as prepaschal and the latter two lines of interpretation as postpaschal.

Remembering that this is merely a sample application of our first criterion of historical reliability, let us begin by studying the latter two interpretations or traditions, the two that are most dependent on the paschal events.

1. The tradition of a Messiah embodied in the figure mentioned in certain passages of Deutero-Isaiah is well known throughout the New Testament. Those passages talk about a *Servant of Yahweh* who suffers for the sins of his people and liberates the latter from their sins by his death.

A few points are in order here, however. Today we talk about the Servant of Yahweh as if it were some messianic personage discussed by four separate poems in the text of Isaiah (42:1-9; 49:1-6; 50:4-11; 52:13-53). But it is highly uncertain that the exegesis of Jesus' own day would have separated those passages from the rest of the Book of Isaiah. What is more, historians rightly point out that the conception of a suffering and executed Messiah was not part of the messianic expectations of that era. In that precise sense it would be a Christian creation.

Now if that is indeed the case, Jesus could easily have appropriated for himself those passages in Isaiah we regard as part of the complex dealing with the Servant of Yahweh, without it necessarily meaning that he identified himself with that mysterious figure and any messianic assumptions attached to the latter. Hence there is no reason why Jesus' allusions to Isaiah—to Isaiah 42:7 in Luke 4:18, for example—could not be prepaschal.

We arrive at the paschal events, however, and the panorama changes—although not immediately. When confronted with the suffering and death of Jesus, for example, it is quite obvious that his disciples did not think of any sort of messianic accomplishment such as that supposedly described in the poems dealing with the Servant of Yahweh. It is the resurrection, and only that, that alters their reading of the Old Testament. Their postpaschal certainty about Jesus' messiahship prompts them to look in the familiar Scriptures for some explanation that will reconcile messiahship with what actually happened. Take Luke's comment about the disciples on the road to Emmaus and their encounter with the risen Jesus: "Then he opened their minds to understand *the scriptures*" (Luke 24:45). We can assume, without fear of error, that this comment alludes precisely to their discovery of the messianic figure of the Servant of Yahweh in Isaiah. Consider the question put earlier to them by their mysterious companion: "Was it not necessary that the Christ should suffer these things and enter into his glory?" (Luke 24:26). It clearly points up how far removed from their thinking was a messianic tradition entailing suffering and immolation, how only the resurrection called their attention to certain passages in Isaiah that we today see as having an obvious relation to Jesus.

Thus the disciples must somehow have come to notice the specific cast of the Deutero-Isaian poems depicting this figure, as well as the latter's messianic character. And they began to notice also how those texts dovetailed remarkably with the sorrowful events of Jesus' passion. So much so, indeed, that the gospel narratives may have accentuated the resemblance vis-à-vis such passages as the following: "I give my back to the smiters, and my cheeks to those who pulled out my beard; I hid not my face from shame and spitting" (Isa. 50:6).

Once Pentecost came and the first Christian community was established, we find that the tradition of the Suffering Servant of Yahweh does not seem to play a very important role in polemics with the Jews about the messiahship of Jesus. So we gather from what Luke has to say in the Acts of the Apostles.[6] The servant poems are cited only once in those debates (Acts 13:47), and there is no association with the sufferings of Jesus' passion and crucifixion.

This contrasts sharply with what happened in the early New Testament church. It is not going too far to say that the tradition of the Suffering Servant was *the* messianic tradition par excellence for interpreting the destiny of Jesus of Nazareth. We can see this in the Pauline school (see Rom. 3:26; 4:25; 8:31-33; Gal. 1:15; 3:13; 2 Cor. 5:21; Col. 2:15; Phil. 2:8, 11; Heb. 4:12; 1 Peter 2:22, 24-25) and in the Johannine school (see John 1:29, 32-34; 3:11; 8:12, 32, 45; Rev. 1:16; 19:15). Both shift the reason for Jesus' death from the (political) antagonism triggered by his preaching to a divine plan wherein suffering is the price that must be paid for the sins of Israel, and of human beings in general, in order to win their redemption or liberation. Thus the killers of Jesus become mere executors of a divine plan of expiatory and redemptive sacrifice. This will become a theme of the New Testament authors[7] and the central interpretation of Christ's death in the early church.

At the source of this clearly postpaschal interpretation are the poems about the Servant of Yahweh, especially passages like this one:

Yet it was our griefs he bore, our sorrows he endured. . .he was wounded for our transgressions, crushed for our faults; he endured the chastisement that brings us peace, and with his stripes we have been healed. . . . Yahweh laid on him the guilt of us all. . . . If he gives himself up in expiation, he will see offspring and lengthen his days; what is pleasing to Yahweh will find fulfillment by his hand [Isa. 53:4-6, 10; Segundo text translated].

From this postpaschal development we can see the theme of the Servant of Yahweh gradually making its way—through Matthew's Gospel especially (see Matt. 26:27; 27:30, 38)—into the events immediately preceding the paschal happenings.

And it goes further than that, even though we cannot be fully sure about many instances. The theme is retrojected into episodes where theological intentions may well go above and beyond narrative purposes. In the baptism of Jesus, for example, the divine voice from above uses words addressed to the Servant (Mark 1:11 and par.). Even further back, we find traces of this tradition in the infancy narratives, particularly in the canticle of Simeon (Luke 2:32; see Isa. 42:6; 49:6).

2. There are serious exegetical difficulties with the messianic tradition of the *Son of Man* in the Synoptic Gospels. On the one hand one of the most certain prepaschal data is that Jesus did use that expression as the subject—in the third person—of many verbs. What we cannot be sure about when reading the Synoptics today, however, is that we have the original form in which Jesus himself used the expression. According to the Synoptics, Jesus employs it as a rather curious substitute for the first person singular ("I"). In Matthew we read: "Who do men say that the *Son of man* is? . . . But who do you say that *I* am?" (Matt. 16:13, 15). Luke simply uses "I" in both cases: "Who do the people say that I am? . . . But who do you say that I am?" (Luke 9:18, 20).

Now if this is the original form, logic compels us to conclude that "Son of Man" could not be an expression recognized as a messianic title by Jesus' listeners. This goes against the view of the majority of exegetes. But the point made by Léon-Dufour is obvious in Mark, and clear though less obvious in Matthew and Luke: "Before being recognized as Son of God [Messiah] at the moment of his death, Jesus, who calls himself 'the Son' or 'the Son of Man,' *deliberately hides his messianic identity*" (Léon-Dufour 1963, 182).[8] Hence he cannot possibly be adverting to it every time he identifies himself as the Son of Man.[9]

However, there is an even more complicated hypothesis about the expression "Son of Man." On the lips of Jesus it could have really designated a third person, a definitely messianic figure distinct from Jesus himself. Note, for example, this statement by Jesus: "For whoever is ashamed of *me* and *my* words . . . of him will the *Son of man* also be ashamed when he comes" (Mark 8:38).[10] This hypothesis claims that the identification of Jesus with the Messiah in the postpaschal redaction of the Synoptics necessitated the identification of Jesus with the Son of Man as well. This accounts for the use of the expression as a synonym for "I" (see Matt. 10:32–33, par. text of the Markan one cited above).

It is curious, however, that the majority of exegetes maintaining this hypothesis do not perceive the contradiction they are falling into by its use, the very contradiction they had hoped to avoid. It is impossible to assume that the gospel redactors were so naive that they did not see how this would run counter to their own assertions. If they permitted Jesus to use "I" or a definitely *messianic title* like the "Son of Man" indiscriminately, that would go against their own assertions that the prepaschal Jesus never proclaimed himself to be the Messiah or wanted to be recognized publicly as such. At the very least we can agree with this comment in the Nueva Biblia Española: "It is doubtful that the expression was interpreted as a messianic title by Jesus' listeners; it never evokes opposition or even curiosity."[11]

Here again, as with the messianic tradition of the Servant of Yahweh, the paschal events change the panorama. And particularly important are the appearances of the resurrected one in his new "glorious body" (as Paul puts it).

It is certainly true that Jesus does not appear to them on the clouds of heaven, as the prophecy of Daniel about the figure of the Son of Man seems to promise. But with his resurrection Jesus attains what might be considered the starting point for such a coming. The (apocryphal) ending of Mark bears witness to this understanding when it tells us: "So then the Lord Jesus, after he had spoken to them, was taken up *into heaven* and sat down at the right hand of God" (Mark 16:19). Luke sees Jesus' ascension in the same way (Luke 24:51), and he adds: "and *a cloud* took him out of their sight" (Acts 1:9). The postpaschal interpretation of Jesus as the Messiah, as Daniel's Son of Man, now comes forcefully to the forefront: "This Jesus, who was taken up from you into heaven, *will come in the same way* as you saw him go into heaven" (Acts 1:11). He will come, that is, among the clouds.

The paschal happenings, you see, do present Jesus as the expected Messiah, but they do not describe him in terms of the glorious coming of a Son of Man. That may well be why the messianic prophecy of Daniel does not play a major role in the debates of the first Christian community with its Jewish contemporaries.

It does have importance, however, in resolving a theological problem: the disproportion between the kingdom of God on earth that Jesus brings, or claims to bring, and the relatively small number of his appearances, which are restricted to a core of his own disciples. What happens is that the glorious second coming of Jesus supplants the imminent establishment of the kingdom of God on earth, which had been preached by the prepaschal Jesus. The term "kingdom of God" begins to fade from the New Testament (see 1 Cor. 1:8; 15:23; 1 Thess. 5:1; Rev. 22:17, 20; etc.), and the process is even evident in the Synoptic Gospels themselves. In short, the postpaschal eschatology associated with the expected coming of Daniel's Son of Man is retrojected on the prepaschal Jesus, particularly near the closing events of his life. There we find promises of a *second coming*, and definitely "on the clouds of heaven."

In the eschatological discourse of Jesus according to Q, we read, "Then if any one says to you, 'Lo, *here* is the Christ!' or '*There* he is!' do not believe it. . . . For as the lightning comes from the east and shines as far as the west, so will be *the coming of the Son of man . . .* and they will see *the Son of man coming on the clouds of heaven* with power and great glory" (Matt. 24:23,

27, 30; see Luke 17:24). It is worth noting that Luke records an almost identical saying of Jesus in the verses immediately preceding his version of the eschatological discourse, but it concerns the coming of the kingdom of God rather than the (second) coming of the Son of Man: "The *kingdom of God* is not *coming* with signs to be observed; nor will they say, 'Lo, *here* it is!' or '*There!*' for behold, the kingdom of God is in the midst of you" (Luke 17:20-21).

When the high priest asks Jesus about his messiahship, Jesus again responds by using the expression "Son of Man" in a sense that is obviously messianic and dependent on Daniel: ". . . and *you will see the Son of man* seated at the right hand of Power, and *coming with the clouds of heaven*" (Mark 14:62; Matt. 26:64). We can assume that this usage originated in a postpaschal and messianic interpretation of an expression that the prepaschal Jesus employed *without that sense*.

There remains for us to study the two most popular strains of messianic interpretation: one concerning the new king, the Son of David (his house or dynasty) and the other concerning the prophet of the last days (Moses or Elijah). As I indicated earlier, they are indefinite about the fate of the messianic figure in question. Hence they are the most likely to have been used before the paschal events with reference to Jesus, both by the people and by Jesus himself in trying to comprehend his mission.

These two lines of hope mingle religious elements with political elements. Indeed the difference between them may lie precisely in the dose of each element to be found in the mixture. The Son of David tradition alludes more to the political aspect. The tradition of the eschatological prophet shows a predominance of religious elements. Let us begin with the former.

3. According to the tripartite Synoptic tradition, Jesus twice lets himself be called the Son of David without retort. One occasion is nothing less than his triumphant entry into Jerusalem (Mark 10:46-52; 11:9-10 and par.). Matthew relates three more instances (Matt. 9:27-31; 15:21-28; 12:22-23).

Thus there seems to be no good reason why we should reject this conclusion:

> It is an established fact, it seems to me, that the Jewish people—at least the people of Jerusalem and Judea—who witnessed the deeds of Jesus and who commonly pictured the Messiah in the lineaments of a ruler of Davidic descent, recognized the messiahship of Jesus in hailing him as the Son of David [Descamps 1954, 66].

And what are we to think about Jesus himself? It is a meaningful question for several reasons. After all, Jesus himself seems to accept that title despite its inescapably political connotations. Indeed he seems to stimulate those hopes actively by phrasing his own preaching in terms of the arrival of a *kingdom* wherein he is the central and decisive figure.

Before we answer the question, however, we must make certain things clear about the very notion of the "Messiah." In *He That Cometh*,[12] Mowinckel rightly points out something about the term's use in the Bible outside the New Testament. "Messiah" (meaning "anointed" in Hebrew) is applied more to the kings of Israel, all of whom were anointed for that office, than to any figure who was supposed to come in the future to inaugurate the final age. So in the Old Testament the term does not usually have any eschatological connotation.

Consider the prophecies that helped to nurture the messianic hopes of Israel once the monarchy was destroyed and for centuries after the Exile. In origin they were prophecies made during the age of the monarchy while the Davidic dynasty was still reigning. In that context they referred to the appearance of an extraordinary king akin to the founder of that royal dynasty (see Isa. 11:1–9). Immediately after the Exile, the prophets Haggai and Zechariah place their hopes for the restoration of the monarchy (and the consequent independence of Israel) on a descendant of David, Zerubbabel (see Hag. 2:20f.; Zech. 4:6f.).

Through the long centuries following the Exile, it became obvious and disturbing that a "political" policy of Yahweh with regard to Israel seemed notably absent. The Jewish people ceased to be a nation and to have a monarchy of its own. The descendants of David disappeared into the population mix.

It was then, says Mowinckel, that there arose a messianic hope in the sense we mean today, the sense already evident in the New Testament. Both in and outside the Bible the sense of despair over historical calculations becomes increasingly linked up with the breaking-in of the final age. That age is to be inaugurated by Yahweh himself through the messianic king of the Davidic house.

The least we can say is that Jesus was disconcertingly ambiguous with respect to that particular messianic tradition. We shall see why in later chapters. He did not lend himself to its *immediate* political consequences along Zealot lines, because it does seem that the crowd really wanted to make him king (according to John 6:14–15). On the other hand he never clearly dispelled its ambiguity.[13]

The best proof of this is the fact that the close circle of people around him, who benefited from his clearest explanations, thought right up to the end that in Jesus they would see literally realized the full restoration of the monarchy and the independence of Israel. Everything that the Synoptics tell us about the misunderstandings of the apostles, the leaders of the Christian churches by the time the evangelists were composing their works, bears the clear mark of being prepaschal.

We are told, for example, that shortly before the paschal events the sons of Zebedee approached Jesus to ask for nothing less than the two highest posts in his kingdom under him. They wanted to sit to the right and left of him when he was on his royal throne. It is clear that this request betokens ambition, or lack of understanding, or both. Luke, you see, often tries to downplay negative features of the Twelve, and in this case he completely leaves out this passage from the Markan tradition, to which Luke is generally faithful. Matthew attributes the request to the mother of James and John rather than to the two apostles (see Mark 10:35-37; Matt. 20:20-21).

This misunderstanding continues right through the paschal events. Luke himself reports the question that the apostles asked Jesus on the very day of his ascension into heaven: "Lord, will you at this time restore the kingdom of Israel?" (Acts 1:6).

In any case, the paschal events eventually cleared away all traces of ambiguity. Two things became clear: (1) The kingdom preached by Jesus had nothing to do with the political independence of Israel or the restoration of its own monarchy; it had to do mainly with the appearance of an absolute power over death, made manifest in the risen one by the paschal experiences; (2) This power constituted Jesus of Nazareth as the Messiah, the expected Son of David.

The first fact is undoubtedly the reason why the term "kingdom of God" (or "kingdom of heaven"), used so typically by the prepaschal Jesus, practically disappears from the rest of the New Testament. With its ambiguity it was no longer necessary, and it was too closely bound up with the monarchy of Israel; after A.D. 70, that Israel would be wiped off the map of the world. It now seemed preferable to use other terms for expressing the same reality.

By contrast, the title *Son of David* now became a crucial expression of Jesus' messianism in postpaschal debates within the Jewish world. The fundamental issue was not the restoration of David's throne, of course, but the resurrection of Jesus. It might be argued that his resurrection hardly seems to have much connection with the messianic hopes invested in the Son of David. The connecting link in this case is the fact that in Jesus' day the redaction of the Psalms was commonly attributed to David himself. What David says of himself in the Psalms seemed to be more than fulfilled in that *other* David, his successor and superior son: Jesus. It is very possible that Jesus himself initiated that line of argument (see Mark 12:35-37), but it might also be a retrojection from the postpaschal period. In any case, we can see the postpaschal use of Psalms to prove the messiahship of Jesus as the Son of David: for example, Psalm 16 (Acts 2:25); Psalm 132 (Acts 2:29-30); Psalm 110 (Acts 2:34-36); Psalm 2 (Acts 4:25-27); and Psalm 89 (Acts 13:22-23).

Moving back from the paschal events, and even granting the great historical reliability of the title "king of the Jews" being affixed to Jesus' cross (according to all four evangelists), we can say that Jesus' discussion with Pilate about whether he was really a king may well constitute a retrojection of this postpaschal messianic interpretation. This would be all the more likely if it included the distinction that Jesus makes (according to John 19:33-37) between two kingdoms deriving from two different powers. Such a distinction was clearly comprehended only after the paschal events, as we have already seen.

The messiahship of Jesus as the Son of David is pushed further back from the postpaschal period. On a level that is already theological, we find it in the efforts of Matthew and Luke to point up, in their respective genealogies of Jesus, his direct descent from David through Joseph (see Matt. 1:1–7; Luke 3:23–38). And when the same two evangelists redact their infancy narratives, they often point up the Davidic descent of Jesus. That literary genre is much further removed from modern historiography than the genre used to narrate the public life of Jesus. It allows the evangelists to be freer with the facts, and hence it is probably responsible for such narrative details as the following: the birth of Jesus in Bethlehem, David's native city; the query of the Magi from the East about the new king; and so forth. When the scribes and priests meet to consider the Magi's query, they conclude that Bethlehem is the appropriate place to find the newborn king on the basis of a prophecy that alludes to the birth of David.

4. The messianic tradition dealing with the *eschatological prophet* is not riddled with the ambiguities surrounding the tradition just discussed. It offers greater assurances of having been utilized in the prepaschal period.

Aside from the references already cited, it is worth noting what happens in the Galilean crisis. The ambiguity of Jesus' royal messianism is resolved by resorting to a messianism of the prophetic type: "And they told him, 'John the Baptist; and others say, Elijah; and others one of the prophets' " (Mark 8:28 and par.). Something similar occurs after he enters triumphantly into Jerusalem and is hailed as the Son of David. His subsequent behavior causes confusion on this matter, but the authorities are still afraid to arrest him: "They feared the multitudes, because they held him to be a *prophet*" (Matt. 21:46).

And the prophetism in question is specifically messianic, it should be noted. Let us take a closer look.

The authority of the monarchy in Israel was always religiously ambiguous because it could appeal to "reason of state" to push through its aims. The tendency is clear as early as the time of Saul. Until the time of the Exile, or the return from it, the prophets of Israel exercised the functions of religious and political criticism vis-à-vis monarchical authority. Theirs was a religious function because they watched over the purity of the Yahwist faith and because they, even more visibly than the royal power, represented a *power* deriving from Yahweh alone. Even though it was not always easy to distinguish the true prophets from the false ones (see Deut. 18:19–22), coming face to face with one of the former meant making a choice *vis-à-vis Yahweh*. The prophets also exercised a political function. Before the Exile they stood as a counterweight to civil authority, pointing up the latter's limitations, omissions, and crimes. That political function was not exercised solely in the area of foreign affairs or international politics; it was also exercised in the area of domestic affairs and politics, in defense of the marginalized and the forgotten.

More attention has been paid to the political function of the prophets in the international arena, where they reminded Israel of its duties vis-à-vis non-Yahwist nations. But the fact is that their political function in domestic affairs was much more important and developed. With the establishment of the monarchy, in fact, equilibrium and social equality among the Israelites rapidly crumbled. So the prophet Samuel had warned them—in what may well be a prophecy *after the event*—when he established the monarchy at the people's behest (see 1 Sam. 8:10–18).[14]

It is symptomatic that prophecy seems to fade out in Israel after the feeble and futile effort to restore the nation when the period of the Exile is over. It is almost as if prophets no longer made sense vis-à-vis foreign rulers who did not respect Yahweh. Moreover, as the old political context faded, a new kind of literature took shape in Israel. Its theme was better suited to Israel's status as a country under foreign domination: that is, the quest for "wisdom," a term which we might better translate as "holiness" or "the spiritual life."

In this sapiential literature we see interest shown in the problems of individuals and their relationship with God, whose providence is assumed to be just. It is definitely depoliticized, at least compared with the earlier thrust of the prophets. History loses the central value it had in an earlier day, when it served as the basis for the activity of prophets. Repeatedly we hear the nostalgic lament that the voice of Yahweh can no longer be heard through his most characteristic representatives.

But the hope does not die. It is "eschatologized": that is, shifted to the end of time. Prophecy will then return to Israel to prepare and usher in the *eschaton*. But how exactly is this turn of events to be envisioned? For some time both informed and popular readings of the Bible had focused on two scriptural passages that could be interpreted as promises of this return of prophecy in the last days. One was a passage in the Book of Deuteronomy that spoke of the coming of a prophet like Moses, who would finally be heeded (Deut. 18:15, 18). The other concerned the return of Elijah, who had been carried up alive into heaven by a chariot of fire (2 Kings 2:11) and thus reserved by God for later purposes.

These hopes were very vague in many respects. I mention only Moses and Elijah here because the image of the eschatological prophet (either the precursor of the Messiah or the Messiah himself) generally centered around those two figures. But this event of the last days was also equated with the return of one or another of the great prophets of Israel. The basic content of the hope was clear in any case: God would *visit* the people of Israel again, after the long absence of prophetism.

One thing seems historically certain. Right around the time of interest to us here, that expectation was heightened by the appearance of various figures, including John the Baptist and Jesus of Nazareth. And one eminently reliable historical datum is that both of them, from the very start, made people wonder if they might not be seeing the eschatological prophet promised by God in one form or another.

There seems to be no doubt that the populace in Galilee and Judea sensed that Yahweh's long silence in prophecy had come to an end with Jesus. Luke is the only Synoptic writer to narrate the resurrection of the son of the widow of Nain, an incident very similar to one involving Elijah (1 Kings 17:17-23). And he then recounts the reaction of the people: "Fear seized them all, and they glorified God, saying, 'A *great prophet* has arisen among us!' and 'God *has visited* his people!' " (Luke 7:16).

Moreover, Jesus gives his disciples a mission similar and complementary to his, thus assimilating them to the extinct line of ancient prophets (see Matt. 5:12; Luke 6:23, 26).

To sum up: the attribution of this particular messianic tradition to Jesus of Nazareth by the multitude, his disciples, and Jesus himself seems clearly prepaschal, even though Jesus himself consistently covers it under what has come to be called the "messianic secret."

Just as many prepaschal data dovetail with this tradition, so we do not notice any blatant change when we come to the paschal events. The crisis of the cross has no specific relationship with the eschatological prophet, but it does with the common fate of prophets. The resurrection becomes the divine endorsement of Jesus as the eschatological prophet, the inaugurator of the last days: the Messiah.

In debates with the Jews about the Messiah, for example, the disciples make express use of the divine promise in Deuteronomy to send a prophet like Moses. In Peter's second address to the people, the idea of Jesus' second coming is linked up with his first. He calls the people to conversion so that God

> may send the Messiah designated for you, Jesus, who is to stay in heaven until the time of universal restoration, of which God spoke through his holy prophets. As Moses said: "The Lord God will raise up for you *a prophet like me* from among your own kinsmen; pay heed to everything he tells you" [Acts 3:20-22; see also Acts 7:37; Segundo text translated].

If we examine the possible retrojection of this particular messianic tradition into the prepaschal narratives, we find various stages of the process in the redaction of the Gospels. Moreover, the main lines of that tradition (dealing with Moses and Elijah) sometimes show up together and sometimes are separate. The essential aim is to show that Jesus, in one form or another, is the messianic prophet of the last days.

The first stage is evident in all three Synoptics. An account of the transfiguration of Jesus on the mountain top (a new Sinai?) is inserted among the prepaschal events. The similarities with the appearances of the risen Jesus, and particularly with his "glorified body," has prompted many exegetes to conclude that a paschal experience has here been shifted to the prepaschal period by the evangelists. That may be the case, or it may be a miraculous, preliminary glimpse of the future (eschatological) glory of Jesus. The main point is that the gospel *interpretation* clearly derives from a postpaschal understanding. Consider one item of undeniable theological value: the transfigured Jesus appears in conversation with *Elijah* and *Moses* (Mark 9:4 and par.). Considering all the other possible candidates (Daniel, Isaiah, David, etc.), we can readily grasp the intention and import of the evangelists in recording this essentially postpaschal event.

A second stage is evident in the episode of Jesus' temptations in the desert, which is narrated by the three Synoptic Gospels. Here again the literary genre is quite different from that employed in the story of his public ministry. The forty days may symbolize the forty years of the Exodus and hence the temptations of Moses. And further, particularly in Matthew's version (which adds "forty nights"), there may be an allusion to the journey of Elijah to the holy mountain (see 1 Kings 18:1–8, esp. v. 8). The hunger that overtakes Jesus may also be an allusion to Elijah. And a further allusion to Elijah, a messianic figure, may be contained in the report that angels ministered to Jesus, just as an angel fed and comforted Elijah.

This process of retrojection reaches its ultimate stage in the infancy narratives. Luke makes a clear reference to the prophet who prepares the way for the coming Lord (Luke 1:76), who should be Elijah in the tradition we are considering. In narrating the early infancy of Jesus, Matthew makes much use of the traditions dealing with the birth, hiding, and saving of Moses that were then circulating among Jews: both those based on Exodus 2:5f. and the more legendary stories that were picked up by such writers as Josephus and that are even closer to Matthew's own text.

All my above remarks on the various messianic traditions and their postpaschal elaboration serve as one possible example among many. They suggest how important it is to distinguish between the prepaschal and the postpaschal if we wish to understand what the evangelists are trying to say.

II

The *second* historical criterion for determining the reliability of our documents entails differentiating the *pre-ecclesial* from the *postecclesial*. This criterion is obviously not wholly dissociated from the first one discussed above.

The evangelists are writing for the Christian *church* (or *churches*), an obviously postpaschal reality. Jesus himself spoke and acted in a different context. If he did try to educate his disciples, it was more so that they would understand him than that they might solve problems for a community that did not yet exist in any strict sense. And that is quite apart from the whole issue, raised by some historians, exegetes, and theologians, as to whether Jesus ever intended to establish an organized community to follow him in his mission.

It seems obvious that much of what we have in the Gospels today was taken out of its original context and addressed by the evangelists to their contemporary churches. It was addressed to church problems, church members, and church authorities. Hence there is a scientific or scholarly need to distinguish between two different contexts: the ecclesial context and what derives from it; the religious, social, economic, and political context of Jesus himself and those things which either derive from it or must be interpreted in its light.

Obviously the latter context is more historically reliable. But we must be aware of the influence of the former (church) context in trying to discern what Jesus' own context was.

The ecclesial context is quite clear in the Gospel of John, for example. We all know that the events narrated in the fourth Gospel are selected and arranged in accordance with the logic of a certain symbolism, which does not mean that those events did not take place at all. Symbols such as water, bread, light, and vine are crucial in trying to understand the structure and preferences of the evangelist's memory. It is not just that those symbols had a *natural* import, so to speak, and were bound up with the cultural needs of a geographically defined church. On a more esoteric level where the redactor of the fourth Gospel was at home, those symbols also had a *sacramental* import. Pagan readers of the Gospel might understand the text perfectly well. But the Christian readers would engage in a second, additional reading of the text in terms of church life. They would realize that bread symbolizes the life procured by *faith*. But, in addition, they could not help but associate the symbol bread with the *Eucharist* celebrated in the church community. And the evangelist makes every effort to ensure that this second reading will *also* make sense.

In the Synoptic Gospels the presence of the ecclesial context is less obvious and deliberate; hence it is more subtle and difficult to detect. Consider the parables, for example. Dodd (*The Parables of the Kingdom*) and Jeremias (*The Parables of Jesus*) are among those who have shown how the parables of Jesus were placed in the service of the postpaschal church and its needs. Originally almost all of them had been part of Jesus' polemics against various listeners (the Pharisees and other religious authorities in Israel) who resisted the kingdom he was proclaiming in one way or another.

Jeremias comments on the parable of the laborers in the vineyard (Matt. 20:1–16). The proprietor gives a basic day's wage to all, even those who have worked for only an hour, and the latter are paid first. When the other workers complain, the proprietor points out he is paying the agreed wage and asks who can question his goodness and right to act as he wishes in the matter. Then Matthew's text offers three morals for the story, one being an addition in some texts: (1) "Do you begrudge my generosity?" (20:15); (2) "So the last will be first, and the first last" (20:16a); and (3) "Many are called, but few are chosen" (20:16b, addition in some texts).

The latter two morals clearly have no logical connection with the content of the parable story.[15] The parable does not suggest at all that the workers of the first hour were rejected or that those of the last hour were chosen. Instead it points up that the recompense was the same for all. But the church soon perceived that Jesus, in speaking of the workers of the last hour, was alluding to the listeners who believed in him and who, by the time the evangelists were composing their work, formed a church, a community of "the chosen" (see Rom. 8:28-30, a text prior in time to the final redaction of Matthew). Thus the parable could be used to make clear to the church the gratitude it owed to God for its unexpected preference. This would shore up its vocation.[16]

The second moral is even more alien to the internal logic of the parable. It was probably suggested by the order in which the proprietor paid the workers, but that is not the point or teaching of the parable. The pay is the same for all, and the order may well be a literary device so that the workers of the first hour are present to protest when the workers of the last hour get paid. This second moral is really a message and a warning to the Christian community, especially to those who enjoy privileges or authority in it. A few verses further on in Matthew we read: "It shall not be so among you. But whoever would be great among you must be your servant, and whoever would be *first* among you must be your slave" (i.e., the *last*, Matt. 20:26-27; see Luke 14:7-11).

It is clear that the first conclusion or moral really sums up the parable: "Do you begrudge my generosity?" It is Jesus' retort to the ill-humored reaction of pious Israelites to his proclamation that the kingdom of God is coming primarily to succor sinners and the poor: that is, people without merit, workers of the last hour.

This example indicates how historical reliability is secured when we managed to separate the later ecclesial context from the context of Jesus himself and the reactions provoked by his words and deeds.

Another example of this same difference in contexts, one which we shall have to consider in much greater detail later, is to be found in the central formulation of Jesus' message: the Beatitudes.

We have two versions of them: Luke's and Matthew's. Comparing the two, we find that both possess a common element and an added element that is different in each. If we eliminate the "you" of Luke and the "in spirit" of Matthew, we get this simple formula: "Blessed are the poor for theirs is the kingdom of God," or, "of heaven," a circumlocution often employed to avoid use of the divine name. Leaving aside exegetical considerations to be explored later, we note that this simple formula can be described as one that is not "ecclesial." It indicates that the kingdom of God comes first and foremost for those who, by virtue of their situation, have most need of it: the poor, the afflicted, the hungry of this world (or, at least, of Israel).

On the other hand it is also obvious that the additions of Luke and Matthew are typically ecclesial. Let us start with Luke's Gospel. It tells us that the Beatitudes are not addressed to the multitude: "And he lifted up his eyes on *his disciples*, and said, 'Blessed are you poor, for *yours* is the kingdom of God . . .' " (Luke 6:20). Employing the second person plural, Luke is clearly addressing himself to the poor and persecuted Christian community of his day. He places words on Jesus' lips that will clarify and explain the critical situation of the church, offering comfort and encouragement to its members.

The catechetical concern of Matthew's Gospel is well known and easy enough to verify. It is the proclamation of a new righteousness or way of acting that Jesus demands of his disciples and that should differentiate them from the disciples of the priests and Pharisees. In the Beatitudes Matthew does not refer to human situations that God pities and seeks to rectify, but virtues that go to make up the elements of a righteousness that "exceeds that of the scribes and Pharisees" (Matt. 5:20). For Matthew, the "situation of hunger" becomes a "hunger for righteousness"; the "poor" become the "poor in spirit"; and so forth. In Matthew, then, the universal teaching of Jesus becomes a part of church catechesis on the new righteousness or holiness that Christians should display. That is what preoccupies the author as he composes his Gospel.

This example of the Beatitudes will help to point up one element of the utmost importance in the shift from the *pre-ecclesial* context to the *post-ecclesial* context.

The early Christian church may have had little structure and many reservations about its own religious character. Nevertheless it clearly constituted an esoteric community to some extent. It was limited and marked off from the rest of the universe, by virtue of its faith in Jesus if nothing else. The earliest pagan testimony we have about it shows that it was a group apart, known for singing hymns to Jesus as God.

The *pre-ecclesial* Jesus, by contrast, did not belong to any group (within which his words and attitudes are to be understood), much less to a specific religious group. He did not act in a specific sphere that we might characterize as *religious*. He was a Jew living in a Jewish milieu, and all the cultural coordinates of that world passed through him. His words and deeds have all the various resonances of the different levels or components of a culture: social, economic, political, and so on. We must remember also that the relative differentiation of these levels is something peculiar to modern cultures of the more developed sort. We should not expect to find something like that in earlier or more primitive cultures, including that of Palestine in the first century A.D.

Today we are so accustomed to looking at Jesus through the (religious) prism of the church that we instinctively look for a specifically and exclusively religious import in all his words and deeds. (To a large extent so did the evangelists themselves.) It is very hard for us to imagine or think that Jesus, when he declared the poor blessed, was simply using a socioeconomic category (having no relationship to moral virtues or religious dispositions) or that the term "kingdom of God," in the ears of his listeners, primarily signified a reality that was at least as concretely political as it was religious.

The specialists in Jesus of Nazareth are usually theologians or biblical investigators. In our specialized world theology and exegesis are generally regarded as disciplines deriving from a *religious* interest and sponsored, in one way or another, by the Christian churches. So it is not surprising that when they do use our second criterion of historical reliability, when they distinguish the pre-ecclesial context from the post-ecclesial context and give primacy to the former, their study of the pre-ecclesial context still tends to be limited exclusively to the *religious* panorama of the Israel in which Jesus spoke and acted.

Thus there has been much study of the variations represented by the different religious groups to which the pre-ecclesial Jesus addressed himself: the scribes, Pharisees, Sadducees, Zealots (insofar as they represented a religious as well as political point of view), Essenes, followers of John the Baptist, and so on. On the other hand there has been far less study of *the rest* of the human context, even though it is just as important for understanding the Gospels and other New Testament writings as well as their historical basis in Jesus of Nazareth.

A few years ago there appeared a book by Fernando Belo entitled *A Materialist Reading of the Gospel of Mark*, which sought to fill in this gap. It aroused a disproportionate amount of debate and opposition, though Belo's use of provocative terminology ("materialist," for example) may well have helped to complicate what could have been a more sensible discussion.

Let me give one example of what I mean. We have already seen that the Beatitudes, in their earliest form, were probably addressed to *the poor*, those who were so in socioeconomic terms (even though the religious factor played a role in their marginalization). Now did Jesus passively expect that happiness or blessedness would suddenly descend from heaven above, so that the poor would cease to be poor and would enjoy their fill? Or did he actually try to alter their lot in real history, by fighting against the power that was marginalizing them? If so, how could he carry on that fight without transferring to the poor a *power* that they did not possess, at the same time weakening those who were imprisoning the poor in their wretched lot?

Here we encounter a tenacious misunderstanding. Thinkers of the stature of Reinhold Niebuhr, who tend to stick to the most serious kind of exegesis, fall into the cultural trap of viewing Jesus as a *religious* reformer. Hence they assume that Jesus, *for that very reason*, renounced *power* completely (Niebuhr 1964, 2:72).[17] But we might well ask in the abstract: Is it possible to exercise *agape*, to fulfill the commandment of the Lord, without exercising power over the causes of evil, be it physical or social in origin?

To get a bit more concrete: if there is any datum implicit in all of the Gospels (including John's), it is that Jesus seriously threatened the foundations of the (theocratic) authority which was responsible for the marginalization of the poor in Israel, and which certainly was not the Roman Empire. If that authority left some room for his public activity, the Gospels unanimously tell us it was because it *did not dare* to put a violent end to it, on the basis of a careful calculation of its political power. The authorities were *envious* of his authority (power) over the multitude (Mark 15:10) and hence were also *afraid* of him (Mark 11:18).

Now no one fears someone who does not exercise any power. Yet it has been said ad nauseam that Jesus was not a revolutionary in any political sense (Küng 1976, 187). Why, then, did the Israelite authorities, whose ubiquitous presence kept them fully informed of all Jesus' activities from the very start, regard him as such, fear him as such, and eventually condemn him to death as such?

One of the thorniest problems in the exegesis of the Gospels is trying to explain how, why, and when the authorities—though still taking every precaution (Mark 14:53f.)—decided that they could now capture and kill Jesus without any excessive risk.

The Gospels clearly suggest that this decisive turn in the situation took place during Jesus' final ascent to Jerusalem, which began with his triumphant entry into the holy city. In a few short days it seems that the religious authorities of Israel were able to nullify Jesus' power over the very same crowds that had acclaimed him as king and Son of David. The multitude would appear before Pilate, demanding Jesus' death. What could have happened to explain this change, which the authorities used to their own political advantage?

Fernando Belo brings out a few facts that have not been given proper stress in exegesis, even though they were not unknown. What is decisive here is the socio-economic context of the Jerusalem population. Jerusalem was a city whose inhabitants made a living off what we might well call religious tourism. Thousands of pilgrims from home and abroad were drawn to the periodic feasts centered in the temple, and the sacred commerce transacted in the temple precincts was economically important.

At one end of the spectrum the priests (generally Sadducees) were an essential component of this basic economic structure. It operated under the Roman authorities, who did not interfere except to collect taxes. The Zealots, at the other end of the spectrum, opposed Roman domination, but they promised an even greater flourishing of this economic structure centered around the temple.

What happens with Jesus? During his last stayover in Jerusalem (which John shifts to the beginning of his Gospel for theological reasons), Jesus does two things that prove to be fatal for his popularity. Why? Because they show him possessing a power that is a real threat to the basic economic structure of the Jerusalem population.

First, and this seems to be the crucial act, Jesus expels the merchants and moneychangers from the house of God: a symbol of the arrival of the kingdom. According to John's Gospel, he condemns all commerce or trade in it (John 2:16; see Mark 11:15 and par.). Second, not only does he prophesy the destruction of the temple and the holy city (Mark 13:1 and par.), but apparently he also arrogates to himself the power to destroy the temple (see Matt. 26:61), or even invites his listeners to do it (see John 2:19). The variant readings, in any case, do seem to point to the confusing and alarming rumors that circulated among the multitude. Without doubt they were connected with the expulsion of the merchants from the temple by Jesus, even if that had been merely a symbolic act followed immediately by the resumption of business as usual.

Here we may well have the historical explanation for the change of attitude towards Jesus by the multitude, a change that the high priests used to their own advantage. It would point up the necessity of not restricting ourselves to a purely religious context if we want to explain many things in the life of Jesus, but rather taking due account of basic facts about the economy, society, and political life of his time and milieu.

Another factor has contributed to the neglect of this broader context and its crucial implications in the study of the historical Jesus: that is, the economistic *reductionism* of the varied analyses that have tried to plug this gap from the time of Engels to that of Belo. Detailed description of the mode of production and its attendant social relationships have gotten lost in pointless detours: Were the Pharisees rich or petty bourgeois? Were the publicans—though they were marginalized religiously and socially—rich exploiters or were they only the exploiters' agents? And in the process these analyses have overlooked crucial data of the sociopolitical level,[18] because that data was framed in religious terms and categories. And, as I said above, Belo's use of provocative terminology does not help to put the debate on a sound footing.

III

I shall deal only briefly with the *third* criterion of historical reliability vis-à-vis Jesus of Nazareth: the literary criterion.

In four New Testament documents we have four *narratives* of Jesus' public ministry, of the events running from his baptism to his death and resurrection. To what extent do these four documents or Gospels permit a reliable history of Jesus to surface? To what extent do they give us access to the historical Jesus?

On the one hand it is clear that none of the four Gospels is a work of *history* in the modern, scientific sense of the term. None of them tries to hide the fact that the narrative conveys an understanding of Jesus that is completely intertwined with faith in him, a faith that it explicitly tries to transmit. This fact, on the other hand, does not mean that the data offered to us is false or almost completely untrustworthy. It does mean that we have to take certain precautions in trying to find out what really happened in connection with Jesus of Nazareth. That is what our study of criteria in this Introduction has been all about.

One of the four documents, John's Gospel, seems to be noticeably far removed from what we today might regard as a trustworthy narrative. Its author or editor dwells mainly on events that the other three gospel narratives inexplicably ignore. One example is the resurrection of Lazarus (John 11), a person well known in Jerusalem. Jesus' action apparently had something to do with his subsequent capture and death (John 11:45–53).

The emphasis of the fourth Gospel on theological symbolism also prompts its redactor to shift events that are narrated by the other evangelists. For example, he has Jesus going up to Jerusalem at the very start of his ministry and driving the merchants out of the temple (John 2:13–22). Is it likely that Jesus, an unknown personage from Galilee at this point, would have enjoyed enough authority to do that? And then there is the soaring theological flight of John's Prologue and some of Jesus' discourses. All of these things have led people to go overboard in discrediting the historical reliability of the fourth Gospel.

While it still poses unresolved problems, two things have brought about a reconsideration of the historical value of many data contained in the fourth Gospel. First, archeology and more recent historiographical discoveries have found that its redactor, for all his free handling of the material and the exact course of events, was an eyewitness to places, customs, and happenings contemporaneous with Jesus of Nazareth. It is very likely that certain concrete points in John's Gospel are more reliable than the parallel treatments in the three Synoptic Gospels: for instance, the precise dating of the last supper and the passion, or the effort of the people to make Jesus king after the multiplication of the loaves.

Second, we cannot minimize the fact that John's Gospel, with its convergent narratives and more or less extensive allusions, offers important confirmation of a large part of the material in the Synoptic Gospels. In other words, we have teachings and deeds of Jesus that are recorded *unanimously* by all four documentary sources in our possession. That is certainly important from the historical standpoint.

The other three Gospels, the Synoptics, are a separate problem. Each Synoptic author has left traces of his own significant and original redactional work, based upon personal characteristics and different ecclesial situations. Nevertheless we see in these Gospels a much greater fidelity to the recollections of Jesus transmitted in writing and by word of mouth in the earliest Christian communities.

Through these three Gospels a large number of episodes and teachings come down to us synoptically: in three similar, though not identical, versions. This again is not negligible from the standpoint of historical reliability. Another goodly portion of the gospel material, sayings or *logia* of Jesus in particular, come to us in a twofold version: through Matthew and Luke. The two seem to have used some written source composed originally in Palestine at some point in time close to the events themselves, and then expanded in Hellenistic settings. Finally, each Synoptic evangelist offers a limited body of material that is peculiarly his own—a fairly important body of material in Luke. The historical value of this corpus is more difficult to evaluate, of course, because we lack precise knowledge of its origin.

The relationships between the three Synoptics are far from clear, and it is hard to explain the reason for their similarities or their differences. Nevertheless the general assumption is that when we have a triple attestation of some word or deed of Jesus, the common source is Mark's Gospel (or some earlier stage of its redaction). When we have two attestations—Matthew and Luke—the assumption is that both took their shared material from a written source called Q, which we do not possess. Presumably Q was composed first in Aramaic and the milieu of Palestine (probably in Jerusalem) and was then translated into Greek and completed in the Hellenistic diaspora with elements of the catechesis of the Christian churches. That leaves the sayings and deeds of Jesus that appear only in Matthew or only in Luke (and a few in Mark, such as Mark 14:51, though it does not refer specifically to Jesus). Undoubtedly they are due to particular traditions received separately by each author. Their origin is difficult to trace. All we have now is an ecclesiastical history that comes much later and is somewhat legendary; it attributes this material to the recollections of certain apostles, for whom Mark and Luke acted as secretaries in some way or another.

From all this we deduce that we have greater historical reliability from the literary standpoint when we are dealing with material transmitted by one of the two most primitive sources: Mark (generally three attestations) or Q (Matthew and Luke).

We also find a marked convergence between this literary criterion and the ones discussed previously. We have already seen the case of the Beatitudes. In the most likely version of them, Q presents a pre-ecclesial version that differs from the redactional work of Matthew or Luke, the latter work being much more influenced by ecclesial needs. Another interesting example of this convergence is offered by Mark's treatment of the Twelve and Jesus himself, which is prepaschal and pre-ecclesial. On this point Luke is clearly influenced by the position of authority that the Twelve have in the nascent church. To some extent Luke drops features of their prepaschal behavior that might give us a bad impression of them: for example, the epithet "Satan" that Peter's protests evoke from Jesus' own lips (Mark 8:33; Matt. 16:23).

Something similar occurs with Jesus himself. Mark, who is followed by Matthew in this matter, presents Jesus on the cross *crying* out the words that have shocked so many exegetes who have a very different idea of what is proper behavior for God-made-human: "My God, my God, why has thou forsaken me?" (Mark 15:34; Matt. 27:46, 50).[19] Not only does Luke ignore this anguished question of Jesus; he also equates his last cry with precisely the opposite attitude: "Father, into thy hands I commit my spirit!" (Luke 23:46).

To this more general literary criterion we must add another one that is more precise and specialized: the *language* used. Here the layman must rely on experts, and I can only point up a few essential elements.

We know that the Gospels and the rest of the New Testament, as we have them, were written in a form of Greek known as *koinē*, which was widely spoken around the Mediterranean at the time. Mastery of style and Greek grammar is not great in Mark, improves in Matthew, and attains a certain measure of correctness and elegance in Luke, particularly in passages due exclusively to his editorial work.

On the other hand there seems to be no doubt that Jesus himself, though he may not have been a total stranger to that more or less international language, spoke the vernacular language of contemporary Palestine: that is, a western variant of Aramaic with Galilean peculiarities.[20] The evangelists record this in Greek, sometimes bringing in the original Aramaic words and translating them into Greek. This is particularly true at points where the Aramaic is necessary to appreciate some misunderstanding or play on words. The cry of Jesus on the cross, "My God, my God!" is recorded in Aramaic by the Gospels ("Eloi, Eloi . . . ") to explain the deliberate or unwitting confusion it evokes in the bystanders, who equate it with an appeal by Jesus to Elijah (see Mark 15:34–36).

Besides these explicit citations of Aramaic, broader knowledge of that language permits today's specialists to detect its presence in some of the more heavy-handed phrases of the Greek "translation."

By itself, of course, the explicit or implicit presence of Jesus' own language does not prove that those words were spoken historically by Jesus. But it does prove trustworthy testimony that we are dealing with an ancient tradition close to the events and recorded in precise form, always in the very same terms. This suggests a conscious desire to reproduce words considered more or less sacred.

This reliability is further bolstered by a curious phenomenon we find in the Greek version of the Synoptics. In some passages we find that the more refined Greek of Luke or Matthew reflects Semitic turns, precisely where the more basic Greek of Mark attains an acceptable degree of fluency. How do we explain this? If we start from the fact that the individual evangelists display a certain freedom in the use of their sources, then there is only one likely hypothesis. In such instances Luke (or Matthew) does not feel personally authorized to offer a free translation, confronted as he is with stereotyped Aramaic expressions that have been transmitted as important ones in Christian catechesis (Léon-Dufour 1963, 194–95). All of which brings us closer to the historical Jesus.

My comments in this long Introduction make no pretense of deciding what is or is not historical in the narratives—or Gospels—we possess concerning Jesus of Nazareth.

I have already indicated that no interpretation or reconstruction of the past is totally free of prejudice or totally objective. Of course it will always be possible to divest ourselves of the most glaring prejudices. For example, Jesus was a first-century Jew. No one in their right mind would attempt to comprehend him *directly* in terms of cultural categories proper to the Greek world, the Far East, or the modern West.

Other prejudices of a more subtle kind are more difficult to detect and combat, however. I am referring to ones rooted in the very reading of the Gospels, in the theological and spiritual traditions of the different Christian churches, or in cultural tendencies that cut across the various denominations. Suppose then an exegete approaches the Gospels, convinced that *all* their authentic content must have to do with a Jesus who was trying to prepare his generation for the immediate end of history. At the beginning of his *Theology of the New Testament*, for example, Bultmann tells us that the only conception of the kingdom that can come from Jesus is one in which God ushers it in without any human intervention or collaboration.[21] Is that a productive key or a reductionist prejudice?

Lest readers think that the problem is being posed solely to Protestant exegesis, let me say something about Catholic exegesis, or at least one strain of it. Insofar as it assumes from the start that Jesus intended to leave behind a church structured by divine right, and reads the Gospels in terms of that perspective, it obviously loses the correct understanding of a large part of the content of the Gospels.

Thus readers should not be surprised to find that the various criteria presented here as the most objective ones do not have the same weight or importance, either individually or in combination, for different exegetes. They are debated and evaluated differently, depending on what people believe they know with certainty about the historical Jesus.[22]

CHAPTER V

Jesus and the Political Dimension

As we have already noted, anyone who seeks to approach the historical Jesus must ask why this person, who seemed no different from anyone else and who never insisted on his own prerogatives, began to arouse interest and passionate enthusiasm among his contemporaries.

Now in our limited world it is hard to imagine any profound interest or passionate enthusiasm that does not somehow entail conflict, that is not conflictive. The conflict may be found on the more abstract plane of ideas, where people staunchly defend some ideas and oppose others. Or it may be found on the more concrete plane of group interests, class interests, national interests, and so forth. Something that does not divide people is not likely to arouse enthusiasm, militancy, and commitment either.

Jesus, true human being, could not escape that law. But if we look at the New Testament documents dealing with him, we find it hard to bring them into agreement on this point.

The evangelists—John included—show us a Jesus who is conflictive in the second sense noted above. He constitutes a threat to certain concrete groups of people. That dovetails with his own assertion:

Do not think that I have come to bring peace on earth; I have not come to bring peace, but a sword [Luke has "division"]. For I have come to set a man against his father, and a daughter against her mother, and a daughter-in-law against her mother-in-law; and a man's foes will be those of his own household [Matt. 10:34-36; see Luke 12:51-53].

And when we read the Gospels stripped of the prefabricated image of "sweet Jesus of Nazareth," at every step we encounter a conscious, voluntary conflict between very definite and well-defined groups. That conflict, far from diminishing, leads to the legal execution of Jesus.

Hence we cannot help but be surprised when we get to the image of Jesus conveyed by Paul (even before the final redaction of the Gospels). His Jesus does not seem to be conflictive. His Jesus unifies: "There is neither Jew nor Greek, there is neither slave nor free, there is neither male nor female; for you are all one in Christ Jesus" (Gal. 3:28). Conflict is there, however, except that Paul situates it on a different level. He is in conflict with those who hold and propagate a different view of Jesus' gospel (see Gal. 1:7–8; 5:7–12). And Paul sees Jesus' death as the consequence of a profound conflict between opposing forces. In Paul's view, however, the opposing forces are not human groups but other great forces in the opposition between the flesh and the spirit: sin-enslavement, the law, and death (Rom. 8:2 and passim).

The contrast between these two very different conceptions of conflict, and hence of the one who introduces it, Jesus, constitutes a serious problem. It certainly has given rise to many misunderstandings, particularly when people have seen one conception as ruling out the other and have failed to notice the underlying convergence that unites the two. So now we must examine each of the two extreme versions of the conflict centered around Jesus. In this volume we shall consider the version of the Synoptics. In Volume III we shall examine Paul's version. And our intention ever remains the same: to move out of the past and construct christologies for ourselves here and now.

If we wish to respond to our initial question as historians, we do possess one important datum that dovetails with the view of the Synoptic Gospels. Even the *non-Christian* historical witnesses of the time insist on one point, which seems to be beyond doubt: Jesus of Nazareth died, after having been condemned by the Roman authorities, as a *political agitator.*

A very different problem, of course, is the "real" truth, not just the historical accuracy, underlying this convergent certainty. The writings that come to us from early Christianity—including the four Gospels—agree that the Romans, culpably or not, took advantage of a legal pretext and executed a sentence that was pieced together and promulgated outside of their own proper sphere of interests. The Gospels agree that Jesus of Nazareth never had any conflict with the Roman authorities; indeed one could document just the opposite. In reality Jesus *was presented* to the Romans as a political agitator, so that they found themselves in an awkward position vis-à-vis their own higher authorities. From the four Gospels we learn that the Romans, despite their vigilance and Jesus' public preaching and activity, never saw in him a political threat or even a potential ally of the Zealots.

If Jesus of Nazareth was a threat, if he agitated anything (politically, so as to merit a political sanction), it was vis-à-vis the religio-political authorities *of Judaism.* In some way, which we must spell out, he hurt their interests, or so they believed. That gave rise to envy and fear at first, then conspiratorial plotting and the capture of Jesus, then sentencing, and ultimately a successful effort to put the Roman procurator on the spot publicly so that he had no choice but to accede to their desire to have Jesus legally executed.

Over against these elements, documented in the Gospels, stands the opposite hypothesis: Jesus was certainly presented and ultimately executed as a political agitator, but it was all a lie, and those who let themselves be taken in by it committed a tragic mistake. Thus Jesus died for reasons that had *nothing to do* with his sentence, with the alleged cause of his death: "The death of Jesus would be, 'historically speaking, a stupid destiny' (Bultmann) . . . exclusively the result of a political interpretation of his activity" (Léon-Dufour 1978, 802).

Insofar as the Roman Empire is concerned, there can be no doubt that Jesus' condemnation to death was the outcome of a self-serving misunderstanding on the part of both Roman and Jewish authorities. All recent attempts to prove Jesus politically linked with the Zealots—Jewish revolutionaries opposing Roman domination for nationalistic and, even more importantly, religious reasons—can hardly be taken seriously. They are threadbare. In terms of the scientific or scholarly approach used in the exegesis of the documents closest to Jesus, we find nothing of that sort in his life. He may have had a disciple, different from Peter (according to Luke 6:15), named Simon the Zealot, and perhaps a second disciple of that persuasion, but that proves very little. Perhaps a few Zealots or former Zealots, feeling confused or defrauded, decided to join forces with Jesus, and he was not adverse to admitting them to the ranks of the Twelve. Nor is much proven by the fact that Jesus did not debate or condemn the Zealots as he did the Pharisees, since the Zealots were more activists than ideologues.

It is very possible that the Zealots thought that Jesus would join them or that he could be used as a tool for their own cause. In particular, they might have thought they could link up with him through the common people. Many poor people probably did divide their sympathy between the Zealots and Jesus, thinking, at least at first, that the intentions of both were about the same.

But one can argue a very different case on an even more solidly scientific footing. Examining the written documents concerning Jesus, we do not find in them the slightest approval of the Zealot cause, even though that opportunity was presented to Jesus (see Luke 13:1). On the contrary, Jesus had friendly relations with the *publicans,* and the latter were the worst sinners in the eyes of the Zealots because they collected taxes and hence abetted the cause of Roman domination.

Other data support this view. Even though neither John the Baptist nor Jesus belonged to the sect of the Essenes, for example, recent investigations after the discovery of the Dead Sea Scrolls have pointed up definite affinities between them. And every point of similarity with the Essenes represents a corresponding estrangement from the Zealots.

In other words, everything that seems more certain historically about the orientation of Jesus of Nazareth's life and message tends to run counter to the hypothesis that he was an *anti-Roman* political agitator. Must we then reject the hypothesis as absurd? Before deciding the issue, we must proceed cautiously because our ordinary use of language here is loaded with traps and clichés.[1]

I

At first glance it seems obvious that nothing about Jesus presented in the Synoptic Gospels, much less in John's Gospel, fits in with our *present-day* idea of a political agitator. Any attempt to read the Gospels from that standpoint seems clearly useless and counterproductive.

But the roots of the problem go much deeper. For one thing, today Jesus is rightly or wrongly considered the founder of a *universal religion,* indeed the most universal that has ever existed in the world if we disregard its internal divisions. To switch him to the history of *politics* would seem to strip him of his historical transcendence and turn him into a petty figure who pretty much failed in his effort to bring happiness to the poor of his country. Moreover, Jesus of Nazareth is also the alleged founder of a *church,* a socioreligious institution that has had to and still has to coexist with different political regimes. In trying to maintain this coexistence, the church has relied on the inevitable argument that it does not belong to the political realm, that its reason for being lies on a different plane, the religious one—however vague the latter concept may be, particularly when it comes to defining the scope of its activity vis-à-vis other spheres. This vagueness has not stopped the survival of the church from being linked up in practice with the peculiar nature of its objective: that is, that it does not seek to compete with other specifically political organizations, projects, and achievements.

Hence we confront problems when we dare today to say that Jesus was a political agitator; to accept the force of this key historical datum, to admit that it was this fact that led him to death, and to affirm that his death was not simply a mistake. When we make such assertions, we are struggling against certain things that somehow escape the control of language, precondition it, and thereby discredit our assertions even before they are subjected to careful analysis. The two words, "political agitator," are made to seem an intolerable distortion and caricature of the figure of Jesus as presented to us in the Gospels—not to mention the politically tame, religio-anthropological version that seems to derive from Paul, with its tremendous theological weight for later generations.

The fact remains, however, that the "official" cause of Jesus' violent death was his being a political agitator, and this should make us stop and think a bit. Is it really possible that it was all due to confusion? Even if we assume that the Jewish authorities were simply trying to blackmail Pilate because of their ill will toward Jesus, why did they feel forced to do away with the latter?

In Section II of the Introduction to Part Two, we discussed the criterion of pre-ecclesial versus post-ecclesial material in the New Testament. We saw that its comments on Jesus tend to have more historical value if they do not directly dovetail with the needs of the early Christian community, since the latter already found itself in different circumstances than those which surrounded Jesus' public ministry.

Now even in the first century (see Acts 24:14), the Christian community was presenting itself as a *religious sect*. Hence it is much more reasonable to assume that such a community would try to pass off the political cause of its founder's execution as a mistake or lie, than to assume that a politically oriented community (such as that of the Zealots) would minimize the specifically political element in the message and activity of Jesus.

While this historical criterion may not be absolutely persuasive, it does dovetail with common sense. Once we accept it, we should not find it too surprising or shocking that Jesus really was a political agitator, to some extent at least. Why, then, do we feel surprise or shock? Is it real or feigned? Let us try to explore the ideological mechanisms underlying it.

Consider the expressions, "political agitator" or "political revolutionary." Each is a combination of adjective and noun deliberately designed for shock value. They are meant to bring out the incongruity between the Jesus described by the Gospels and some historical interpretations of him that seem to be fantastic caricatures.

Let us begin with the nouns. Both "agitator" and "revolutionary" have acquired clearly pejorative connotations in general usage, and in the specific context under discussion here. This is only intensified by the already pejorative connotation of the adjective "political." The labels "revolutionary" and "agitator" are usually applied to people who have had some superficial impact on the political scene but ultimately went down to defeat. If things had turned out differently, and no matter what value one might or might not attribute to politics, those very same people would end up being designated by more high-sounding terms: statesman, legislator, liberator, and so forth.

It is indicative that none of the latter functions are usually associated with Jesus of Nazareth, at least not on the level of politics. If Jesus did operate on that level, then he clearly must be numbered among the losers. If he thought up laws and imagined different structures for society, they were never implemented. If he won over the people, it was only for a short while; when they realized they had been deceived about his project, they called for his death. If he tried to liberate the multitude from the heavy yoke of alienating sociopolitical structures, the multitude soon realized that the obligations involved in winning and maintaining that liberation might well be even heavier than the old burden.

So if we assume that the political aspect of Jesus' life and message must be taken seriously, that he was indeed a revolutionary, then we can only say that he was a failed revolutionary. The label would fit him insofar as his plan to establish a new order remained an unfinished project. Indeed the label "agitator" would fit him even better, if we choose to focus on the political aspect as the key to his activity. The net result of his activity was agitation, one of those seismic waves of messianism that periodically swept over Israel in that era, subsided in failure, and ultimately led to the tragic destruction of Jerusalem (A.D. 70) and the dispersion of the Jewish people.

The implicit force of the above argument lies in the obvious ridiculousness of interpreting Jesus in such terms—that is, as a failed political figure—when his significance *on the religious plane* can hardly be doubted. He has had profound and enduring influence on the Western world and, through Western civilization, on the rest of the world.

Yet there is a flaw in this clichéd argument that could be challenged, though I am not going to dwell on it here. As I tried to point out in Volume I to some extent, the weak point of that argument is that it tends to equate, in historical and sociological terms, the message of Jesus of Nazareth with what we call the "Christian religion." Remember that the cultural vacuum left by the fall of the Roman Empire and the invasion of barbarian peoples led to the creation of a strange synthesis. It was an amalgam of elements found in the gospel message with other elements very much at odds with that message but needed to incorporate the masses culturally and sociopolitically into the vacuum left by the Roman Empire.

That is precisely what we find in the so-called Christian religion.[2] We find an amalgam rather than a careful, trustworthy exegesis and implementation of Jesus' teaching. And, paradoxically enough, what is today called the "Christian religion" is a *far more politicized* version of the gospel message than any of the denigrated political rereadings that are being made today.

Let us get back to the label "agitator" as it is applied to Jesus. In ordinary usage an agitator is also one who takes advantage of conflicts existing in a given society and exacerbates them for his or her own purposes. That is how the person agitates, and one of the most common forms of such agitation today involves taking advantage of class struggle, the kind of social conflict present in our developed societies.

To bring up the issue of class struggle in connection with Jesus is to indulge in caricature in order to discredit a political rereading of the Gospels in *two* ways: (1) by showing how anachronistic it is to use the term "class struggle" for the situation in first-century Palestine; (2) by the even more anachronistic and incredible tack of attributing both the term and the *fact* of class struggle to Marxism, as if such conflict were essentially and peculiarly its own creation.

When we eliminate the traces of caricature, however, we find that we must admit one thing about Jesus as he is depicted by the Synoptics from the start to the finish of his ministry: with the central proclamation of his message, Jesus is someone who not only seeks but manages to sharpen the main conflicts latent in Israelite society. The mere proclamation of the proximity of the kingdom, as something that will bring blessedness to the poor and woe to the rich, not only points up the opposing situation of the two groups in Israel but also undermines the very foundations of the peaceful coexistence that had been typical between them.

People talk about how absurd it was for him to be killed for political reasons. They fail, or choose not, to notice the first visible effect of his preaching in Galilee and of his arguments in defense of the poor. What was it, according to the Synoptic Gospels? It was a conspiracy between the ideologico-religious authorities (the Pharisees) and the political authorities (the Herodians) to get rid of him: "The Pharisees went out, and immediately held counsel with the Herodians against him, how to destroy him" (Mark 3:6).

Does that not mean that the conflict, already in Galilee, had reached the point where those at odds with the group protected by Jesus felt so threatened that they were ready to plan his assassination? And this would bring together factions that had never come together as allies on other occasions for other purposes. Here we surely have one sign—we shall see others—of the radicalness of the conflict aroused by Jesus. It prompts groups to disregard traditional conflicts between themselves that had been going on for generations. Even Herod and Pilate become friends behind Jesus' back, and their new-found collaboration became proverbial.

Are we not told later, as clearly as can be, that Jesus utilized the power of the poor, those who knew he was on their side and against their oppressors (see Mark 11:14; 12:12; 14:2; etc.), as a counterweight to the power of the Israelite politico-religious authorities in Jerusalem? Once again in Jerusalem age-old enemies, the Pharisees and the Sadducees, united against Jesus. Their intramural conflict had become far less important than the conflict that Jesus introduced between the common people and them. Even then they did not dare on several occasions to make open use of their authority, to seize Jesus and do away with him. They must watch for the right moment and take advantage of it, seizing Jesus by night to take him off for judgment before the people know what has happened. That is a measure of the power that Jesus had acquired through the conflict which he himself provoked, and for which he risked everything and was willing to face the ultimate consequences.

In order to say that only a tendentious rereading of the Gospels can make a political agitator out of Jesus, one must be profoundly ignorant of the most explicit gospel testimony. If Jesus did not *agitate* the political scene in Israel, then we must label the Gospels false in their most obvious prepaschal data.

The only sensible explanation for such weird blindness is that one is understanding the word "politics" in its most restricted and impoverished sense: as merely the intent to seize power. To be sure, the term "political agitator" very much lends itself to that interpretation. Jesus was not a political agitator in that sense, nor in any sense that would exclude a religious dimension from politics.

So now we must move on to consider the adjective "political" in the phrase "political agitator," which is used to disqualify any notion of Jesus' being interpreted in that vein.

II

When the adjective "political" is applied to Jesus, it takes on the overtones of caricature. And the reason is due largely to a misunderstanding, which may be intentional or not. There is a tendency to equate what we call the "political" sphere today (i.e., a specialized sphere of human activity) with the basic political dimension that has accompanied humanity ever since it began to live in organized societies.

Before we focus on that specific point, which is crucial for the following chapters,[3] we must recall one thing we discussed in Section I of the preceding Introduction. Jesus presented himself in the lineage of the ancient prophets of Israel, and the latter, according to the Old Testament, clearly participated in the political sphere, even as we understand that term today. It is also a fact that the people of Israel saw in Jesus features of the ancient prophets, of two in particular: Elijah (see Mark 8:28; Luke 9:19) and Jeremiah (Matt. 16: 14).

Let us look at what can be called the Elijah cycle (1 Kings 17-2 Kings 1). With the exception of some minor episodes (e.g., 1 Kings 17:7-24), almost the entire cycle depicts Elijah taking a stand against the politics of Ahab, the king of Israel (and briefly against the politics of his son and successor, Ahaziah). Against the reason of state wielded by the king and the resultant syncretistic alliances, Elijah stands for the Yahwist religion in all its purity and intransigence. Generally his conflicts with the king are an inextricable mixture of politics and religion.

Many, to be sure, try to take advantage of the constant inclusion of the religious factor to deny the *political* activity and significance of Elijah, implying that any and all political activity, as such, would necessarily have to be secular. Elijah, however, does not limit himself to reminding the king of his religious and cultic duties. To begin with, he always looks for political means that will put pressure on the king (see 1 Kings 18:11-40). To deny the political content of this approach—and here I mean political even in our modern-day sense—would be equivalent to denying the political character of the current conflict in Northern Ireland simply because the division was religious in origin.

There is more, however. Elijah opposes the politics of Ahab, not only with the use of political power, but also on nonreligious matters, fighting for a just domestic policy in defense of the weak (see 1 Kings 21:1-24). The episode concerning the vineyard of Naboth,[4] which struck deep roots in the memory of the Israelite people, certainly helped to identify Jesus with Elijah in the popular mind—as much as, and perhaps even more than, the fact that Elijah was supposed to make a personal return at the end of days.

Even in this matter, of course, the demand for political justice is made to Ahab in the name of Yahweh. It does not cease to be religious because it is also political, but neither does it cease to be both simultaneously. And the same holds true, for example, for the Beatitudes that Jesus addressed to the poor, the hungry, and the afflicted.

In the tradition of Matthew, the prophet Jeremiah is associated with Jesus. Jeremiah was even more political than Elijah, if that is possible, but that did not prevent him from operating in the religious realm as well. He appealed to the mandate and approbation of Yahweh to justify his actions. Like Elijah, he forthrightly links the political future of the kingdom of Judah with a liberating change in specifically sociopolitical structures (as opposed to specifically cultic or religious structures):

> Thus says Yahweh: Do justice and righteousness, deliver the oppressed from the hands of the oppressor, do not trample underfoot the alien, the orphan, and the widow; and do not do violence or shed innocent blood in this place. Because if you put this word into practice, then there shall continue to enter the gates of this house kingly successors of David on the throne, riding on chariots and horses, along with their servants and their people. But if you do not heed these words, I swear to you by my own honor—oracle of Yahweh—that this house will end up in ruins [Jer. 22:3-5; Segundo's text translated; see Jer. 38:17-18].

Going much further than Elijah, however, Jeremiah's judgments touch upon matters that we today would regard as strictly political, matters in which one can see only expediency rather than any moral judgment. The kingdom of Judah is being attacked by the king of Babylon, for example. Jeremiah announces that all should leave Jerusalem and surrender to the Chaldeans, or else face death (Jer. 21:8-9). He suggests (Jer. 21:10), of course, that a plan of Yahweh lies behind this imperative, which in itself is a strictly political decision.[5] But the fact remains that here the prophet cannot even invoke an argument grounded on social morality, as he could in the previous case.

Jeremiah is unable to offer objective proofs of this alleged will of Yahweh, and so he is judged on the only plane that is humanly reasonable: the political plane. His adversaries get him thrown into prison for allegedly deserting to the Chaldeans (Jer. 37:13) or for being a vulgar agitator who is distracting people from their political duties: "Let this man be put to death, for he is weakening the hands of the soldiers who are left in this city, and the hands of all the people, by speaking such words to them. For this man is not seeking the welfare of this people, but their harm" (Jer. 38:4).

There is no little significance in the fact that Jesus, in the eyes of his contemporaries (of Matthew at least), seems to reincarnate the fate of the ancient prophets, of Elijah and Jeremiah especially. And in the case of the ancient prophets the revelation of God and the divine will were inextricably bound up with structures and decisions that political representatives have always considered, with good reason, to be part of their specific responsibility.

Obviously this does not prove conclusively that our reading of the message and activity of Jesus must *also* be political. It simply enables us to set aside the phony scandal, often evoked for transparently ideological reasons, involved in the assumption that Jesus' condemnation to death was due to sheer misunderstanding and an unwarranted political interpretation of something that was meant to be *solely* religious.

III

The Gospels themselves offer us the example of the Old Testament prophets as a key to the understanding of Jesus. That should spur us to form a clearer overall picture of the relationship between the religious and the political. By "religious" here I mean, at least, the way religion was lived by the prophets and Jesus; by "political" I mean politics in both its broader, more universal sense evident in every age and the more restricted sense we understand today. Only then can we properly evaluate the nature of the impact produced by Jesus of Nazareth and avoid the snares of ordinary language usage and its clichés.

Before we examine the various potential or necessary relations between religion and politics in general, we must draw one further conclusion about the political role of the prophets because Jesus presented himself as one of them and because the church in turn presents itself as continuing the work of Jesus.

The position of the prophets in Israel was always an uncomfortable one. The Old Testament offers abundant testimony of their isolation and subjection to persecution, and the New Testament assumes that all prophets suffer the same fate: "Blessed are you when men hate you, and when they exclude you and revile you, and cast out your name as evil. . . . Rejoice in that day . . . for so their father did to the prophets" (Luke 6:22–23; see Matt. 5:11–12). And according to a tradition picked up by Jesus, almost all the authentic prophets of Israel had to pay in bloodshed for the right or duty to exercise their prophetic mission. Jesus tells us that such was the case with the last of the prophets, John the Baptist, and that such must be the case with the Son of Man (see Matt. 11:14; 17:12).

This distinctive destiny among all the *religious* functions calls for some explanation. The only sound explanation is that prophetism comes into conflict with *established authority and power*. It threatens the latter and the latter responds with violence, provoking the death of the prophet. And there can be only one good reason why the reason of state systematically comes into conflict with prophetism: because the latter intervenes and interferes in the sphere of the former, even though the claim and power of prophetism have their ultimate origin and validation in the religious sphere.

Looking at the opposite side of the coin, we find one proof of the same point in the rapidity with which the church, when forced to coexist with political regimes not imposed by it, declares its neutrality vis-à-vis those regimes and silences any and all prophetism.[6] The representative of Jesus the prophet is no longer another prophet like him but the priest, the pontifex. And the characteristic activity of the latter, as centuries of church history make clear, was to establish the respective competence of the two spheres: politics and religion.[7] This was done painstakingly and often violently, as the struggles between popes and emperors indicate.

Speaking in Christian terms, however, we can say that such a delimitation of competencies is never viable. Love, *effective* love, is the commandment of Jesus, and anyone can see that such love is conditioned by all the *systems* that affect human coexistence, from the psychological and interpersonal to the social and international. Hence it is obvious that *all* those systems must be subject to the same supreme criterion, insofar as the Christian is concerned.

Such, in fact, is the case. No one who holds the Christian standpoint finds it surprising that the religious sphere should decide what is useful or harmful in the educational field, what is moral or immoral in such cultural manifestations as art, dress, and communications, and what is just or unjust in the social distribution of wealth and other privileges. Why, then, do we find a strange exception being made when it comes to the political sphere?[8]

A disclaimer must be added to what was said at the beginning of the last paragraph. A considerable number of Christians do think that religion is purely an individual or interpersonal affair, that it has no business interjecting itself into other fields. At first glance the mainline Christian churches unanimously condemn this sort of individualism and structural indifference. Consider the Social Gospel movement, the social teaching of the Catholic church, and the responsibility that the churches feel (perhaps too belatedly) in the face of genocide or deep-rooted political abuses that have become systematic. All of these things would prompt one to assume that Christianity of a more responsible sort is not willing to restrict the gospel criteria for religious activity to the individual and interpersonal spheres.

But no sooner do we leave those spheres and move out into the more general and political spheres conditioning effective love than we find growing inhibitions in the teaching of the church, however inconsistent they may appear to be.

We are told, for example, that the Christian contribution does not lie in structural change of an economic, social, or political sort but in the conversion of the human heart, that the former without the latter would be futile and deceiving. To prove this, people take a tack that relates more directly to our present subject: they go to the Gospels to prove that Jesus of Nazareth and his message were concerned solely with this conversion of heart in our interpersonal relations.

It cannot be denied that there is an overwhelming amount of evidence to support such a contention. The vast majority of Jesus' practical teachings, even those that Matthew and Luke locate in his central discourse, consistently deal with how we are to act with other *persons* (or with God). Only a small portion of his teachings deal with how people are to act vis-à-vis *groups:* the scribes, the Pharisees, the priests, the poor, sinners, and so on. Moreover, even those groups seem, at first glance, to be identified by Jesus in terms of behavior of their *individual* members rather than in terms of their structural situation or impact.

It is well worth the trouble, in the process of elaborating christologies, to go back and feel the strong literary emphasis placed on the interpersonal realm in the Gospels, especially that of Matthew. In six sections Matthew describes the new Christian righteousness that is superior to the righteousness of the Pharisees. The last two sections, dealing with a basic attitude of gratuitousness, go like this:

> You have heard that it was said, "An eye for an eye and a tooth for a tooth." But I say to you, Do not resist one who is evil. But if any one strikes you on the right cheek, turn to him the other also; and if any one would sue you and take your coat, let him have your cloak as well; and if any one forces you to go one mile, go with him two miles. Give to him who begs from you, and do not refuse him who would borrow from you.
>
> You have heard that it was said, "You shall love your neighbor and hate your enemy." But I say to you, Love your enemies and pray for those who persecute you, so that you may be sons of your Father who is in heaven; for he makes his sun rise on the evil and on the good, and sends rain on the just and on the injust. For if you love those who love you, what reward have you? Do not even the tax collectors do the same? And if you salute only your brethren, what more are you doing than others? Do not even the Gentiles do the same? [Matt. 5:38–47; see Luke 6:27–35].

What is said about the scribes and Pharisees, whose righteousness is declared inadequate for entering the kingdom of heaven? One verse or two (if we include verse 13) of Matthew 23 does allude to the structure they have established in Israelite society: "They bind heavy burdens, hard to bear, and lay them on men's shoulders; but they themselves will not move them with their finger" (Matt. 23:4). But for one or two verses that might have a structural sense we find eighteen verses in the same chapter where the two groups are characterized by hypocrisy in their individual or interpersonal behavior. They cross sea and land to make a single convert, and then make him twice as bad as they are (v. 15). They say that swearing by the temple or the altar means nothing and is not binding, but that swearing by the gold of the temple or the gift on the altar is solemn and binding (vv. 16–18). They pay tithes on mint, dill, and cummin but disregard justice, mercy, and faith, thus straining out a gnat and swallowing a camel (vv. 23–24). They clean the outside of cup and plate, but inwardly they are full of extortion and rapacity (v. 25). Like whitewashed tombs, they look fine on the outside, but inside they are full of uncleanness, hypocrisy, and iniquity (vv. 27–28). They build and adorn tombs for the prophets, but their behavior shows them to be the children of those who murdered the prophets (vv. 29–31).

The problem is that this evangelical *climate*, with all its imaginative allure, is transposed without further ado to our context two thousand years later. One further point deserves mention. That particular climate is especially evident in Matthew's Gospel and its preoccupation with the new justice or righteousness of the Christian. We see it, for example, in his "virtuous" version of the Beatitudes. And for many centuries in the history of the Roman Catholic church, indeed up to the liturgical reform that followed Vatican II, Roman Catholics were familiarized with only one of the Synoptic Gospels, that of Matthew. Readings from Matthew's Gospel dominated the liturgical year. Readings from Luke and Mark, from Luke in particular, would have offered different perspectives and emphases, as we shall see in later chapters. They would have thrown a different light on what might be called the alternative between interpersonal morality and structural morality.

Be that as it may, a more general observation is the important point here. *Faith*, in Paul's sense, consists in entrusting our destiny to God. It thus liberates us *from* the temptation to seek security in the law and *for* the work of achieving the most perfect possible love with the instruments provided by our own age and circumstances. Over the course of two thousand years the factors conditioning the effectiveness of love have obviously changed a great deal. Vatican II itself offered abundant evidence of such change. Many ills in antiquity, it noted, could be eliminated or diminished by action in one particular field: for example, almsgiving in the economic field, curing in the health field, and better interpersonal and group relations in the social field. But now, it stressed, dealing with those ills increasingly depends on interaction between all fields, all social groups, and ultimately all nations.

Now there is only one activity that typifies politics as a distinct sphere. Politics brings together the threads of all the other fields and weaves them together to serve the common welfare, using the proportionate power needed to ensure their appropriate unification. Thus all the planes where religion intervenes and offers guidance must ultimately open out to this more universal—political—dimension of love.

The scope and quality of education, for example, exceed the good will and competence of educators themselves. They will depend, in large measure, on the balance achieved between expenditures for military defense and other types of expenditure in the national budget, and this is an eminently political question. Better distribution of the national product can no longer depend on some type of social assistance. To a large extent it is subject to the workings of the international market, and so it will ultimately depend on the political priorities established within the interplay of market forces. And so it goes for other areas as well.

When it comes to the Christian understanding of love, therefore, what valid reason do we have for excluding from consideration the field in which the most crucial decisions affecting love's exercise will be made? Would it not be much more logical to take Jesus' remarks, couched in apparently more interpersonal terms in line with his own era, and translate them into political terms? To push the point further: Even in Jesus' day didn't his remarks have a more explicitly and crucially political point than we are usually inclined to admit? Why? Because the political dimension, even when less apparent and less endowed with its distinctive elements, is a crucial factor wherever an organized human society exists, even though that society may be less complex and developed than our society today.

Admittedly the modern growth of the political sphere and its complexity poses a problem. To some extent it has given rise to a specific class of people: the professional *politicians*. Increasingly we tend to make a distinction between them on the one hand, and people in other fields who may have a profound political influence in a broader sense of the word.

Actually the distinction could be applied pretty far back, as we have seen. The Old Testament prophets obviously belong to the second category just mentioned. The Israelite kings and many members of their court belong to the first category, even though their traits as professional politicians might not be as sharply defined as they are today.

In line with what I said in Volume I of this work, both groups obviously act in accordance with some basic anthropological faith, elaborating some system of means, some ideology, to implement it.

As we saw in Volume I, the means employed end up influencing one's initial faith. Let us take a case from the Old Testament. A professional politician like Saul might well begin with the same anthropological and even religious faith as a politically influential person from another field, such as Samuel the prophet. The profoundly tragic, rather than criminal, fate of Saul lies in his ability to appreciate and manipulate political means. As time goes on, he increasingly sets store on the reason of state. Samuel's activity in the religious sphere proves him to be a political figure in a real and crucial sense. But he remains amazingly indifferent to the calculations that Saul must make as king of Israel: that is, as a professional politician in the strict sense of the word (see 1 Sam. 10–31).

This basic mechanism or process has grown with the increasing complexity of the political sphere. In his own day Saul was the ruler of a barely organized monarchy. He could oversee and handle the reason of state on his own. Today professional politicians must rely on a huge number of collaborators and helpers, whose specialized competency can be judged only approximately and on the basis of long-term results, given the enormous complexity of the factors involved.

But the complexity of political life today, similar to the complexity of every other sphere of life, cannot be used to argue that religious faith and its derivatives must call a halt before political options. Once again we cannot help but suspect that this unwarranted pretension is based on an overvaluation of one specific sector for strategic reasons. In other words, the church is sacrificing its prophetic function for the sake of maintaining its religious structures that have been designed for the masses.

Be that as it may, the above observations may permit us to say something pertinent about Jesus of Nazareth, something that will pave the way for a proper understanding of his message in the following chapters.

I tried to show in Volume I that a *divine revelation*, one which founds a *religious* faith, cannot stay on a purely religious plane or be maintained there, unless it is nothing more than some sort of sacred magic (a sacred ideology rather than a faith). God can only be revealed in connection with values that are humanly meaningful, and those values must be manifested historically on one or more of the planes where the human being stakes the meaning of its life and the possibilities for happiness. Strictly speaking, then, we can say that there is no divine revelation that does not take its course through preferences and concrete realizations on the plane of interpersonal relations, education, economics, politics, and societal life. The revelation of Jesus does not, could not, constitute an exception.

On the other hand it is obvious that Jesus of Nazareth was not, and could not be interpreted as, a professional politician. Jesus purports to reveal God, and how God sees and judges the human endeavor, in order to give it its most authentic sense of meaningfulness. In an earlier time in Israel, the teachers of wisdom did the same thing, focusing on individual conduct. So did the prophets, only they stressed how God saw Israelite society as a whole and thus offered a political vision grounded in religious faith. As we shall see in the following chapters, the documents in our possession dealing with Jesus incline us to view his life as a prophetic effort, as a revelation of God couched in preferably political categories.

This inclination finds confirmation in the fact that the authorities who oppose and ultimately execute Jesus display the same mixture of religion and politics. The poor and *politically* marginalized people in Israel were put in that position by authorities who claimed to be acting in line with God's supposed vision of the relationship between conduct and social *status*. In making a frontal assault on that vision, Jesus was certainly attacking the political structure of Israel. On the basis of divine revelation he was destroying the foundation of an authority structure that was political in the name of an idolatrous conception of God, that was conveying a false image of God.

Perhaps—only perhaps—these observations will obviate misunderstandings and help my readers to understand my exegesis of the Synoptic Gospels in the following chapters.

CHAPTER VI

The Central Proclamation of Jesus

The Synoptics are not so structured that a first reading immediately brings out what Jesus is proposing that is new, interesting, or even shocking to his contemporaries when he abandons the anonymity of thirty years and begins his ministry. Three crucial occasions do combine, however, to form what might be called a circle of meaning that brings us closer to the heart of the question: (1) The Markan source offers us a summary of Jesus' initial preaching in Galilee after he had been baptized and returned there to start his ministry. (2) Q, the common source of Matthew and Luke, presents Jesus' answer to the crucial question that John the Baptist asks as to whether Jesus is *he who is to come*. Jesus' answer is a description of his mission, its results, and obstacles to it. (3) Q also offers us the solemn opening of a discourse or sermon (on the mount in Matthew, on the plain in Luke) in which Jesus apparently shows us God's view or judgment of Israel's reality. That view or judgment will then serve as the inspiration for all of Jesus' own activity.

Let us take a little look at the circular concatenation of the three passages.

The Markan summary of Jesus' initial preaching goes like this: "The time is fulfilled and the kingdom of God is near; change your outlook and believe in the good news" (Mark 1:15 and par.; Segundo's text translated).

The kingdom of God is "what is to come," and now at last it is arriving. The time has come; it is near. Besides that, there is a need for conversion, for a radical change in outlook or attitude. So either the kingdom has not been expected or people's expectations had gone off in a different direction. In either case, the proximity of the kingdom is not automatically a piece of good news, something people can readily believe in and hope for without having to experience a profound change.

The second passage (2) has to do with a doubt that overtakes John the Baptist regarding Jesus: "Are you he who is to come, or shall we look for another?" Jesus responds to this question by pointing to signs of the proximate arrival or presence of the kingdom: "Go and tell John what you hear and see. The blind receive their sight and the lame walk, lepers are cleansed and the deaf hear, and the dead are raised up, and the poor have good news

86

preached to them. And blessed is he who takes no offense at me" (Matt. 11:2–6; Luke 7:22–23).

The term "kingdom of God" does not appear in this passage as it did in the previous one, but it is obviously implied in the question about *he who is to come*. The person *who* is to come is somehow identified with *what* is to come (with him) once the time is fulfilled: that is, the kingdom. The former introduces the latter. Therein lies the crucial nature of the question asked by John the Baptist's disciples. Must they wait or look for another to usher in the decisive reality, the kingdom of God?

Jesus answers them by pointing to "signs of the times" associated with himself and his activity. Those signs share a common characteristic: the most disadvantaged are being helped in their need. In all the instances cited, except for the last one involving the preaching of the good news to the poor, Jesus' help is thaumaturgic in form. The last sign stands out for several reasons. Let me mention only two here. In the first text we saw that the good news consisted in the arrival of the kingdom. So that is what is being preached precisely and specifically to the poor, the only group in the list distinguished by its social condition rather than by some physical condition. In all likelihood this ties in closely with the beatitude or blessing with which the passage ends. Jesus foresaw that at least some of the signs of the kingdom's arrival would cause scandal rather than joy. It is hard not to equate the scandal with this specific proclamation of the good news to the poor.

Finally, this intrinsic relationship between the poor, the good news, and the arrival of the kingdom shows up clearly in the third passage cited above, the one dealing with the Beatitudes, particularly when we read the Beatitudes in what must have been the Q version: "Blessed are the poor (the mournful, the hungry), because the kingdom of God is theirs" (see Matt. 5:3f.; Luke 6:20f.). The kingdom is coming for them, to make them happy, to rid them of their poverty, affliction, and hunger. Luke's version, which is closer to the original, and his redactional work explain even more clearly why the coming of the kingdom constitutes good news only for the poor. His version adds the note that this news can only be bad for those whom the kingdom finds laden with wealth and goods (Luke 6:24f.). Only conversion (to the cause of the poor), hence a change in values, could logically turn the arrival of the kingdom into an occasion for joy, into good news.

It is within this article, which closely associates three terms ("kingdom," "the poor," and "good news"), that the prophetic content of Jesus' proclamation moves. This, in other words, is his message and the key to his outlook, ministry, and death. So we must now take a closer look at those terms.

I

Especially noteworthy is the fact that the key terms in this meaning-circle are *political*. "Evangel" or "good news" is neutral in itself, of course. It is more like a container specified by its contents: in this case, by the other two terms ("the poor" and "kingdom"). It, too, is political, or becomes political, insofar as it indicates a positive relationship between two terms that point to a political structure. It states that the kingdom will constitute something beneficial and blessed for the poor specifically.

The previous chapter, I hope, paved the way for a clearer understanding of what I mean here by "political," and in what sense the terms "kingdom" and "the poor" belong to that category. Obviously they are not political *as opposed to* religious. Quite the contrary is true. They are all the more crucially political precisely insofar as their underlying motivations are religious.

It is no part of our purpose here to forget that the term "kingdom" is qualified by the phrase "of God"[1] or that the poor in question here may well be, at least in principle, the very people who are also called *the poor* "of Yahweh" in various passages of the Old Testament.

Jesus' listeners understood one thing perfectly: while the force behind the kingdom (or those poor) was the force of God, the reality of the kingdom was something to be achieved on earth, so that society as a whole would reflect the will of God: "Thy *kingdom* come. Thy will be done *on earth* as it is in heaven."

Let us set aside the question of the poor for a moment, however, and try to recapture what the prophetic proclamation of Jesus—and perhaps of John the Baptist (see Matt. 3:2)—on the arrival of the kingdom signified in Israel.

Right off we discover something simple but suggestive. Jesus appears on the scene proclaiming the arrival of the *kingdom*, and disappears from the scene after having been accused of introducing a kingdom and being its *king*. All four Gospels agree that the reason given for Jesus' death, the charge inscribed on his cross, was "Jesus of Nazareth, the King of the Jews" (John 19:19-22; Mark 15:26; Matt. 27:37; Luke 23:38). Three years (according to the majority of exegetes) were not enough for Jesus to dispel the ambiguity of the term and prove that he was using it in a *purely* religious sense!

Is it not more logical to assume that he accepted and shouldered this ambiguity, this double meaning, from start to finish? Even in choosing the term, Jesus could not have been unaware of the *political* content it *already* had in the minds of the people. As we have already seen (see pp. 54-55), they were looking for the restoration—and certainly the political restoration—of the Davidic throne. The three Synoptics attest that Jesus did not make the least effort to dissipate the misunderstanding—if it was a misunderstanding—when the crowd in Jerusalem hailed him as David's successor and their king (Mark 11:10 and par.).[2] Even when the authorities specifically asked Jesus to clarify the matter, the Matthean tradition tells us that he answered as follows: "Have you never read, 'Out of the mouth of babes and sucklings thou has brought perfect praise'?" (Matt. 21:15-16; see Luke 19:39-40). If one chooses to assume that this is a postpaschal interpretation, or a redactional interpretation of Matthew, that would only lend even greater weight to the argument.

We have a tendency to exaggerate the obtuseness and incomprehension of Jesus' disciples, to whom we are indebted for the comprehension and transmission of difficult and subtle teachings. But we cannot overlook their testimony, which is clearly prepaschal, that even they themselves *never* separated the religious content of the word *kingdom*, as used by Jesus, from its political content. Note what Matthew and Mark tell us about the mother of the sons of Zebedee (Matt. 20:20-24) or James and John themselves (Mark 10:35-41). Matthew may have been trying to exculpate the disciples themselves, whereas Mark is not reluctant to introduce elements that put the future authorities of the church in a bad light. In any case, either the disciples or their mother asked Jesus that they be allowed to sit on his right and left in his kingdom—a *political* petition if there ever was one! This request does not evoke smiles from the other disciples; it evokes envy and indignation. This surely indicated that they all were thinking in identical terms about *power* in the future kingdom.

Even more significant, however, may be something we find in Luke. He tends to leave out anything that might cast discredit on the first authorities in the church, and so there is no mention of the above incident in his Gospel. But he recounts a similar incident as taking place on the very day that Jesus ascends into heaven. Whatever date exegetes may ascribe to that event, it obviously took place after the whole crisis of meaning produced by Jesus' death and resurrection. It is generally understood that the cross radically disqualified any conception of the kingdom that was not based on gratuitous self-giving and did not exclude all use of power. It is also assumed that the resurrection experiences of the disciples were eschatological experiences of the definitive victory of the kingdom through a new and unexpected means. But Luke tells us that the disciples remained perplexed by the fact that there had been no *political* fulfillment of the kingdom: "So when they had come together, they asked him, 'Lord, will you at this time restore the kingdom of Israel?' " (Acts 1:6). Even more curiously, Jesus does not upbraid them for the crude misunderstanding embodied in that question. On the contrary, his response seems to lend support to it: "It is not for you to know times or seasons which the Father has fixed by his own authority" (Acts 1:7).

I have repeatedly stressed that the religious plane and the political plane are not contradictory ones, particularly in Jesus' context. There is no question of choosing between them, of opting for one realm of meaning instead of the other. What is obvious is that we cannot easily accuse the authorities of Israel of condemning Jesus on false pretenses when his own disciples, who were at his side and were taught privately by him, shared the very same point of view.

Historically speaking, we can say that it would be much more logical to examine to what extent the political (i.e., politico-religious) content of the coming kingdom concretely threatened the structural situation of these authorities and thus prompted them to defend themselves by having Jesus executed.

II

The above remarks hardly exhaust what might be said about *the kingdom* in the preaching of Jesus of Nazareth. But they do lead us to examine its relationship with the second of the three terms mentioned earlier: "the poor."

The kingdom of God is not announced to everyone. It is not "proclaimed" to all. That is not due to a decision made by Jesus; it is due to the very essence of the kingdom. It is not so much that Jesus establishes differences so that he gets a hearing from some and not from others, even though he was capable of making significant discriminations alongs those lines (see Mark 4:10–12 and par.). Far more important is the fact that *the kingdom itself* cannot be preached indiscriminately as *good news*, as *gospel*. The kingdom is destined for certain groups. It is theirs. It belongs to them. Only for them will it be a cause for joy. And, according to Jesus, the dividing line between joy and woe produced by the kingdom runs between *the poor* and *the rich*.

A person would have to be very blind not to see that this characteristic differentiation, which the kingdom of God sets up between sociopolitical groups in Israel, is the source of an antagonism that is intrinsically *political*. Once we notice this, however, we have every right to assume that we have found in it the key to the violent death of Jesus, the prophet charged with preaching this kingdom, for explicitly political reasons.

As we have seen, the expression "kingdom of God" in itself was a religio-political term capable of arousing the passionate and favorable interest of *all* Israel. The restoration of the throne of David, which was associated with the expression, could at most only indirectly threaten the exclusively religious, sacerdotal authority held by the party of the Sadducees. Right from the start of John the Baptist's preaching, however, the proximity of the kingdom seems to be connected with conflict and judgment. We must not forget that we are dealing with a prophetic proclamation in all its radicalness and conflictivity:

> You brood of vipers! Who warned you to flee from the wrath to come? Bear fruit that befits repentance. . . . Even now the axe is laid to the root of the trees. . . . I baptize you with water for repentance, but he who is coming after me. . . . His winnowing fork is in his hand, and he will clear his threshing floor and *gather his wheat into the granary*, but *the chaff will burn* with unquenchable fire [Matt. 3:7–12].

In the Baptist's preaching, however, it seems that the criteria behind this judgment do not operate by way of political conflict so clearly, even though various social abuses are mentioned in Luke's version of his preaching. It is quite possible, of course, that the Synoptic writers were not faithful to the vision of John the Baptist. But insofar as we can compare John's preaching with that of Jesus, it would seem that the imminent catastrophe of a divine judgment prompts John to stress a change in attitude and outlook on the part of individuals so that they might escape God's wrath. Although Jesus continues to express himself in eschatological terms, he seems to allow for a time in which the changes that must take place are more profound, complex, and societal in nature. While the conflictive aspect of the kingdom is radically the same, the dividing lines of the governing criteria cut through broader structures.

Of all the Synoptics it is Luke who most clearly perceives and explains this aspect of conflict in Jesus' proclamation of the coming kingdom. He redacts the Beatitudes in line with the source as addressed exclusively to *the poor*, the hungry, and the mournful. But he is especially anxious to indicate and stress the corresponding negative side: the kingdom of God is a piece of *bad news* for the concrete groups that stand opposite the poor in the social spectrum. Its arrival sounds the death knell of the privileges that have so far been enjoyed by the rich, the satisfied, and all those who have been able to laugh in the world as it has actually been structured (see Luke 6:24–25).[3]

Even though the woes found in Luke's version may not have been uttered expressly by Jesus, they clearly dovetail with the logic of the general conflictivity that Jesus introduces or heightens in his prophetic proclamation of the kingdom. This conflictivity is evident both in Mark and in Q as well.

Following a consistent thread, we shall see that the list of groups given preference by Jesus grows, and that its political cast becomes increasingly clear and obvious. Paradoxically enough, the aspect of political conflict becomes increasingly crucial and decisive as the line of preference shifts from social groups to others that would have to be classified in much more directly religious terms.

Even the most consistently apolitical exegetes find themselves forced to point up the kingdom's clear *preference* for certain groups that are rather clearly characterized in the Synoptic Gospels. And since the term "kingdom of God" and any mention of its immediate addressees tend to disappear from the New Testament writings after the paschal events, giving way to a more unifying universalism such as that of Paul, both elements would seem to enjoy a high degree of historical trustworthiness.

Let me offer one example among many possible ones. Hans Küng writes:

No amount of discussion can conceal the fact that Jesus was a *partisan for the poor*, the mourning, the hungry, the failures, the powerless, the insignificant. . . . The absolutely unpardonable thing was not his concern for the sick, the cripples, the lepers, the possessed; not the way he put up with women and children around him; nor even his partisanship for the poor, humble people. The real trouble was that he got involved with *moral failures*, with obviously *irreligious and immoral people*: people morally and politically suspect, so many dubious, obscure, abandoned, hopeless types existing as an ineradicable evil on the fringe of every society. This was the real scandal [Küng 1976, 268–71].

Here scandal means conflictivity, political conflictivity (as we shall see). So why should anyone, Hans Küng in this case, try to evade that conflictivity by appealing to the allegedly impartial transcendence of Jesus? Earlier in his discussion he writes:

> Jesus apparently cannot be fitted in anywhere: neither with the rulers nor with the rebels, neither with the moralizers nor with the silent ascetics. He turns out to be provocative, both to the right and to the left. Backed by no party, challenging on all sides: "The man who fits no formula" [ibid., 212].

If that is so, why was he considered dangerous by some but not by others? Küng wants to put Jesus above and beyond it all:

> He belongs neither to right nor left, nor does he simply mediate between them. He *really* rises *above* them: above all alternatives, all of which he plucks up from the roots. This is his *radicalism*: the radicalism of *love* which, in its blunt realism, is fundamentally different from the radicalism of an ideology [ibid., 262].

Now anyone can set up a long list of alternatives that one can say that Jesus was truly *above*: for example, Roman domination versus the political independence of Israel. But did Jesus set himself *above and beyond* the alternative of the Pharisee and the publican praying in the temple, with everything that each symbolizes as a structure group?

Let us leave that issue aside for the moment and consider the list of human groups preferred by Jesus in his proclamation of the kingdom of God by word and deed. In Küng's text cited above, the list starts off with the poor, the hungry, and the afflicted and then is filled out with many other categories. In reality, however, its sense in human terms is probably the very same. Religious and moral categories are added, but we immediately suspect that those latter categories were added to camouflage the political option that is so clear in the first set of categories. In his own day Jesus said: "Blessed are *the poor*, for theirs is the kingdom of God." One could hardly have criticized him for such a view without appearing to be inhuman. So when his adversaries tried to undermine his prestige, they preferred to depict him as "a friend of tax collectors and sinners" (Luke 7:34; see Mark 2:15–17 and par.). One does not have to be too keen to suspect that here we are dealing with the very same preference for the very same group of people.[4] The change of label in designating them alludes to the ideological reasons used to keep the majority of people in Israel suffering under the weight of heavy burdens (Matt. 23:4) and deprived of the benefits of social equality.

Later on I shall examine the theological grounds for this religious discrimination and Jesus' attacks on it. Right now I want to explore the hypothesis I offered above about opposition to Jesus in Israel: that the more religious in tone and cast it seems to be, the more *political* is the underlying issue at stake.

In any society a huge majority of dispossessed and marginalized people constitute a threat to the small minority that enjoys authority and its accompanying privileges of all sorts. In the face of such a threat from the majority, how is the minority to shore up the division of labor that ensures its authority and privileges? The *political* means are many and varied, ranging from the cruder technique of providing the authorities with an overwhelming military force to the more sophisticated one of convincing the marginalized that their plight is due to divine decree.

Insofar as the Israel of Jesus' day is concerned, people now often succumb to an anachronistic cliché. They tend to equate the decisive *political power* with the most visible and powerful political institution in the Palestine of Jesus' day: the Roman Empire. But all serious historical investigations have indicated that the Romans, at least in that particular province of their empire, limited themselves to the exercise of two political functions: maintaining order with their legions and collecting a general tax through a corps of local officials known as publicans.

Now either of these two factors explains the *internal* social structure of Israel in Jesus' day, which derived from factors that antedated Roman domination and was preserved independently of that domination. Although we could go further back (see Sam. 8:10-18), let us simply focus on the return of Israel's cultural and religious elite from the Babylonian Exile. In the biblical narratives we can readily detect a growing chasm between that elite and the rural population that had remained and intermingled in Palestine during the Exile. Remember that the Exile affected only the most prominent people in Israel.

The possessors of religous culture referred to those who had remained in Palestine as the "people of the land," using the term in a pejorative sense. The term took in the majority of the population. Deprived of their leaders and representatives, they did not represent a threat to the foreign invaders, so they were left in Palestine as a source of manual labor, under governors who represented the Babylonian Empire.

This population was undoubtedly religious. But because it was deprived of priests and its cultural elite and because it intermingled with neighboring peoples, it deviated noticeably from Yahwist orthodoxy. When direct foreign domination ended and the exiled nucleus returned, the latter naturally took over power from the former, although it maintained relations of vassalage with the successive empires under which Israel lived down to Jesus' day. But this elite took over power more by religious title than by political title.

Viewed in societal terms, Palestine continued to be a *theocracy* even when it had lost its kings and become a political colony or province of foreign nations. The division of social classes or groups was religiously sanctioned. Only a minority knew the (religious) law and fulfilled it (or its external obligations at least). Legal purity and impurity served the ideological function attributed to prestige, money, or power in other societies. The poor were called sinners, and they ended up regarding themselves as such.

It is in these political terms that we must read and understand the Lukan parable of the Pharisee and the publican (Luke 18:9-14). As is quite obvious in the parable, the publican represents the vast majority of "sinners," whereas the Pharisee represents the elite, the few who are not like the rest. And the figurative details of the parable make clear that an exploiting minority—as Jesus would put it—has nothing to fear from a majority that goes around with its eyes down, beating its breast and calling itself a sinner. Political danger could come only from someone who would open the eyes of that majority, call it "justified," and at the same time label the dominant majority an impenitent and unpardonable sinner.[5]

This is just one example, among the many we shall have occasion to examine in the following pages, of how a tension conceived and expressed in religious terms becomes the dominant or overdetermined contradiction in a specific society such as that of Israel.

To put it another way: someone who is systematically destroying the *real* authority of the dominant group in a theocracy—even if, or rather precisely because, he is doing that in *religious* terms—becomes a fearful *political* adversary. Framed in the domestic context, the social structure, of Israel, Jesus is much more markedly *political* with his religious message than are the Zealots in their activity. The activity of the latter is more directly concerned with subversion, but it is directed against a power that is greater, yes, but also more extrinsic to the situation.

Jesus never for a moment gives up his central intention of revealing God and the import of that revelation for human existence *as a whole*. But in so doing, he clearly makes use of a political *ideology*; and here I mean "ideology" in the sense I defined the term in Volume I. Jesus makes himself heard and understood by involving himself, in God's name, in the sociopolitical tensions of contemporary Israel and soliciting the interest of his listeners there in both the positive and the negative sense. It is thus that he acquires disciples and adversaries.

III

In the end all four Gospels attribute the violent death of Jesus to the religio-political authorities, who saw him as a threat to their own power. Could Jesus not have dispelled the misunderstanding, if such there was, by changing his language or by spelling out more clearly the religious rather than political thrust of his message? Or is it possible that he did not perceive the political implications of that message?

In line with the historical hypothesis I have adopted and the consistent thrust of everything we have seen in the above sections, we see a Jesus who is fully aware, not only of the general consequences of the antagonism he accentuates, but also of its political consequences.

To be sure, it is not easy to reach a decision about the historical reliability of the three predictions that Jesus makes in the three Synoptic Gospels about a violent and fatal end to the conflict.

As I indicated in the Introduction to Part Two, one argument against their historicity is the fact that they could be prophecies *after the event*, predictions placed in Jesus' mouth after the paschal events had taken place. This becomes almost a certainty with the latter half of the last prediction, which practically summarizes his passion step by step. The same would apply to the prophecy of the resurrection and its dating "on the third day."

One thing favoring the historicity of the three predictions, of their general content at least, is the fact that they constitute a unique case in the redaction of the Synoptic Gospels. A parallel passage in those Gospels rarely appears in identical form, using the very same words in the same order. We know how freely the Synoptic writers dealt with the repetition of events they found in their sources: for example, the multiplication of the loaves. They summarize them, omitting this or that detail or placing it somewhere else in the chain of events. But here we have three passages that dovetail noticeably. Even though the Synoptic writers place different episodes or *logia* between the three predictions, they are in remarkable agreement on situating the first prediction after Peter's confession of faith in Jesus as the Messiah.[6]

All of these facts, surprising to any exegete familiar with the similarities and variants of the Synoptics, suggest that here we are dealing with something more than a mere postpaschal addition.

Where in all likelihood we are dealing with a prophecy after the event, we do find the usual traits of Synoptic redaction: great overall similarity with many variations in detail. Such is the case with prediction of the details of the passion (mocking, scourging, crucifixion, etc.) and of the resurrection (on the third day). That leaves us with the exceptional aspect: material that is extraordinarily identical in vocabulary and details. The only significant variant has to do with the third prediction in Luke's version. Instead of Jesus being delivered twice, once into the hands of the high priests and scribes and then into the hands of the Gentiles (Romans), only the latter is mentioned in Luke.

What are we to think of the central nucleus of Jesus' three predictions about his death as recorded in the Synoptics? Remembering that the antiquity of a tradition is a criterion of historical reliability, we can say that the extraordinary similarity of the three versions suggests an obligation of literal fidelity to one's source. And such an obligation occurs only when the source is transmitting an old and almost sacred memory[7] very closely bound up with the words of Jesus himself. This antiquity is hard to refute or deny. So even though we may admit that the early Christian community had Jesus making predictions of his violent death that he himself never formulated, the way they relate this violent death with the ministry of Jesus—so close to the actual events—is far from being historically insignificant. Much of what I will say now is based on my assumption that these predictions go back to Jesus himself. But my remarks would apply just as well if the predictions were considered postpaschal, because of their antiquity and identical formulation.[8]

Moreover, we might well voice the question raised by many other exegetes, including Hans Küng, about the exclusion of such prophecies on the grounds that they are postpaschal: "Does this mean that Jesus never thought that he might lose his life? This is a different question. Would he have been so naive as not to have had any presentiment of what finally happened to him?" (Küng 1976, 320).[9]

That question merits only one answer: no! It also suggests we should try to explore the logic that would have naturally led Jesus to foresee his future as inevitable. In other words, we must try to discover and explicate the cause and effect relationship between Jesus' preaching and activity on the one hand and his violent death on the other. To whom and for what reason did that preaching and activity become intolerable, so that they felt compelled to undertake a *political* action that they themselves regarded as complicated and dangerous.

All the purely religious accusations that might be directed against Jesus fall ridiculously short, it seems to me, unless we add the political dimension. Or, to put it even better, unless we keep in mind the political dimension intrinsic to them.

Suppose Jesus did publicly violate the Sabbath on occasion. Suppose he twisted the law and its authoritative interpretations. Suppose he declared himself to be the Messiah. Suppose he was regarded as a blasphemer, directly according to the Johannine tradition, indirectly by forgiving sins and placing himself above the law according to the Synoptics.[10] Even all those things would hardly constitute acts capable of provoking the process that led to Jesus' violent death. On this plane, of course, we could be the victims of our own secularized context, where a *purely* religious reason rarely serves as the sufficient cause of important and risky political events. When that does prove to be the case, we tend to talk about *fanaticism*. Must we then impute such fanaticism to the religious authorities who sent Jesus to his death?

The best way to answer that question, it seems to me, is to examine carefully the central nucleus of Jesus' three main predictions of his eventual passion. In that way we may be able to see how he himself viewed his conflictive situation.

In line with what has been said so far, the nucleus of those predictions can be reduced to the following assertions: (1) *He must suffer many things and be rejected by the elders, the chief priests, and the scribes and be condemned to death.* (2) *The Son of Man will be delivered into the hands of men* (and they will kill him; Matt., Mark). (3) *We are going up to Jerusalem, and the Son of Man will be delivered* (to the Gentiles; Luke) *to the chief priests and the scribes; they will condemn him to death and deliver him to the Gentiles* (Matt., Mark).

Three important points in this nucleus merit careful consideration. *First,* the mention of Jerusalem in the third prediction as the appointed place and destination for a process culminating in the predicted events helps us to situate the three predictions *before* Jesus' (only or last?) ascent to the holy city. Moreover, the fact that the first prediction is invariably situated immediately after Peter's messianic confession in the Synoptics enables us to locate it *after* Jesus' ministry in Galilee, which in all probability was ended by a crisis. Note that the context of Peter's confession tells us that it was a private conversation between Jesus and his apostles, and clearly suggests that not all of them shared Peter's certainty.

Second, we are surprised to note in the three predictions the absence of the group with whom Jesus, according to the three Synoptics, had his most serious, ongoing battles: the *Pharisees*. To be sure, some elders or members of the Sanhedrin would be Pharisees. Nevertheless, the explicit omission of the Pharisees is surprising because they are always present in Jesus' most important religious controversies.

Third, noteworthy is the fact that at least two of the predictions put stress on the religious authorities in Jerusalem: the *high priests*, accompanied by their functionaries, the scribes. To this religious bureaucracy, if you will, the first prediction logically adds mention of the elders, the consultative body that gave force to the decisions.

Let us now try to discern the meaning and import of these three elements, assuming that the three predictions, thus stripped of postpaschal additions and reduced to their nucleus, go back to Jesus himself. But remember that the results of our study would still hold weight even if they were to be regarded as the fruit of observations by the early Christian community rather than predictions that could be attributed directly to Jesus.

With regard to the *first* point, two Synoptic writers (Mark and Luke) tell us that as early as Jesus' ministry in Galilee, a province under Herod's jurisdiction, the enemies of Jesus were conspiring to do away with him.

That is how we should interpret the warning some Pharisees gave to Jesus, according to Luke: "Get away from here, for Herod wants to kill you" (Luke 13:31-33).[11] We have little data to confirm the likelihood of such an intention in Herod himself. But Mark, probably more trustworthy on this point, informs us that there was a conspiracy against Jesus almost from the very beginning of his ministry in Galilee and that *Herodians* were involved in it. After two bitter debates between Jesus and the *Pharisees* on the observance of the Sabbath, we are told: "The Pharisees went out, and immediately held counsel with the Herodians against him, how to destroy him" (Mark 3:6).

Remember what I said above. No matter what the existing legislation may have been, a religious subject such as the observance of the Sabbath could hardly have led to the violent death of Jesus unless there existed some group that was sincerely fanatical in religious matters. So we must ask ourselves whether such a group did in fact exist. The answer is yes. Such a group did exist, and it was made up of the Pharisees.[12] In the circumstances narrated by

Mark, that group could very well conceive a mortal hatred of Jesus rooted in religious reasons. The first conspiracy seems to confirm that hypothesis, particularly when we take two things into account: (1) controversies were numerous and violent in the Galilean context; and (2) the chronological dating that Mark gives to the conspiracy, like other Markan dates of that sort, may not be absolutely correct.

One thing is certain. For all their importance and prestige, the Pharisees lacked the power and authority to get rid of Jesus. Not inclined to go in for individual assassination for whatever reason, they had to ally themselves with others who possessed power and authority, *political* power and authority.

When Mark writes that "the Pharisees went out" of the synagogue to conspire, he seems to be suggesting that their allies were to be found in the outside world. It is unlikely that respect for the holiness of the place—the synagogue was not a temple—prevented the conspiracy from being planned inside it. However that may be, and even if we assume that the Herodians did not frequent the synagogue, that does not mean that they were areligious or antireligious. It is just that other interests were dominant in their minds. Commenting on Mark 3:6, the Jerusalem Bible tells us that the Herodians were "*politically* minded Jews" (my italics).[13]

Mark does not tell us what reasons the Pharisees might have offered to establish a common ground with the Herodians for their fight against Jesus. We can only assume that they presented the *political consequences* of Jesus' religious preaching. There was Jesus' conception of the kingdom of God and its strange preferences. There was his effort to topple the barriers of the law and place the latter in the service of the human being. This was not simply heresy. It could well be viewed as an incitement to subversion. We may hear an echo of this near the end of Jesus' life, when he is depicted as an agitator from Galilee: "He stirs up the people, teaching throughout all Judea, from Galilee even to this place" (Luke 23:5).

Perhaps the Herodians were not interested, or perhaps they could not convince the superficial hedonist that Herod seems to have been. Even more likely, the reasons offered by the Pharisees may have seemed a bit too subtle to authorities whose power was grounded not on religious factors but on the armed support of the Roman Empire.

The important point here is that the same scheme would apparently be repeated in Jerusalem because the same forces were present, and there the radicalness and antagonism would become explosive. That is fairly obvious in the reply that Jesus sends to Herod, according to Luke. He knows that his destiny will be played out in Jerusalem, and for the very same reasons (see Luke 13:33). Why? Because it is there, and only there, that there is an intrinsic linkup between (prophetic) religious interpretation and reason of state.

With regard to the *second* point, we should not be surprised to find that mention of the Pharisees disappears from the predictions concerning the events that are to take place in Jerusalem. And it is certainly not because there were no Pharisees there or because they were not at least as numerous and important in Jerusalem as they were in Galilee.[14]

The reason is that the protagonists have changed, even though the same basic scheme of conspiracy and plotting reappears. Why? Because in Jerusalem a new group, with more intelligence and power, will perceive what the Herodians were unable to gauge in Galilee: the *political* danger of Jesus.

The Pharisees disappear from the predictions because they have already fulfilled their ideological role as embodiments of religious fanaticism. Indeed that group plays both an illustrative and curious role. Rooted in his vision of God, Jesus delivered his most decisive blows against them. They are his enemies par excellence. Or, if you prefer, they are the enemies par excellence of the God that Jesus reveals to be the center of the coming kingdom. To characterize them and to attack their whole religious viewpoint, Jesus uses a label that has stuck to them ever since in the language of the West: *hypocrites*.[15]

This characterization calls for reservations, however, or for distinctions at least. The word covers a range of attitudes from plain *lying* (conscious misrepresentation) to *bad faith* (consciously responsible in origin but unconscious in its further developments).

It is true that Jesus attacks them on both counts. According to Matthew, Jesus attributes the religiosity of the Pharisees in general to their desire for prestige (hypocrisy as lying): "They do all their deeds to be seen by men. . . . They love the place of honor at feasts and the best seats in the synagogues, and being called rabbi by men" (Matt. 23:5-6).

Only once does Mark present Jesus hurling the accusation of hypocrisy at the Pharisees, but this time the charge refers to something far more radical. It concerns the profound deformation of a religion that is professedly from the heart but that has imperceptibly turned into something contrary to its own initial roots. Legalistic fanaticism has led them to an overall fanaticism in which the law itself is no longer recognized and traditions have taken its place (hypocrisy as bad faith). The very word "tradition" implies the gradual, unwitting clouding of their capacity for judgment (see Mark 7:1-6; Matt. 15:1-7).

Everything we know about the Pharisees from the Gospels and extrabiblical sources shows them to be a sincere and fanatically religious group. (Sincerity and fanaticism very often accompany the ultimate stages of bad faith.) Theirs is a terrible legalism. And if they are guilty of hypocrisy, it goes far beyond any conscious distortion motivated by their quest for privileges. It ultimately stems from *hardness of heart* (the heart being the seat of judgment), which is translated into an insensitivity to the evident needs of their neighbor, an insensitivity excused by appealing to higher, divine precepts. In Volume I of this work, I briefly considered Jesus' attack on that conception of God, and I shall return to it later. Here I shall simply summarize Jesus' position in the words of Mark's Gospel: "The sabbath was made for man, not man for the sabbath" (Mark 2:27).

Now there is one essential point that must be understood in the light of my preceding observations: the Pharisees had an important function in Israelite society. And this was true despite the fact, or more accurately because of the fact, that they had practically no political authority at all. There can be no doubt that this function was intimately bound up with their *prestige*, their moral authority (which Matthew attributes to their religious motivation). All Israel saw them as the group that represented the law interpreted with intellectual authority and taken seriously (to the point of fanaticism).

In that sense they represented what Jesus himself called the "traditions" of the ancestral past, all the things most deeply and distinctively rooted in Jewish nationality and culture, the touchstones for appeals to any grandiose national unity.

Aside from prestige, the Pharisees profited little from the sociopolitical structure of Israel. For that very reason, however, they sanctioned it with greater authority and objectivity through their interpretation of the law. Remember that the *status* of every individual and group in Israel derived from the law and its interpretation. The sick, the marginalized, the ignorant, the poor, those trapped in moral dead-ends: all found in those interpretations of the law the divine sanction and hence justification for their sorry situation in society. On the surface, then, the Pharisees seemed to be the most neutral and disinterested representatives of divine "justice" and its division of social roles on earth. In reality, however, they wittingly or unwittingly constituted the most powerful ideological tool available to the real authorities. Through them the real authorities could introject divine justification of their own position into the victims of the prevailing system.

That is why the religious discrediting of the Pharisees—an essential part of Jesus' preaching—was rightly viewed as the more subversive political activity. It was not that people felt he was sliding improperly from one plane to the other. Rather, they saw with ever-increasing clarity the political consequences of a message that continued to remain intrinsically religious. Indeed it was obviously much more subversive, because it was much more effective, than any attempt to use political means to attack the authorities who dominated the social system of Israel.

Those authorities, then, represent a new phase in the struggle undertaken by Jesus, and they take center stage in his prediction of a sorrowful future. The Pharisees cease to be the decisive nucleus in Jerusalem, the seat and stronghold of the real authorities. There Jesus' attack on them reaches its real political targets: the elders, the high priests, and the scribes.

That brings us to the *third* point in our study of Jesus' predictions. When it comes to spelling out the enemies who will put Jesus to death, those predictions mention *the high priests and the scribes* on two occasions, and *the elders* as well on one occasion. For the moment we shall disregard what might be the meaning of the "men" into whose hands Jesus will be delivered, according to the prediction considered to be earlier.

First of all, the combination of elders, high priests, and scribes designates the components of the great Sanhedrin in Jesus' day: that is, *the authority* that passed judgment on all religious matters and even on many civil matters. The only civil matters outside their jurisdiction were those of a serious nature that naturally concerned the Roman authorities as well. In such matters the Roman authorities assumed jurisdiction.

Secondly, the combination of "high priests and scribes" designates precisely what we today would call the Jewish *clergy* of the time as opposed to the Jewish laity.[16] The scribes, somewhat akin to our theologians or moralists, were *ordained*—by the laying on of hands[17]—to carry out that function. Their work was concerned primarily with interpreting the law and applying it to practical cases not covered by its letter. In short, the combination of "high priests and scribes" comprised the officially constituted *religious authority* of Israel, which was indisputable as such.

Finally, when mention is made in Jerusalem of all these components of the Sanhedrin, there is an allusion to their dominant (but not sole) religio-political tendency. They serve as the basic support and most visible embodiment of the *priestly party*, the party of the *Sadducees*. It is true that the Pharisees, a lay group in itself, counted many scribes in its ranks. So we read of "the scribes of the Pharisees" in Mark 2:16, and more properly of "the scribes and the Pharisees" in Matthew 5:20. But the priestly or Sadducean party was dominant, particularly around its bastion: the temple.

There were theological differences between the Pharisees and the Sadducees, of course. For one thing, they disagreed on belief in the resurrection of the dead (see Acts 23:1-8). But rather than being a sincerely religious sect in opposition to the Pharisees, the Sadducean party seemed to be much more concerned about their own power and its benefits than about the purity or profundity of their religious opinions.[18]

Like the Herodians, the Sadducees were politically minded Jews, closely linked to the other fonts or bulwarks of power and authority: Herod, the Romans, and the Jerusalem populace in the service of the temple. In this alliance of interests, however, they could defend themselves, not only by appealing to religious reasons invested with official authority, but also by using their own power to exert pressure on other authorities that were merely political.

Thus the perspicacity of the Pharisees in detecting the political aspect of Jesus' preaching would have a much more decisive impact on the Sadducean party in Jerusalem than on the Herodian party in Galilee. Sadducean differences from the Pharisees would play no role. Here the crucial fact was that the Sadducees had much more tangible things to lose with the kingdom of God proclaimed "with power" by Jesus. The latter could not have been, and was not, unaware of the political impact of his message or of its fatal conflictivity when it touched upon such concrete interests. That is why there is such likelihood that the predictions are his.

It is this complex of motivations, much more human and down to earth than those at stake in his arguments with the Pharisees, that would decide his fate in Jerusalem. This may help to explain the second prediction, considered by many exegetes to be the earliest and most creditable as a prepaschal pronouncement: "The Son of man will be delivered into the hands of *men*" (Mark 9:31).

In all likelihood this statement contains a grammatical form known as the divine passive. It is a way of not using the name of God directly when God is the active subject of the verb. So we could rephrase the sentence to read that in Jerusalem God *will deliver* the Son of Man into the hands of *men*.

Interpreting the second prediction that way, we see that it is closely connected to Jesus' exclamation on the cross, his very words most likely: "My God, my God, why hast thou forsaken me?" (Mark 15:34).[19] The touchstone of Jesus' religious revelation would be the moment when human self-interests are made manifest and threatened, when the vaunted religious authorities have to make clear the human mechanisms they obey, when those who claim to have faith *in God* must reveal the ideology that underlies their treatment of the *human being* (see 1 John 4:20).

Thus the essential nucleus of the three predictions, uttered in the middle of Jesus' ministry, sheds a clear light on the significance that Jesus gave to his message. It explains why Jesus, once he was in Jerusalem, did nothing to dispel the fatal misunderstanding that would necessarily picture him as a political agitator; it explains why he did the very opposite, in fact. He makes no effort to dispel the misunderstanding because there is no such misunderstanding. When he is delivered into the hands of men, it is because his message has reached its natural goal, because it has been completely comprehended.[20]

So closes the circle. From start to finish, from his adversaries to Jesus himself, everyone and everything make clear that the revelation of God in Jesus was intrinsically political, without ceasing thereby to be religious: that is, to appeal to a faith truly such.

God cannot communicate with humanity except by taking up, in the limited way that is part and parcel of everything in history, the language of human meaningfulness and values on one or another of the planes of existence. The political plane is no more unworthy than any other plane of serving as the vehicle for God's revelation. It does not compromise or obscure the religious content God wishes to interject into it any more than any other plane does.

As we come to the end of these two chapters, we might do well to go back to our original question: Was Jesus a *politician*?

To say that Jesus was not a professional politician, that he was not the author or proponent of any political ideology, may constitute a historical mistake that is far more serious than a simple anachronism.

After all, what is a politician or a professional politician in our day? Someone who uses or creates, in an open, explicit way, a system of political means in order to place them in the service of a *faith*, a certain conception of the meaning of the human being and its social life (be it religious or not). And do we not find the very same two dimensions in the activity of Jesus?

Shall we say that persons are all the more professional politicians insofar as they hide the values served in order to concentrate solely and exclusively on the means? If so, then Jesus obviously cannot be regarded as a politician in that sense. But to say that is to discredit the political function and go directly against our own use of language. Do we not apply the designation of great politicians to those who have earnestly tried to explicate and propagate most clearly the values that they served? And do we not label as "political hacks" those who are concerned solely to win power, without knowing or caring why or wherefore?

Of course one might persist in applying the label "politician" only to those who have actually exercised power. But that runs counter to the widespread and long-standing historical recognition of the political importance of people who gave direction to the political action of others without ever exercising power themselves.

Finally, some will say that today, at least, people cannot seriously envision orienting their political activity in line with the gospel of Jesus. That is quite true, if the phrase "gospel of Jesus" is taken literally. But what, at bottom, is the reason that people cannot use Jesus' gospel to orient themselves politically? People may say that Jesus can only offer general principles, that real-life politics calls for concrete means—ideologies—that act as a lever on history. But here is the anachronism: in his own day Jesus was supremely concrete, to the point of forcing his political enemies to put him to death as the only means of evading his power.

Why, then, should we call abstract *today* what was *then* concrete and effective? Is it not because *we are no longer creating christologies*—to use the latter word in a positive sense? The effort to fashion one, single christology, to turn into a tract what in Jesus was concrete situation, project, and life, can evade the problem of time only by way of abstraction. A faith without ideologies does certainly avoid the "danger" of calling Jesus a politician. But the price of this secure neutrality is the insignificance of Jesus for humanity and the impossibility of faith.

CHAPTER VII

The Proximity of the Kingdom

In this chapter I shall move in concentric circles to deal with basic points raised in the two preceding chapters. Nevertheless, this chapter will not be a summary or religious correction of their political thrust.

In the two preceding chapters I tried to open up my readers to two crucial points, to get them ready for all their implications.

First of all, I raised this question: How is it that an ordinary human being with no religious authority whatsoever, a lay person in the fullest sense of the word, began to arouse interest in his contemporaries? And how did he do this without preaching about himself? How did he manage to wangle through the complex, power-laden religious structure of Israel and arouse the concrete, passionate interest of his contemporaries? When we let go of tenacious clichés and pose the problem in rigorous, historical terms, we soon realize that this interest derived from the fact that the preaching of Jesus dealt very concretely with the human lives of the Jewish people and that this interest, right up to the very end (a political end if there ever was one), was the logical result of the conflictivity triggered by Jesus himself, not by some juridical mistake. To put it in other words: the force and power of the message preached by the historical Jesus certainly did not derive from the fact that people, from the very beginning, saw in him the founder of a new religion.[1]

The second point may seem to be opposed to the first, though it is not. It is simply this: even though the message and activity of Jesus had concrete consequences of a political nature, they never ceased to be religious at the same time. And the religious aspect was not an accidental admixture. There is no question of choosing one end of the spectrum or of adding one aspect to the other to balance the two dimensions. What I have been trying to show up to now, and what I will continue to try to show in the following pages, is that *everything* said and done by Jesus of Nazareth had inherently political dimensions, not merely hypothetical applications, that he expressed his religious message in a political key and in that way manifested God. Hence it is only by grasping the political thrust of expressions (in their rightful context) that seem to be merely religious that we will comprehend the true intention of

Jesus and come to an authentic (religious) interpretation of his message.

If we are to continue our exegesis of who and what Jesus was in history, we must first tear down the hermeneutic assumption that we must choose between the political and the religious.

Assuming these two points as my working hypothesis, I shall now try to interpret the overall message of Jesus of Nazareth. We shall be going back over points already examined, to be sure. But now we shall see that they are not isolated or exaggerated applications to spheres other than the religious one, but, rather, authentic centers that spell out and make comprehensible all the rest.

If my analysis of faith in Volume I was correct, then we know that an authentic *religious* faith is not such because it deals with a specific plane bearing the label "religious." Religious faith will always be transmitted in an anthropological key: on one of the value-planes where the human being seeks to give meaningfulness to its existence. The religious is not one of those planes; it is a quality of faith. The political plane is not the only or the privileged plane for conveying religious faith, of course. But my readers should realize by now that everything we can know about Jesus of Nazareth from history proves that this was the plane where the historical Jesus played out his meaning-laden destiny from start to finish of his ministry.

I

I have already cited Mark's summary of Jesus' initial preaching in Galilee: "The time is fulfilled, and the kingdom of God is at hand; repent [have a change of outlook], and believe in the gospel [good news]" (Mark 1:15; see Matt. 4:17). Luke's version of Jesus' preaching at the start of his ministry in Galilee offers a striking similarity of motifs to the episode of his appearance in the synagogue of Nazareth (Luke 4:16–21).

Several questions come to mind right away as we read this basic résumé: What exactly is this kingdom of God that is at hand? Why and for whom does it constitute a gospel, a piece of good news? And why does this good news require repentance, a change of outlook, in order to be believed?

If we refrain from imposing on those questions the prefabricated solutions of our theology, we will find the answers in the Synoptics themselves, particularly in the two that depend on Q: Matthew and Luke. The fact is that we find the first elaboration of Jesus' summarized preaching in Galilee in what Matthew calls the Sermon on the Mount and Luke calls the Sermon on the Plain. And we find it expressed even more concretely in the declarations of blessedness, the *Beatitudes,* that lead off those sermons.[2]

We find something surprising here, however. Both Matthew and Luke seem to show respect for words of key importance in Jesus' message. They give them a typical and solemn form, and they place them in the same basic meaning-context. Nevertheless they have Jesus saying very different things! We need not have comparative recourse to the common source of their statements and what we can know about it. Reading the Gospels in any accurate translation is enough to bring out this disorienting difference. According to Luke, Jesus declared Christians blessed in their real-life *situation* of poverty, hunger, and affliction: "And he lifted up his eyes on his disciples and said: 'Blessed are you poor . . . ' " (Luke 6:20). According to Matthew, Jesus declared happy those people (Jews? Christians? human beings?) who possessed "poverty of spirit," a "hunger for justice," and a whole series of such *virtues* (see Matt. 5).

Jacques Dupont has pointed out how a theological motif—the inerrancy of Scripture—prevented exegetes from recognizing this obvious difference and asking which version was the correct one. Sheer logic suggests that one writer or both must have understood what Jesus said in an improper way, that is, in a sense different from that meant by Jesus himself.[3]

How are we to explain this scandalous difference on such a central point? We sense that some obstacle inherent in this specific point of Jesus' message must lie behind this difficulty in recording its correct tenor. Now if we follow the redactional course of this passage in its broad outlines (Myre 1977, 75–104), we come up with the following.

1. Numerous examples in both the Old Testament and the Gospels themselves indicate that the most current and normal form of beatitudes is a statement in the *third person*: blessed are those who . . . Now the fourth Beatitude in Q (and Luke), which came out of a different context, probably contained a prediction of future persecutions, similar to those of Jesus, which would fall upon his followers. This special Beatitude, as it appears in Matthew's text (5:11), which here resembles Luke, logically requires the *second person* plural: "Blessed are *you* when. . . . " Faced with three Beatitudes in the third person and one in the second person, Luke must have chosen to unify them all by adopting the second person, fully realizing that he was transposing the Beatitudes to the church. As the continuer of Jesus' work, the church would be poor, hungry, afflicted, and persecuted. But there can hardly be any doubt that the original must have had the form we find in Matthew. The first three Beatitudes in Q must have been in the third person plural: Blessed are those who. . . .[4]

2. We have just seen how Luke tried to bring the first three Beatitudes into harmony with the fourth. Matthew tries to do the same thing by placing the three Beatitudes (plus four other explanatory ones he adds) in the service of a *general theme* he uses to center the Sermon on the Mount. It is a program for a *righteousness* that "exceeds that of the scribes and Pharisees" (Matt. 5:20). To speak of righteousness is to talk about a pathway of virtues.[5] According to Matthew, then, Jesus declared blessed those who possessed the principal virtues that go to make up Christian righteousness, which is in turn the culmination of authentic Old Testament righteousness. The *situations* of the original Beatitudes were, in this case, transformed into so many *virtues:* poverty into "poverty of spirit," hunger into "hunger for justice," and so forth.

3. Now if we bring together these two different redactional dislocations and set them aside, we will have the probable text of Q, the source common to Matthew and Luke: "Blessed are the poor. . . . Blessed are those who mourn. . . . Blessed are the hungry. . . . " In other words, the declaration of blessedness is addressed to people caught in a certain *situation* that is not peculiar to the Christian community and that always entails neediness and pain.

What is so difficult, then, about the first three Beatitudes in the form just indicated? Jesus' statement is simple and clear. Why did it have to be applied or explained in such tortuous and roundabout ways that only serve to reduce the amplitude of the Beatitudes?

As we begin to try to answer such questions, we must remember that the issue at hand is nothing more nor less than defining what exactly is involved in the *kingdom of God* that arrives with Jesus. The Beatitudes do precisely that. Not only do they declare blessed three categories of people; they also bring out the why and wherefore of such a declaration. That gives us two more points to add to the above.

4. The poor are happy or blessed for the simple reason that "theirs [not *yours* as Luke has] is *the kingdom of heaven.*" The poor define the kingdom because they will be its owners. It comes for them. So true is this that those in the opposite situation can logically give only one response to the announcement of the kingdom's arrival: a mournful "yikes!" of pained surprise. The kingdom will bring to an end everything that afforded them recompense, that made it worthwhile for them to struggle to achieve their present situation; hence it will vitiate the meaningfulness and value of that situation.

5. The kingdom also comes to change the *situation* of the poor, to put an end to it. As the first Beatitude tells us, the poor possess the kingdom of God. That is not due to any merit of theirs, much less to any value that poverty might have. On the contrary, the kingdom is theirs because of the inhuman nature of their situation as poor people. The kingdom is coming because God is "humane," because God cannot tolerate that situation and is coming to make sure that the divine will be done on earth. Poverty must cease to wreak destructive havoc on humanity. Thus the latter part of the second and third Beatitudes spells out the import of the latter part of first Beatitude. The kingdom will ensure that the mournful will be able to laugh, that the hungry will get their fill: in short, that the poor will cease to be poor.

Here we have something that has proved to be profoundly scandalous for theology, however little reflection has gone into it. I am not talking about Jesus' preference for the poor. Even the most conservative theologians agree that Jesus, though addressing himself to all, gave a privileged place to the poor in his message and his actions.[6] In Chapter V we noted the mechanisms whereby theology can accept this clear preference without reaching the terrible conclusion that Jesus is thereby promoting some sort of class warfare.

Right now let us try to pinpoint the specifically theological stone of scandal in the Q version of the first three Beatitudes (which would be the reason for the divergent versions of Matthew and Luke). We must try to recapture the "scandal of the cross" of which Paul writes, you see, because the Beatitudes addressed to the poor and the cross constitute two different stages on one and the same road.

The difficulty of theologians is brought out as clearly by Jacques Dupont as by anyone else, so let me use him here. After arriving at the aforementioned conclusions about the editing history of the Beatitudes, Dupont asks and answers the following question about the majority situation of the poor in Israel:

Must we conclude that one need only belong to the mass, more or less indifferent in the matter of religious practice, to ensure oneself a share in the happiness of the kingdom? *Obviously not!* Weiss explains: "Poverty or social oppression do not yet constitute a reason for proclaiming those human beings blessed. It is necessary, in addition, that *they be consciously aware* (empfinden) *of their misery.* When the authors of the Old Testament, of the Psalms in particular, write about *the poor,* they naturally assume that in their suffering these human beings place their sole hope in God. However far removed they may be from the irreproachable conduct of those who pass for models of piety, these *sinners* have not let the spark of the religious life be extinguished within themselves. The representatives of righteousness deny them salvation. They know that they will not share in the future world, that they will face the great day of judgment with empty hands. Nevertheless they still cling to the God of the promise with their terribly frail and fragile hope" [Dupont 1954, 435; citing Weiss 1906, 240; my italics].

It is a very nice passage, to be sure. But the Old Testament is not the New Testament, the Psalms are not the gospel message, and it is not certain that the Psalms always talk about the "poor of Yahweh" in that sense.

I am not being anachronistic when I say that this theological difficulty in grasping the most obvious thrust of Jesus' words may be responsible for the curious fact that Matthew and Luke offer us two divergent versions of such an important and central text. Dupont himself cites a Christian work of the early centuries known as the *Pseudo-Clementine Epistles.* In transcribing the Beatitudes, the *Pseudo-Clementines* "adopt a specific viewpoint and do not mention Matthew's specification ('in spirit')." When it comes to the question "of knowing if the poor will be saved even if they were impious, Peter responds: 'Not at all. The indigence of the indigent person is no good if that person covets what does not belong to him or her . . . ' " (Dupont 1954, 412).

It should now be obvious to my readers that the theological scandal of the Beatitudes lies in the fact that there is a period after "the poor." In their clearest and most ancient sense, they tell us that there is an intrinsic and positive relationship between the kingdom and the *situation* of *every* poor person, between the happiness brought by the kingdom and being poor *(period!)*. Any and all added comment is speculation; it does not come from Jesus. Dupont arrives at the very same conclusion *exegetically* and then denies it *theologically,* though his denial is completely illogical after all his work to establish the original import of the Beatitudes.

The context of the Sermon on the Mount suggests to us that if the Beatitudes in their original form (as reconstructed for Q) go back to Jesus himself, their natural addressees were the poor of Israel. Not simply or mainly because the preaching of Jesus of Nazareth was limited to the territory of Palestine (see Matt. 10:5-6), but because their very terms and origin allude to Old Testament tradition. Limitation does not imply exclusion, however. Pronouncing them in our context today, would Jesus use the very same terms, disregarding the fact that among the poor today we find good and bad people, Christians and atheists? Would their situation once again take precedence over moral and religious conditions?

In his exegesis André Myre draws the logical conclusions for which Dupont paved the way with his exhaustive study of the Beatitudes:

Hence it is the intuition Jesus has of *his God* that governs his life and makes him choose *those to whom he is going to speak about God.* It is quite obvious that Jesus does not turn to some social or religious group that had prepared itself in some special way to receive God, that had the requisite religious dispositions for it: a tiny remnant of especially pious people chosen out from a worldly mass destined for perdition. *Inner dispositions have nothing to do with Jesus' choice.* Jesus addresses himself to the lowly, the socially marginalized, the sick, the disadvantaged, the poor people who are victims of injustice, those kinds of people who have no hope in this kind of world. He announces to them that God loves them. And it must be stressed: this option, this proclamation, *has nothing to do with the moral, spiritual, or religious worth* of those people. It is grounded exclusively on the horror that the God known to Jesus feels for the present state of the world, and on the divine decision to come and re-establish the situation in favor of those for whom life is more difficult. *Jesus reveals God, not the spiritual life of his listeners* [Myre 1977, 80-81].[7]

Here we have the great paradox, the unexpected finding: the more the Beatitudes allude to the simple, anguished situation of the poor, the afflicted, and the hungry, the more *political* they turn out to be; but, at the same time, the more they are dissociated from any intrinsic relationship with the moral, spiritual, or religious dispositions of human groups, the more *religious* they become. For it is thus that they enable us to probe much deeper into the "heart" of God, into the mystery of God's will on earth. And only thus do we glimpse the realm of values for which God opts and then makes the object of God's reign.

II

What we have seen so far about the addressees of the Beatitudes, and of the kingdom itself, is not idle speculation; nor is it based solely on the hypothetical reconstruction of the source common to Matthew and Luke.

Before we move on, let us note an important documentary fact. I said earlier that Luke, unlike Mark and Matthew, does not present a summary of Jesus' preaching in Galilee at the start of his ministry there—unless we count as such Jesus' preaching in the synagogue of Nazareth, which is narrated solely by Luke and situated by him at the start of Jesus' Galilean ministry.

In that episode Jesus avails himself of a biblical reference, taken from the Book of Isaiah, on which he is to comment. He chooses a passage, reads it, and then goes on to say: "Today this scripture has been fulfilled in your hearing" (Luke 4:21). We seem to hear an echo of the other summaries of his preaching: "The time is fulfilled." And what do we have in Luke instead of the assertion that "the kingdom of God is at hand"? What is the "good news"? We find the answer in the text chosen by Jesus from the Book of Isaiah (61:1–2): "The spirit of the Lord is upon me; therefore he has anointed me. He has sent me to announce *good news to the poor,* to proclaim liberation to the captives and recovery of sight to the blind, to liberate the oppressed and proclaim a year of favor from the Lord" (Luke 4:18–19; Segundo text translated).

Here again, as in the Beatitudes, the poor are the recipients of the good news because the mission of the Anointed One is directed to them. And it is their painful situation that moves Yahweh to intervene. Here again there is no mention of the moral or religious qualities of the poor, the captives, the blind, and the oppressed. Although many readers take it for granted, nothing says that the blind who curse their blindness will remain in it. To make the parallel clear: the "year of favor from the Lord" is for "the oppressed" [8] just as the kingdom belongs to the poor (period!).

Once again, and this time unmistakably, the sociopolitical situation seems to take precedence, at least on the level of expression, over moral and religious qualities; no mention is made of the latter as possible factors conditioning the good news. The parallel with the source of the Beatitudes could not be more evident.

Now, however, we begin to go down a road where interpretation of the announcement of the kingdom, though it remains essentially the same in the Synoptics and thus confirms what we saw in the previous section, begins to show the seeds of different christologies that have been creatively adapted to different audiences. In the material recorded solely by Luke, therefore, we find the confirmation and explication—in a specific direction—of the Beatitudes that Jesus addressed to *the poor.* We have just seen one instance of this, and we may now look for others.

We know that Luke addressed his Gospel to readers of Hellenistic culture. Unlike John, he was not led to abandon the Synoptic backdrop in so doing. But he was led to play down aspects relating almost exclusively to the Jewish world and to play up anthropological aspects common to any and every society of his day and hence more directly accessible to his readers.

In that respect we are impressed by the considerable space that the specifically Lukan material gives to the sociocultural theme of poverty versus wealth. Here Luke clearly differs from the other two Synoptics. He also differs from the image we today have of the two terms and perhaps from our conception of wealth in particular.[9] That is not really surprising. The growth of capitalism has created a type of *rich* person unknown in Jesus' day, in Palestine at least: a person who accumulates and deals in capital funds, no matter what *lifestyle* that person may display before us. Today we tend to associate wealth more with power. In Luke's time a rich person was characterized more by a particular way of spending money after acquiring it.

Having noted these precautions, which should be kept in mind as we proceed, we can now gauge the peculiar importance that Luke attributes to the *social* aspects of poverty and wealth.

With regard to *the poor,* first of all, Luke's vocabulary is more precise than that of the other two Synoptics. It suggests that he is particularly attentive or sensitive to various forms of *poverty*. Thus he differentiates: the poor who lack all the necessities (the *ptochói* of the Beatitudes and of the parable of the rich man and Lazarus); the poor who have only the bare necessities (the *penichrá* widow who puts her mite in the moneybox of the temple); and those who are in need of some of the necessities (the *endeés* who, according to Luke in Acts, did not exist in the early church because of the sharing of goods practiced by it).

Insofar as *the rich* are concerned, Luke shows an extraordinary interest in their situation, both in itself and in relation to the message of Jesus. This is evident from his frequent references to them. Besides the two passages he shares with Mark,[10] and the "woes!" he addresses to them in his contrasting version of the Beatitudes, Luke writes no less than eight times more about the rich in his own special material.

In one case Luke merely explains why the rich young aristocrat, who had asked Jesus how he might enter the kingdom of God or gain eternal life, went away sad in the end: "for he was very rich" (Luke 18:23). In all the other cases, however, we are dealing with whole passages that are to be found only in the Lukan tradition: the conversion of Zacchaeus (Luke 19:2); the advice to invite to the dinner table—a favorite theme of Luke as we shall see—people who cannot return the invitation (Luke 14:12–14, which ends in the form of a beatitude: "You will be blessed"); the parable of the rich man and Lazarus, the poor beggar (Luke 16:19–31); and, finally, the parable of the foolish rich man (Luke 12:16).

If we add to that Lukan passages which deal with the theme in some way (e.g., the so-called parable of the prodigal son), we can say that *almost all* the material which Luke contributes to the Synoptics deals more or less directly with these two opposed situations of human existence: poverty and wealth. Now it will always be possible for someone to minimize this finding by attributing it to the personal curiosity or sensibility of the redactor of the third Gospel: like the innocuous hypothesis that Luke was a physician because of his detailed description of different illnesses or cures. In exegetical terms, however, and in the light of the central place occupied by the Beatitudes, it is safer and more scientific to assume that Luke's interest in poverty and wealth derives precisely from the confluence of various strands of testimony about the message of Jesus recorded in the traditions of the early churches on the one hand, and from the Hellenistic church context of Luke on the other—two roads that start from the same point: the Beatitudes of Jesus.

From our standpoint Luke's interest in the theme is all the more noteworthy insofar as Luke does not display any formulated or unconscious prejudice *against wealth*. Unlike the Fathers of the church, who in later centuries would conclude that "no one can become rich without injustice," [11] Luke has nothing to say about the moral and social problem of the *origin* of wealth. More naive, perhaps, he thinks solely about its *use*.

For the evangelist that use, when it is normal, centers around the supreme "social" moment: the *meal table*. Luke always uses the middle voice (Zerwick 1957,171) of the Greek verb for "enjoy," indicating that he means "enjoy oneself" in the context. And he envisions the two great joys of the dinner table: food dishes and company. That is what the rich of the parable enjoys while poor Lazarus goes hungry at his gate (Luke 16:19, 21). In his abject poverty the prodigal son recalls the meals provided the hired servants in his father's house. When he returns home, his father welcomes him with a festive meal, a banquet, thus arousing envy in the elder brother (Luke 15:16, 23-25, 29, 32). The future banquets of which he is assured constitute the foolish calculus of the man who has passed the threshold of wealth (Luke 12:19) but is destined to die that very night. According to Matthew, the difference between John the Baptist and those living in royal palaces lies in the quality of their garments. Luke adds the image of delights enjoyed by the latter, undoubtedly alluding to the delights of the royal table as well.

Logically enough, the *sumptuous* character of banquets (see Luke 16:19) is in proportion to the size of one's wealth. But the pleasures of a shared meal are not a possibility reserved exclusively for the rich. They can also be enjoyed by those who share the modest means they possess. It is in the latter sense that we should interpret Luke's typically frequent references to Jesus' presence at some banquet, rather than picturing him as participating in the banquets of the truly rich. According to Luke, Jesus is invited three times by a Pharisee and he accepts the invitation. According to Mark 2:15, Levi offers Jesus a simple meal; Luke turns it into a banquet. The connection between sharing meals and joy is also brought out by Luke with reference to the early church, despite the relative poverty of the latter (see Acts 2:46; 14:17), and he links the absence of both in the second and third Beatitudes.

Most importantly of all, it is Luke who does most to spell out the connection between the pleasures of a shared meal and eschatological realities (though the general opinion is that he tends to postpone the latter whereas the other two Synoptics expect them in the immediate present). Even though the datum itself may be postpaschal, one thing that shows up clearly is the importance Luke attributes to what went on at Jesus' last meal with his apostles before he suffered (Luke 22:15). Luke records more material than do Mark and Matthew as to what was said and done at that meal. Moreover, Luke stresses the "earnest desire" of Jesus "to eat this passover with you . . . for I tell you I shall not eat it again until it reaches its fulfillment in the kingdom of God" (Luke 22:15-16; Segundo text translated). Luke's Jesus does even more to point up this continuity. It is only in Luke's Gospel that Jesus uses the opportunity of a common meal to define the kingdom precisely in terms of a banquet: "And I assign to you, *as my Father assigned to me, a kingdom, that you may eat and drink at my table* . . ." (Luke 22:29–30).[12]

Of all that Lukan material, however, it is the parable of the rich man and poor Lazarus that is of special interest to us because it spells out in unmistakable terms the Beatitudes as Luke must have read them in Q. To grasp this connection, however, we must slough off not only postpaschal additions but also the theological presuppositions of later centuries.

First and foremost, it is a parable dealing with the changes to be ushered in by the arrival of the kingdom of God. The fact that at the end Lazarus is depicted in Abraham's bosom (Luke 16:22) is a clear allusion to the eschatological banquet. The fact that death must intervene between the present situation and the future one (that will be ushered in by the arrival of the kingdom) is clearly a recognized trait of Lukan theology, one based on the realization that the eschatological kingdom of God is slow in arriving. The parable is certainly not focusing on the different destinies of two human beings as they move from life in this world to eternal reward or punishment, as later theology would claim. This is made quite clear from the discussion between the rich man and Abraham, as we shall see.

Both the situation of the anonymous rich man and that of poor Lazarus are described in a way that surprises us, even after what we have just seen about the Lukan material. The day-to-day lives of these two men, who will end up with such different destinies, are described without the slightest reference to their moral or religious circumstances. Though one might be tempted to assume it, nothing says that Lazarus is patient, pious, or has placed his trust in Yahweh. And though we may feel antipathy toward the rich man, we are not told that he is pitiless, cruel, blind to the misfortune of others, or impervious to Yahweh's law. Moreover, if we try to detect moral insinuations in the parable's description, which underlines the opposition between them as much as possible, we find that the rest of the parable soon sets us straight. The reasons given for their opposite fates after death rule out any moral judgment. As in the Beatitudes (even in Luke's version), the parable describes two *situations,* not the interior life of the parties in question.

What, then, accounts for their diametrically opposed situations after death, with the arrival of the kingdom? The answer is clear, decisive, and theologically scandalous. Abraham gives it to the rich man: "Son, remember that you in your lifetime received your *good things,* and Lazarus in like manner *evil things;* but *now* he is comforted here, and you are in anguish" (Luke 16:25).[13]

That answer is surprising and disconcerting from a theological standpoint because moral or religious reasons are totally absent. Poor Lazarus is participating in the eschatological banquet simply and solely because he is one of the poor.

Here we evidently have an almost literal reproduction of the first Beatitude, this time in vivid images, and even of the other two Beatitudes, which make it still clearer that the kingdom of God is coming to invert situations: so that those who now weep can laugh and those who are hungry now can have their fill. Fully in accord with Luke's view, those who are laughing now will end up weeping, and those who have their fill now will end up hungry, because the advantage of the rich will end with the arrival of the kingdom.

With good reason we could say that in this parable Luke restores to the Beatitudes their universality, stripping away the ecclesial limitedness his editing had imposed on them. Here the original Beatitudes again ring out in their most radical tone. And so we can reiterate André Myre's comment on the Beatitudes, this time inserting a more specific allusion to this parable:

> And it must be stressed: this option [for Lazarus], this proclamation, *has nothing to do with the moral, spiritual, or religious worth* [of Lazarus]. It is grounded exclusively on the horror that the God known to Jesus feels for the present state of the world [and of Lazarus in it], and on the divine decision to come and re-establish the situation in favor of those for whom life is more difficult. *Jesus reveals God, not the spiritual life* [of the rich man and Lazarus] [Myre 1977, 80–81].[14]

III

These observations on the peculiarly Lukan material—and here "material" is meant in both the nominal and the adjectival sense—sought to bring out the extent to which the supposedly original form of the Beatitudes is linked up with other important elements of the third Gospel. But Luke's material moves us away from the Palestinian context that dominates Mark, Matthew, and even Luke himself when he is dependent on the two sources common to the Synoptic Gospels.

We have already seen that Q probably presented the Beatitudes as addressed to (Jewish) human beings in situations of poverty, affliction, and hunger. The key word here is *poor* people, and the other two words spell that out. We also saw that Luke, by inclination or by virtue of his context, stressed two points in his own explanation: the privation of food at table and of the social relations associated with the meal table. In his version the "weeping" mentioned in the Beatitudes seems to be the result of that privation.

A question is in order here, however. Can we identify the "weeping" of the poor simply and solely with their hunger, or does it also allude to other dimensions of poverty that were of less interest to Luke? In trying to answer that question, we are immediately confronted with two difficulties.

1. We do not know if Jesus really uttered the Beatitudes, even in their most primitive version (Q). When memory tries to recall a deceased person, it sometimes confuses deeds with words. Moreover, in the ancient world it was a common and accepted procedure for historians to put words and whole discourses into the mouths of eminent personages that they had never uttered, because the words explained the meaning of their actions. It made the narrative more vivid than it would have been if the historian had simply offered an explanation of his own. So although our Q source is closer to Jesus than any of the actual Gospels, it is not an adequate guarantee that Jesus actually *pronounced* the Beatitudes. The Beatitudes could have been a formula used by the Christian community to recall and explain how Jesus acted and why he chose to be mainly concerned about certain people—the people who were his friends, those to whom he spoke about the kingdom as a piece of good news. [15]

2. Even if we assume that we have correctly reconstructed Q, we are still faced with a Greek translation of another Q in Aramaic. So whether or not Jesus is the author of the formula of the Beatitudes, what original term lies behind the translation that turns the *poor* into the possessors of the kingdom?

Let us start with an assumption that is not required by sheer logic in order to sustain the point I am going to make, as my readers will see. Let us assume that the Beatitudes do not represent the exact words of Jesus himself, that they embody what witnesses understood about his general attitude, his preferences, and his friendships. In that case we must say that the Gospels do not depict Jesus with excessive frequency among the poor, understanding the latter term in the markedly economic sense that Luke gives to it and exemplifies in the image of Lazarus. [16] Moreover, Luke himself agrees with Matthew (and Q) insofar as he cites a very old and creditable accusation against Jesus. He tells us that Jesus' enemies accused him of being "a glutton and a drunkard, a friend of *tax collectors* and *sinners*" (Luke 7:34; Matt. 11:19). This fits in much better with what the Synoptics narrate, as well as with a good part of the preaching that they attribute to Jesus.

Is there a *term* in the original language of Jesus, then, that combines both notions: the day-to-day difficulties of economic poverty *and* the social rejection suffered by those who were publicly considered sinners?

Such a contemptuous term did in fact exist in Israel. A literal translation of the Aramaic term would be "the people of the land." I am not going to explore the historical origin of that term. [17] The point of interest to us here is the likelihood that it is this term that was translated into Greek as "the poor," for want of an intelligible Greek equivalent. The word actually alludes to a whole group of marginalized people, in whom economic poverty is combined with moral reprobation.

Poverty entailed the usual lack of general education and culture. In that age and context it entailed a lack of religious education in particular. This translated into a fervent faith, but one marked by theoretical impurities and negligent practices. In John's Gospel the Pharisees allude to this reality when they say: "But this crowd, who do not know the law, are accursed" (John 7:49). The evangelist could have used two Greek words for what is translated here as "crowd." One, *laós,* is positive or neutral. The other, *óchlos,* is pejorative. According to John's Gospel, it is the latter pejorative term that was used by the Pharisees and high priests.

There can be no doubt, then, that one single concept lies behind the two words, the *poor* and *sinners,* and that the "weeping" of the second Beatitude may allude to it. We will have ample opportunity to prove that in what follows. Here I shall limit myself to one example.

Jesus' friendship with sinners does not contradict his message about the kingdom of God; it is inextricably bound up with that message. One of the most scandalous statements in the preaching of Jesus, recorded by Matthew (ordinarily the most prudent of all the evangelists), refers specifically to the relationship between the most blatant public sinners and the kingdom: "Truly, I say to you, the tax collectors and the harlots go into the kingdom of God before you" (Matt. 21:31). Notice that there is a strict parallelism between that statement and the first Beatitude (according to Q) if the *poor* and *tax-collectors* and *harlots* do, in fact, constitute one and the same group.

Going (before) *into* the kingdom[18] is really a declaration of blessedness, a beatitude that could logically be expressed as follows: "Blessed are the tax collectors and the harlots. . . ." And "before" establishes a special relationship between this group and the kingdom, a relationship of belonging, so that we could end this Beatitude in a strictly parallel way: "because theirs is the kingdom of heaven," if only by way of priority.

Having reached this point, we can abandon the exegetical hypotheses we started with. They are no longer necessary. It really does not matter whether the Beatitudes were uttered by Jesus or whether they simply sum up his way of acting and relating to people. And it really does not matter whether the Aramaic term, "the people of the land," is or is not behind the Greek word for "the poor." If we concede that the Beatitudes do sum up the preaching and general behavior of Jesus, then we must broaden the concept of the economically poor, not to include virtues, of course, but to include the weeping of those marginalized as sinners.

André Myre stresses the necessity of amplifying the concept of the poor in the behavior of Jesus:

> Jesus stays apart from the great centers inhabited by the educated and the people of good position (because they have less need of hope and

know how to make out for themselves in life). Jesus goes to the places where he will find the poor people who have no resources against the powerful. That is what he does with the tax collectors or publicans, who are despised and anathemized (Matt. 2:15-17). He announces that God loves them more than Pharisees, who are certainly good people and have less need of help (Luke 18:9-14). He is accused of being a glutton and a drunkard, a man who hangs around in bad company (Matt. 11:19). He does not hesitate to say, though it scandalizes good people, that prostitutes will be among the first into the kingdom of God (Matt. 21:31). Jesus has to make a choice. Not being able to address himself to everybody at the same time, he refuses to concern himself with those people whose affairs are going well. He mixes with those who have lost everything (Luke 15:4-7). It is the sick, not the healthy, sinners rather than the just (Mark. 2:17), who need him. So he will go out to them, cure them, tell them that God loves them so much that he pardons them and wants to be their king. In his own life, then, Jesus incarnates an important line of force in the Old Testament. He gives God a face. He reveals God [Myre 1977, 80].

All that is quite correct. But in offering this summa of Jesus' preferences and thus broadening the concept of *the poor*, one may not perceive the radical politico-religious change involved when it comes to the *sinners* specifically.

The most important thing to realize here is that Jesus did not add the group, sinners, to the poor, the sick, the hungry, and the afflicted, embracing them with the same sort of compassion. *The poor themselves are sinners.* If we view them in terms of their material *situation* and their marginalized place in society, they are poor. But if we view them in terms of the alleged *reason* for their poverty and marginalization, they are sinners.

In other words, declaring them sinners is a way of offering the *ideological* reason for their poverty, of hiding and justifying it. Here we find ourselves right in the middle of a political conflict, and the power of one of the groups lies in its interpretation of the law, in its religious conception.

One example from the Synoptic Gospels will suffice to show how this conception plays its part in the ideological mechanism of repression operative in Israelite society.[19]

Take the account of Jesus' conversation with a rich young man (Mark and Matthew), or rich aristocrat (Luke), about *salvation*. The young man asks what he must *do* to possess (or inherit) *eternal life*, that is, to enter the kingdom (Mark 10:17-23 and par.).[20] In his reply Jesus first mentions the commandments.[21] When the young man claims to have fulfilled them, Jesus adds that something still is lacking in the young man: not for him to be "perfect" or heroic in his virtue, but to "complete" or fulfill the requisite conditions. When he hears from Jesus that he must give away his goods to the poor and accept discipleship, the young man goes away sad because "he was very rich" (Luke 18:23). I will save for a later chapter my discussion of the meaning of this *conversion* that is required, apparently, even of those who have fulfilled the commandments.

Right now we are interested in the commentary of Jesus, and even more, in the comments of his disciples. Remember that the latter certainly were chosen from among the poor and that they were often attacked by purists as being sinners. Jesus looks around and says to his disciples: "How hard it will be for those who have riches to enter the kingdom of God!" (Mark 10:23 and par.).[22] Note the total astonishment of his disciples and their revealing question: "Then who can be saved?" (Mark 10:26 and par.). If entry into the kingdom is so difficult, or even humanly *impossible* (Mark 10:27 and par.), for the rich, who have every chance and resource to be righteous, how will it be possible for those whose poverty necessarily converts them into sinners?

Jesus' disciples have heard, or palpably experienced, the Beatitudes addressed to the poor, the group to which they belong. Yet they continue to be oppressed by the dominant ideology, which justifies their expulsion from the future kingdom even as they are now expelled from Israelite society.This should make clear one thing that often goes unnoticed: the capital importance of including the category of sinner in that of the poor to whom the kingdom belongs.

Thus the God revealed by Jesus is not just a compassionate God committed to those who suffer. It is not just that God will take more and more groups of afflicted people into his eschatological kingdom. Out of *fidelity* to self,[23] God is obliged to fight against the ideology that uses religious law as a tool of oppression.

Jesus' revelation of God is simultaneously political and religious. He transforms the accustomed notion of God's law, and the corresponding notion of sin, to turn it against the oppressors of his people. To say it once again: the more political is the key in which we read and interpret the Synoptic Gospels, the more we discover the profoundly religious character of Jesus' preaching. Along with a new "politics" goes a new notion of God. As Jesus puts into practice the strategy of the kingdom of God, new features of the divine countenance come to light.

CHAPTER VIII

The Demands of the Kingdom: Conversion and Hermeneutics

One question brought up in the previous chapter was not answered. What exactly is the change of outlook, the conversion, that Jesus is talking about when he says, "Change your outlook and believe in the good news"?

Although christologies are often presented as if they can, the fact is that we cannot answer that question if we disregard the liberation strategy of Jesus. We cannot operate on the assumption that *conversion* is some general thing meaning the same for all and demanded of all alike, that it has nothing at all to do with the specific, concrete political necessities of the kingdom of God.

One of the most serious obstacles to reading and understanding the message of Jesus and its logic is failing to recognize that Jesus' proclamation of the imminent arrival of the kingdom sets up three different groups in Israel and that the demands and recommendations of Jesus' message are divided up among them in very different but understandable ways. First and foremost, the kingdom of God establishes the "natural" addressees of the good news, as we saw in the previous chapter. Second, it inevitably sets over against them another group of people. Caught up in the active mechanisms of oppression, this second group can only react with pained surprise to the coming of the kingdom; for them it is a woeful event. Finally, the liberative, conflictive strategy of Jesus creates a third group: his disciples. They are brought together by Jesus "to be with him, and to be sent out to preach" (Mark 3:14) the same message that Jesus is proclaiming about the coming of the kingdom.

Of course we are aware of the postecclesial focus of the Synoptics, of Matthew in particular, and how it affects their treatment of these exigences and recommendations, which differ for the three groups just indicated. The Synoptics turn them into counsels or conditions addressed to the Christian community. They become an exegetical nightmare of incoherence because heroic demands are intermingled with statements of universal compassion.

This intermingling is particularly noticeable in the way that Matthew structures the major discourses of Jesus, where recurring key words provide the

119

guiding thread. Aside from the context, a key word brings to mind some other occasion where it was introduced into Jesus' teaching and may even have been addressed to a different group of people. The same is true of the way that the parables are used, as we have already noted. Originally employed in polemics with the scribes and Pharisees, they are used to further the growth of the early Christian community, the church.

The material we have been examining so far should enable us to turn all this Synoptic data into a more logical and diversified message. We will be able to pinpoint differences and organize the data more sensibly if we remain sensitive to the existence of a political conflict. Already underlying the situation, it was brought out into the open by Jesus as he sought to introduce the kingdom into the concrete life of the poor.

I

If the *good news* of the kingdom's arrival is not such for all, then we must logically assume that his call to conversion, in its most immediate and radical terms, is also addressed to a specific group in Israel. It is not without reason that conversion is a precondition for *believing* in this good news because such conversion is what makes the news *good*.

Dovetailing with this view is the reply that Jesus gives to the disciples of John the Baptist. The approach of the kingdom is obvious in the works of Jesus, or should be. Jesus tells John's disciples: Blessed are those who do not see the approach of the kingdom as a scandal, as something to be rejected.

A good portion of the teachings of Jesus are specifically designed to combat the causes, real or alleged, conscious or unconscious, for rejecting the kingdom. Many of the *parables,* so typical of Jesus' way of teaching, deal with this issue. And I need hardly point out that these figurative, highly original narratives are much more likely to have been transmitted correctly in the gospel versions, in their essentials at least, than other sayings, counsels, and discussions of Jesus.

Focusing exclusively on the Synoptics, Joachim Jeremias *(The Parables of Jesus; Rediscovering the Parables)* discerns thirty-eight parables.[1] Setting aside the postecclesial morals added to many of them, we can say with a great deal of certainty that at least twenty-one of those parables deal with the reasons why Jesus' opponents end up being scandalized with his preaching about the imminent arrival of the kingdom. Thus they are attacks on the oppressive religious ideology of the Israelite majority and, for that very reason, a revelation and defense of the God who has chosen sinners and the poor as the preferred recipients of the kingdom.

First we have a set of parables that urge people to be *on the watch* for the unexpected arrival of the crucial event. Although these parables were adapted by the Christian community to refer to the Lord's second coming or the death of the individual, there can be no doubt that they were originally polemical parables.[2]

With them Jesus destroys false feelings of security. Those who belong to the religious establishment feel so secure that they think they can turn their backs on the kingdom. They feel that the kingdom is not designed to overthrow the values around which they have organized their social life and its privileges. Jesus sets them straight about their mistake.

Less concerned with specifically Jewish social structures, Luke sees accumulated wealth as one of these false securities. It is in this context that we should frame the parables of *the foolish rich man* (Luke 12:16–21)[3] and *the faithless steward* (Luke 16:1–9). In them eschatological urgency enables a person to discover the true meaning of wealth, even of ill-gotten wealth. It should be shared with others so that one can make friends for oneself among those who possess "eternal habitations": that is, the true recipients of the kingdom. We know who the latter are: the poor, those who cannot pay their debts.[4]

Closer to the historical Jesus, Mark and Q indicate a shift in the reason given for "watching." From the socioeconomic thrust of Luke we move to a politico-religious reason. If anything, the latter dovetails even more closely with the conflict-ridden strategy we have noted in Jesus' proclamation.

Thus the householder in the parable of *the thief in the night* (Matt. 24:43–44; Luke 12:39–40) will lose his household treasures because he did not make sound preparations for the unexpected arrival of the Son of Man and the kingdom. That this householder represents the Israelite authorities is made clear by the immediately following parable about *the steward* (Matt. 24:45–51; Luke 12:41–46). Set over his master's household and servants, he is supposed to "give them their food at the proper time." But the master delays, and the steward takes advantage of the delay to "beat his fellow servants." The arrival of his master takes him by surprise, and he is punished severely. He is put with the hypocrites (Matthew) or with the unfaithful (Luke). Among this first set of parables, we have here perhaps the only explicit allusion to religious authority as a tool (hypocrisy-ideology) of oppression. Be that as it may, a similar context is indicated in the parallel parable of *the doorkeeper,* which comes from the Markan source (Mark 13:33–37 and par.).

Finally, the excessive tardiness of the bridegroom gives a false security to the foolish attendants in Matthew's parable of *the ten maidens* (Matt. 25:1–13). Here again we are not dealing with sheer imprudence that is cruelly punished. When the bridegroom returns, the maidens knock on the door as friends or relatives who assume they have a right to participate in the nuptial banquet. This assuredness proves to be hollow. The bridegroom turns them away with the unexpected retort: "I do not know you."

Now let us move from these parables to the explicit message of Jesus and try to find out the exact nature of the false security portrayed in them. Even in the eschatological preaching of John the Baptist we find a warning that people are not to rely on some divine obligation toward the "children of Abraham" (Matt. 3:9),[5] Jesus goes even further, if that is possible. He calls them "children of the kingdom," as if to say that the kingdom would naturally seem to belong to them. This sense of security is theirs as they wait for the kingdom, causing them to equate the waiting period with the kingdom itself. Too late they will awake to reality, seeing people who are not children of Abraham seated at table with him (as was the poor Lazarus): "Many will come from east and west and sit at table with Abraham, Isaac, and Jacob in the kingdom of heaven, while *the sons of the kingdom* will be thrown into the outer darkness" (Matt. 8:11; see Luke 13:28–29).

This first group of parables, however, is only the start of the whole polemic. A *second* group of parables carries it much further. Like the Beatitudes, this second group sets up an opposition between two groups of people. One is made up of those who are not on the alert because they feel secure towards—or against—the kingdom. The other group is made up of those who feel that they are excluded from the kingdom: sinners and the poor. It may well be that they are not on the watch for the kingdom either for that very reason, yet they do not become the target of Jesus' attack.

We have already seen in the previous chapter that Luke's parable of *the rich man and poor Lazarus* is an almost exact reproduction in vivid images of the first Beatitude and the first woe. Luke typically stresses poverty as an extreme social situation, whereas the more prudent version of Matthew addresses the Beatitudes to the possessors of certain virtues that serve as preconditions for the happiness promised with the arrival of the kingdom.

The same editorial opposition between Luke and Matthew (in their reading of Q) with regard to the Beatitudes can be found in the parable of *the banquet* (Matt. 22:2–13; Luke 14:16–24). Once again the arrival of the kingdom finds its natural guests unimpressed; they make light of it (Matt. 22:5). Then comes the second decisive and effective invitation: to those on the byways and lanes, to "the poor, the maimed, the blind, and the lame" (Luke 14:21). Nothing is required of them. They are compelled to come in (Luke 14:23), even though it is known that they include "both bad and good" (Matt. 22:10). Now remember that a parable is not an allegory where each detail has its own symbolism. So we must not assume that divine spite is all that is behind the blessings—or the invitation—conferred on the poor. That will be made crystal clear in the three following parables of the second group. In this parable logic requires that one of the favorite themes of Jesus be sacrificed: God's *original* preference for those who are suffering. But that only brings out all the more clearly the polemical intention underlying it. It is obviously an attack on those who let the moment pass them by because they think they are invited *by right* to God's eschatological banquet. And those people are the supposedly righteous people of Israel.

As far as the socially marginalized people who actually take part in the banquet are concerned, Jesus does not idealize them (as we shall have occasion to see). They are both good and bad. If they do enter the bliss of the kingdom as poor people, *without any moral precondition whatsoever,* they do so because of their inhuman situation that is an affront to God: because they have been left on the sidelines in the religiously established society of Israel.

This close-fitting parallelism with the blessings and curses of the Beatitudes helps us to detect the odd finale that Matthew appends to this parable, which both he and Mark found in Q. Actually it is not so odd when we recall that Matthew had already drawn back from the *imprudence* [6] of the original Beatitudes, even though other passages in his Gospel clearly indicate that he knew what their original tenor must have been. We see him converting the *situations* alluded to in the Beatitudes into virtues that impose conditions on the happiness announced by Jesus and brought by the kingdom.

That is what happens at the end of the parable of the banquet, and it prompts Joachim Jeremias to talk about a *different* parable: the parable of *the wedding garment*. Now even if Jeremias is correct, the very fact that Matthew appended this parable to the parable of the banquet proves that Matthew was afraid of the amorality of the banquet parable. The king has had the dregs of humanity sit down at his banquet without any selective process whatsoever. Then, according to Matthew, he goes around and checks them out, expelling someone who did not have the fine clothes appropriate for a wedding reception.

The incongruence of the king's attitude is patent. One can hardly make such demands on poor beggars dragged in off the streets. But as he did with the Beatitudes, Matthew wants the symbolism to preclude the false presumption that might arise, according to him, if no moral qualities befitting the kingdom were demanded of the invited guests. Once again the political feature is lost, and with it the deeper revelation of God's heart: that is, God's love for those who are suffering, *for the sole reason* that their situation is inhuman, that they are being oppressed and marginalized in their society.

As I indicated above, the following three parables in this second group reveal to us the deeper divine intention behind God's establishment of the kingdom on earth. They might be called the parables of God's "joy," because that word is central in all three of them. Moreover, the three of them go together in Luke's version. Two of them are found solely there: *the lost drachma* and *the prodigal son*. The third is common to Luke and Matthew: *the lost sheep* (Luke 15:4–32; Matt. 18:12–14). [7]

Let us start with the two specifically Lukan parables. We have a woman who has lost one drachma (of the ten she possesses) and a father who has lost one son (while the other son has remained faithful to him). The two parables stress the fact that worry, concern, and effort are focused on what has been lost in order to recover it. Again we can detect a polemical thrust against the religio-political authorities of Israel. They take advantage of a religious pretext—human perdition—to disregard and neglect sinners and the poor, who are left unnoticed on the margins of society, in misfortune and disgrace.

This is even more obvious, if that is possible, in the parable of the prodigal son. Everything suggests a preference for the lost son that is nothing less than scandalous: his father catches sight of him at a great distance, runs to meet him, and counters his expressions of penitence with lavish gifts and a banquet that he had never given his elder son. Clearly the father is expectantly looking forward to his son's return without imposing conditions on him: "He was lost, and is found." In what state? With what moral dispositions? It does not matter. The fact that he had been lost is sufficient reason for the father's joy.

The polemical note against the Israelite authorities shows up especially in the effort of the elder son to keep his prodigal brother out of the joyful merrymaking because the latter "has devoured your living with harlots" (Luke 15:30). Against this argument the father has only one thing to say: "He was lost, and is found."

God's bold preference for those who are suffering acquires a new feature in the parable of the lost sheep, which can be added to the above two parables. Without the sheep doing anything, the shepherd (God) goes out looking for it. Why? Nothing suggests that it is the best or most valuable sheep in the flock. Nor is there any indication that it had turned around and was heading back home after straying away. It is lost and in trouble: that is all. But that is enough to make the shepherd leave the rest of the flock, go out to find it, lay it on his shoulders, and celebrate with a party when he returns home with it. Here again, as in the case of the drachma and the prodigal son, we are being shown what brings more joy to God: "Just so, I tell you, there will be *more joy* in heaven over one sinner who repents than over ninety-nine righteous persons who need no repentance" (Luke 15:7; Matt. 18:13). It is to bring more joy of this sort to God that the kingdom is coming. This is why Jesus has been "sent only to the lost sheep of the house of Israel" (Matt. 15:24), as will his followers and disciples be sent after him (Matt. 10:6). The tradition which derives from Mark offers its own parallel version of this same mission: "Those who are well have no need of a physician, but those who are sick; I came not to call the righteous, but *sinners*" (Mark 2:17 and par.).[8]

It is here that we come to the crucial point of Jesus' attack. Up to now it has been directed against the religious authorities for failing to have the sentiments of God and hence being in opposition to God's kingdom. If the kingdom is coming, they imagine it is coming to benefit the righteous and reward them all the more. Surely it could not be coming to bring happiness to sinners and the poor! In thinking along those lines, argues Jesus, they betray their ignorance of God. God's joy lies in rescuing sinners and the poor from the misfortune and marginalization in which they find themselves and in restoring their humanity to them.

Now strong as that attack on the authorities might be, one could claim that Jesus is still admitting that the poor are sinners in need of pardon and a physician. Unlike the righteous, these sinners would still be required to take the first step of undergoing conversion, of turning to the God who is so anxious to declare them blessed with the arrival of the kingdom. So though Jesus' attack is radical, it merely shows us two opposed groups and God's unexpected preference for one of them. One of those groups is made up of the poor, the lost, the sinners; the other is made up of the rich, the righteous, and those who have no need of conversion.

The final parable in this second group, dealing with *the children in the market place,* derives from Q (Matt. 11:16-19; Luke 7:31-35). It depicts Yahweh complaining that his religious representatives in Israel have never been in tune with the divine sentiments expressed by the prophets, no matter what approach the latter might use. Consider the last two prophets, John the Baptist and Jesus. Both went unheeded, the former heralding the gloomy foreboding of the coming divine judgment, the latter heralding the joy that the kingdom would bring to sinners and the poor.[9]

As yet, however, Jesus has not pinpointed and picked apart the mechanism used by one group (the rich and righteous) to oppress the other group (sinners and the poor). A trace of suspicion rises in our minds. Is there perhaps a certain irony in Jesus' references to the righteous and sinners? Are the "righteous" really righteous? Are the "sinners" really sinners? Who in Israel is really in need of urgent conversion?

II

That brings us to a *third* group of polemical parables, which reverse the prevailing value-judgment in Israelite society as to who are sinners and who are righteous. These parables tell us that those who think they have no need of a physician are the ones most in need of a physician, that those who think themselves righteous are sinners through and through.

Jesus thus begins to take apart the whole ideological mechanism which, as we saw in the previous chapter, links the two groups together in a basic way. We see that the erroneous interpretation of God's judgment, and of the law that grounds it, both hides and justifies the oppression of one group by the other.

The opposition between the two groups is already evident in the parable of *the two sons,* which is exclusive to Matthew (Matt. 21:28-32), although in this case the values of the two groups are exactly the reverse of the ones expressly indicated. What characterizes the first son, who represents the sinners, is his open refusal of the order he receives from his father (God), but then he repents and obeys it. What characterizes the second son, who represents the supposedly righteous, is his public profession of his intention to obey his father, but in the end he does not.

At first glance the polemical thrust of the parable seems obvious: the supposed righteous are really sinners, whereas the supposed sinners are relatively righteous because they have done the will of their father (God).

To say that, however, would be to force the sense that Jesus intends to give to the parable, as we see from the extraordinary commentary which immediately follows it. The fact is that *all* are sinners. But whereas one group of people, knowing themselves to be sinners, can easily be pardoned, the other group of people, passing themselves off as righteous, are *incapable of conversion.* Their sin is not only greater but somehow unpardonable. Jesus brings this out by noting how the two groups reacted to the accusatory preaching of John the Baptist. The sinners believed him. As for the supposed righteous: "John came to you in the way of righteousness, and you did not believe him, but the tax collectors and the harlots believed him; and even when you saw it, you did not afterward repent and believe him" (Matt. 21:32). *Sin,* in its most radical, crucial, and unpardonable sense, has switched from one group to the other; it is now among "the righteous who have no need of repentance."

Even clearer on this point is the Lukan parable of *the Pharisee and the publican* (Luke 18:9–14). In the temple the Pharisee stands and thanks God for the righteousness that separates him from sinners. And lest there be any doubt, he alludes specifically to the publican he sees there. Separated from the Pharisee by a good distance, both physical and moral, the publican is fully aware of his marginalization. Not daring to lift his eyes, he beats his breast and asks God's pardon for a sinfulness he cannot deny.

And the paradoxical conclusion? The "just" man goes home without justification. The sinner goes home, if not made righteous, at least *pardoned.* And, when you come down to it, how could God *pardon* someone who is a *just and righteous* person?

Let us pause for a moment to appreciate fully the conflict-laden—and certainly subversive—impact of this teaching presented by Jesus. He does not merely side with sinners and the poor in a definite and public way. He says that the upholders of justice and righteousness are sinners in a far worse sense. They are unpardonable sinners because the righteousness they think to be theirs closes them off from any possibility of conversion.

The audacity of this value-reversal within the socioreligious structure of Israel is lost on us today. We assume that what happened in the synagogue cannot be repeated in the church. We also assume, just as mistakenly, that the church no longer plays any role in the existing class struggle because of its transcendence and its mission of reconciliation. Finally and most importantly, we fail to appreciate what is triggered when the marginalized people of society, in the name of laws and virtues, discover that they have been deceived by people who, in God's eyes, are unpardonable criminals and sinners.

Not only do the other three parables in this group stress the much greater sinfulness of those who consider themselves righteous and in no need of conversion. They also make clear that their sin is not just a religious crime, that it concretely comes down to creating an oppressive relationship with other human beings.

In the Introduction to Part Two I have already discussed the parable of the *laborers in the vineyard* (Matt. 20:1–16). Restoring the original overall sense of this parable, we see that the owner of the vineyard chooses to be good or generous. He gives all his workers the same wage, even though some of them have worked longer than others.[10] The resentment of the workers of the first hour toward this decision prompts the owner to make this retort to one of them: "Friend, . . . do you begrudge my generosity?"[11]

Here we see why Jesus' proclamation of the "Lord's year of grace" (see Luke 4:19)—in strict parallelism with the Beatitudes—was to prove scandalous to some and provoke their resentment. The year of grace meant that every fifty years ownership and freedom were once again shared out equally among all the Israelites. This was done gratuitously. In other words, it made no difference how people had worked or administered their goods. Every fifty years people would recover their basic human possibilities.

The scandal derives from the fact that the privileges resulting from the division of labor are always attributed to virtuousness. It is assumed that they are grounded in the will of God. Oppression thus becomes sacred, even penetrating the minds of the oppressed. But the God of Jesus does not think that way, refuses to play that role. The envy or "evil eye" with which some regard this equitable distribution in the divine project is viewed as blameworthy by the God of Jesus. Here we see clearly the criterion that God uses to judge what is sinful: not what is contrary to the law, but what is contrary to the *human being*.

In the parable of the laborers in the vineyard an apparent sense of justice or fairness lurks behind the resentment of the workers of the first hour, who would prefer to see their fellow workers of the last hour go without basic necessities. Even that sense of justice disappears completely in another parable from the Markan source: *the murderous tenants of the vineyard* (Mark 12:1-12 and par.). Here again we have intermediate authorities: tenant farmers. In the parable studied above we already came across the image of the vineyard, a symbol of Israel. In this parable we are clearly aware of the conflict-ridden tension between the owner of the vineyard and his tenants. Hearing this parable, Jesus' audience could not help but recall Isaiah's parable about the vineyard, which ends with the solemn words: "For the vineyard of Yahweh Sabaoth is the house of Israel" (Isa. 5:7; Segundo text translated).

Unlike Isaiah's parable, Jesus' parable is addressed not to the people but to the authorities of Israel. They are accused of having rejected all the servants sent to demand payment of the rent,[12] that is, of the special fruits for Yahweh under Israel's care. When the proprietor finally decides to send his own son and heir for that purpose, the general intention of the tenants is expressed with full clarity: "This is the heir; come, let us kill him, and the inheritance will be *ours*" (Mark 12:7 and par.).

In this parable we do not have the clear-cut opposition between two camps that is evident in all the other parables of this group. But here Jesus' polemic against the religious authorities of Israel is even more radical. Dismantling the mechanism of oppression they use, he accuses them of nothing less than wanting to *take possession* of Israel for their own advantage. There is no doubt that the listeners at whom this parable was directed got the message: "When the chief priests and the Pharisees heard his parables, they perceived that he was speaking about them. But when they tried to arrest him, they feared the multitudes, because they held him to be a prophet" (Matt. 21:45-46 and par.).

Finally we have another parable in the same vein in Matthew's Gospel: *the pitiless debtor* (Matt. 18:23-24). In it the servant of the king who owes the latter a large sum is undoubtedly a subordinate ruler (somewhat akin to the tenants of the preceding parable) of some province, whose revenues he may have appropriated for himself (Jeremias 1966, 164). Once again we find a strain that is characteristic of Jesus' parables. The debt of this person entrusted with power and authority is pardoned, independently of his moral or spiritual dispositions. It is pardoned simply and solely because he cannot pay it. But the pardoned servant takes advantage of his right to oppress another servant who owes him the small sum of one hundred denarii, a sum which he finds impossible to pay. The subordinate ruler sends the servant to prison. The king sets the situation right. It is the first servant, the "wicked" servant and sinner, who will go to jail.

Delegated authority is not meant to be used to take personal advantage of the law, but rather to realize the values of the supreme authority, God. God's criterion and maximum value, demonstrated vis-à-vis the enormous debt of the first servant, is concern and compassion for the human being, and particularly for those who are suffering. Jesus' polemic here against the oppressive ideology of Israel's religious authorities, who have been unfaithful to their responsibilities, recalls the explicit accusation he levels against those "ideologues": "You . . . have neglected the weightier matters of the law, justice and mercy and faith" (Matt. 23:23).

There is a change in the ontological value-premises with respect to the two camps into which Israelite society is divided in Jesus' day. This should logically entail a parallel change in the epistemological premises *on the basis of which divine revelation (i.e., the law) is interpreted.*[13]

This ultimate destruction of the oppressing ideological apparatus shows up in a *fourth* and final group of polemical parables. They are characterized by a theme that is also elaborated in explicit discussions, as we shall see in Section III of this chapter. This major theme of Jesus' message concerns the hermeneutic key to interpreting God. According to Jesus, that key entails attending to the human being and placing oneself in the service of humanity's full and complete humanization.

From that standpoint the fundamental conversion of those to whom the word of God has been revealed involves shifting from the notion of privilege to the notion of responsibility, ceasing to regard oneself as an end and considering oneself a means. One is working with a mistaken hermeneutic key if one considers God's revelation as an acquisition. That key unwittingly causes "hardening of the heart." The other person—and inevitably the poor person in the end—comes to take a secondary place vis-à-vis the divine treasure one thinks one possesses. Using that criterion, one no longer understands anything of revelation, however careful and scientific one's reading of its written word may be.

The first three parables in the fourth group are designed to combat this radically distorting preunderstanding: the Q parable of *the talents* (Matt. 25:14-30; Luke 19:12-27), the Markan parable or comparison of *the salt* (Mark 9:50; Matt. 5:13; Luke 14:34-35), and the Lukan parable of *the fig tree* (Luke 13:6-9).

There is a common strain in all three: value never resides in the thing in itself, in something that can be the object of possession; it lies in some usefulness, some "fruit" that can be expected from the thing.

The parable of the talents introduces the image of money, stressing the danger of regarding it as wealth *in itself*. That is the mistake of the servant who got one talent. Preoccupied with its intrinsic value, he buries the talent, preferring not to jeopardize this acquired wealth even though the acquisition is only temporary. The argument against him comes from his own lips when he tries to justify himself: "Master, I knew you to be a hard man, reaping where you did not sow, and gathering where you did not winnow" (Matt. 25:24). The master expects to receive something that he did not give as such but that lies buried in the mechanism that should produce it (in this case, the money).

The parable of the salt stresses the uselessness of keeping and respecting (rather than throwing away and stepping on) something that is worthwhile only when its own being is lost in the transformation of something else that truly matters: food, in this case. Moreover, Matthew places this parable or comparison at a very important point in his Gospel: between the Beatitudes of the kingdom and Jesus' revelation of the new law ("But I say to you . . .") governing a new righteousness ("greater than that of the scribes and Pharisees"). Situated thus, the comparison functions as a hermeneutic key designed to prevent the mistake of interpreting the second law and its righteousness as the first law was interpreted.[14]

The parable of the barren fig tree stresses the time allotted for conversion, which coincides with the period of Jesus' preaching. This period for bearing fruit, granted by Jesus to those who have limited themselves to possessing what has been given by God, has been snatched from the will of God as it were. For God is tired of seeing the divine plan stalled, the plan to place what has been given to Israel (the law and the prophets) in the service of its truly intended recipients.

Who are those recipients? That is made clear in the parable of *the sheep and the goats:* the image of the final judgment (Matt. 25:31–46). The recipients are obviously the poor. Starting out in need of the most concrete and material basics, they thus become the unacknowledged recipients of what Israel was supposed to be: multiplied talents, salt that seasons, a fruitful fig tree.

Contrary to all the previsions of those who possessed divine revelation, God's judgment is based not on the law promulgated, studied, and elaborated over centuries, but on the help offered "the least."[15] But this does not and cannot signify the abolition of the law and the prophets, that is, of divine revelation (see Matt. 5:17). Perceived human needs thus become the key to interpreting what revelation is trying to say to human beings.[16]

This hermeneutic dislocation, which aims at dismantling the *ideological* apparatus of oppression in Israel, ends with the Lukan parable of *the good Samaritan* (Luke 10:29–37). Two groups, with their opposite interpretations of God's will, reappear here that are always present, if only implicitly, in the polemical parables of Jesus: (1) the Jews who represent the authority of the law (the priest and the Levite); (2) the marginalized sinners of Israel. Since the time of the return from exile, the Samaritans constituted the most despised part of the people of the land, indeed to the point where they were considered pagans for all practical purposes.

Here again we find an inversion of values in accordance with the heart of God. It is the Samaritan whose acts will make him the representative of God's party and will, of the correct interpretation of God's law. The official representatives of that law, on the other hand, fail to recognize it.

How was the Samaritan able to *get it right?* The answer, which is theologically subtle, is to be found in the *context* in which Luke places the parable. A lawyer tries to put Jesus to the test, asking him the same question that will be raised by the rich young man: "What shall I do to inherit eternal life?" Jesus asks him a question in turn: "What is written in the law?" The lawyer's answer, accepted as correct by Jesus, offers the twofold commandment taken from Deuteronomy (6:6) and Leviticus (19:18): *love for God and neighbor.*[17]

The lawyer feels compelled to make clear that his question has to do with a more intricate problem. Assuming that there are no difficulties in interpreting the first part of the commandment, he asks Jesus about the second part: "And who is my *neighbor?*"

Jesus replies with a parable and then asks the lawyer a maieutic question. It is a curious question if one considers the problem posed by the lawyer: "Which of these three, do you think, proved *neighbor* to the man who fell among the robbers?" There is only one answer the lawyer can give: "The one who showed mercy on him."

Jesus' final question is curious because it does not seem to dovetail with the question that was raised in the first place: Who is my neighbor? that is, Whom should I love? Jesus seems to evade the question by defining "neighbor," not as someone whom one ought to love, but as someone who does truly love.

We must remember that the term "neighbor" originally meant someone *close* to you (Latin *proximus*), and that is how it was used by the law. The proximity of family, tribe, or nation limited and defined the reciprocal obligations of love. Among countless prescriptions note, for example, the ones governing loans to fellow Israelites and loans to foreigners (Deut. 23:20–21). The lawyer would know by heart all the various definitions and distinctions made by the law regarding proximity and the respective obligations of love. Hence the difficulty of his question.

It is here that the real surprise comes with Jesus' answer. Jesus tells him that proximity cannot be fixed beforehand. It is not a *consequence* of the law but rather a *premise.* Being a reciprocal relationship between persons or groups, neighborliness *is fashioned* precisely through human love. A heart sensitive to others, a loving heart, finds *neighbors* wherever it gets a chance to approach a needy person with love. And only those who start from this *prejudice* in favor of the human being—even though they may be pagans or atheists—understand the law and the will of Jesus' God.

This view utterly disqualifies the other (epistemological) premise of adopting a neutral attitude and trying to find out what God wants by resorting to what has somehow or other managed to get set up as divine word, law, or revelation.

III

Here we have the radical change of outlook that Jesus demands of one of the groups highlighted by his preaching: those in Israel who declare officially what the will of God is and hence what people are to think of the message of Jesus. This conversion means moving from the oppressive security of the letter of the law to the liberating insecurity of having to opt for the poor, even in the face of God's very word. Only being in tune with the poor and their interests will open one's heart to the correct interpretation of God, of the law and the prophets, and ultimately of Jesus himself.

It seems almost incredible that in the elaboration of christologies greater attention has not been paid to Jesus' systematic dismantling of the oppressing religious ideology. It is hardly an excuse to say that the parables, having been deflected from their polemical use, are difficult to interpret today as properly theological teachings. And I would add: all the more *theological* insofar as we discover the *political* function of the theology that the parables attack. But alongside the parables we also have the properly theological polemics that occupy a central place in the most primitive Synoptic Gospel: that of Mark.

I am not going to repeat the detailed exegesis of those polemics that I offered in Chapter II of Volume I. Here I simply want to bring out the main points. My readers will have no trouble noting the close parallelism between these debates and the groups of parables we have been studying in this chapter. The only difference, logically enough, is the literary genre. Whereas the parables express their content in a much more vivid way, the theological controversies offer us more detailed, subtle, and certain rational data on the subject under discussion.

Jesus is asked what can licitly be done during the sabbath rest (see Mark 2:23–3:5). Jesus denies that it is possible to resort first and "directly"—without prior criteria—to a reading of the law. The Sabbath and its prescriptions have not been established for its own sake, but so that the human being can "do good" to human beings. Hence the law is truly understood only by those who, in reading the law of sabbath rest, relativize its prescriptions and interpret them, or transform them if need be, to benefit someone in need.

Not only does Jesus point out that (human) legalistic traditions have been taking the place of God's authentic commandments. He also asserts that even the latter, considered "apart from" the human being, do not constitute the will of God as a generator of moral values (see Mark 7:1–23). God does not come to human beings with pre-established moral recipes. He wants them to establish their morality in accordance with their intentions—freely, from within themselves, and accepting the risk entailed. And to say it once again: only those whose intentions are based on love correctly understand the useful sense of the commandments. Being in tune with God's intentions, they relativize those commandments accordingly and suppress them when necessary (as in the case of the commandment regarding pure and impure foods).

Even more radical is Jesus' argument as to how one is to recognize the revelatory presence of God in history, operative in people like Jesus. Luke tells us that Jesus is healing a mute (Luke 11:14-16). Could this constitute a divine intervention? Jesus' adversaries are not convinced. They need some less ambiguous, more certain criterion. Jesus could be working the cure—freeing a possessed person, according to the contemporary outlook—with the power of the prince of devils rather than that of God. It is better to ask Jesus for a direct, unmistakable sign from heaven. They think that is the way accreditation came in the past to those who were recognized in the law and by the prophets as being sent by God.

Insofar as direct signs from heaven are concerned, and even assuming they are possible, Jesus refused to offer them (Mark 8:11-13). Heaven is mute for those who do not already possess a criterion for recognizing its voice in the human events that have an effect on human beings. The presence of heaven on earth—that is, something historical as a revelation of God—can be recognized only by those who already have a pre-judice as to what constitutes the good of the human being (see Matt. 12:38-42; Luke 11:29-32).

What about the possibility that Jesus is curing with the power of the prince of demons? Following the same line of argument, Jesus offers a scandalous response: in the last analysis there is no point in differentiating God from Satan in cases such as this one. If Satan starts curing people, starts restoring to human beings the spoils of their lost humanity (see Luke 11:22), then *he is working against his own interests* and helping those of God. Whenever and wherever a human being is freed from some obstacle to the attainment of its full humanity, God comes out the winner (Mark 3:22-27). Before human beings resort to God to find a sure criterion of the divine presence in history, therefore, they should first develop their own sensitivity and judgment regarding the human being and its needs (see Matt. 16:1-4; Luke 12:54-57).

This is the obligatory hermeneutic circle, one which makes our fellow human being the criterion for recognizing and hearing God (talking about our brother or sister). And it is the attempt to evade this required circle that is described by Jesus as the unpardonable sin or blasphemy (Mark 3:28-30). It does not mean that God cannot pardon it if the person repents. Unlike other sins for which the compassionate God will grant pardon, however, the sin of making God an accomplice in, and a reason for, the oppression of the human being urgently calls for *conversion*.

It should be apparent that the polemical parables and these theological debates converge to form the overall strategy of Jesus in favor of the poor. He will dismantle the ideological mechanism wherewith the poor themselves turn the popular religion they practice into an instrument of oppression that benefits those with power in Israel.

The stance of Jesus vis-à-vis the conflict of opposed interests in the society of his time and country is not that of a man who places himself *above* them or *transcends* them. Far from it! The (eschatological) reconciliation sought by his message will entail the unmasking and accentuation of that conflict and its hidden mechanisms, in order to turn its victims into conscious, active subjects in the struggle. [18]

And Jesus—*perfectus homo*—achieved that with the limitations of any and every human enterprise, as his death for political reasons proves. Those reasons do not obscure or muddy his religious message, his radical revelation about the heart of God. On the contrary, they provide us with the key to understanding his revolutionary message about that God and the criterion for gauging the decisive character of that revelation in realistic terms.

CHAPTER IX

The Demands of the Kingdom: Prophetism and Conscientization

We have already seen that Jesus' preaching calls for conversion on the part of those in Israel who are opposed to the kingdom. This demand for conversion follows a strict logic and ultimately defines what the kingdom is, by contrast if you will.

We face a different situation when we attempt to study Jesus' preaching to sinners and the poor on the one hand, and his own disciples on the other. The contours become blurred. We confront statements, recommendations, and precepts that are hard to reconcile.

In other words, just as it is easy to see what Jesus is attacking, so it is difficult to grasp what he wants to construct with his *collaborators* for the benefit of those who are the recipients of the kingdom. The reason for these antinomies may lie in the vagueness and multiple meanings of the term "kingdom of God" as well as in the elaboration of that concept in differing christologies, even within the Synoptic testimony itself.

Consider one example. According to Matthew, Jesus said: "Come to me, all who labor and are heavy laden, and I will give you rest. Take my yoke upon you . . . for my yoke is easy and my burden is light" (Matt. 11:28-30). At first glance it would seem that those who labor and are heavy laden in Israel are sinners and the poor (as in the parable of the banquet), the victims of a rigidly inhuman interpretation of the law made by those who "bind *heavy burdens,* hard to bear, and lay them on men's shoulders; but they themselves will not move them with their finger" (Matt. 23:4).

But all exegetes recognize that "taking the yoke" was a common figure of speech in Israel for discipleship. Thus Jesus would be inviting sinners and the poor, for whom the kingdom is coming without conditions or distinctions, to become his disciples. And if they do, he promises them a light burden by comparison with the heavy burden laid on their weary shoulders by the Pharisees and the doctors of the law.

134

Now there can be no doubt that *at least* Jesus' disciples are the ones to whom are addressed the prescriptions of the "law of Jesus," which is supposed to be the source of a righteousness exceeding "that of the scribes and Pharisees." This clearly is the thinking of Matthew as it appears in the Sermon on the Mount (Matt. 5:20). To describe this "greater" righteousness, Matthew depicts Jesus using the same basic expression six times: "You have heard that it was said [in the law] . . . but I say to you" (Matt. 5:21, 27, 31, 33, 38, 43). And each time Jesus uses the latter phrase, he makes the moral obligation of the law even more demanding than it was. Thus he equates adultery of desire with actual adultery, and insult with homicide. Jesus' law, in other words, is even more demanding, an even "heavier" burden, than the law taught and interpreted by the scribes. Jesus could hardly be inviting those laboring under the weight of the burden placed on them by the scribes to take an even heavier burden on their shoulders!

It is no accident that we find this clearcut example of a contradiction in Matthew's Gospel.

Up to this point we have been looking in the three Synoptic Gospels for the most trustworthy basis on which to ground our understanding of Jesus of Nazareth: who he was and how he acted. Despite significant differences in the redaction of key passages (e.g., the Beatitudes), we have seen that in one way or another the three Synoptic writers bear unmistakable witness to a politico-religious conflict that pits Jesus, the defender of sinners and the poor, against the ideological and material authorities of Israel. We have also seen that the three Synoptics agree in their clearcut depiction of the theology that Jesus sets over against that of the authorities in order to destroy their ideological weapon used for the oppression of the people. The logical consistency of all that—plus the significant fact that their redaction was done for communities no longer facing the same conflict, with the possible exception of Matthew's redaction—is the best guarantee of its historical reliability.

So we have a nucleus of data that is relatively certain and generally common to all the Synoptics. Nevertheless we must not forget that *the three Synoptic Gospels constitute so many christologies*. Each one interprets Jesus differently, endowing his mission with distinct features. That should not surprise us, once we realize that this *mission* is the reality being lived by the evangelists in their Christian communities or churches at the very moment they are redacting their Gospels.

On this basis we might venture a general hypothesis. Once we have defined the group opposed to Jesus and his demand addressed to them as conversion, we are left with two other groups. They are united, negatively if you will, by Jesus' defense of them and by his assertion that both groups (sinners and the poor on the one hand, his disciples on the other) will enjoy blessedness or happiness in the kingdom. So we could say that the definition of these two groups and their reciprocal relations begins to produce, even in the Synoptics, three different christologies with their respective ecclesiologies.

I

Present-day exegesis tells us that the redactional work of Mark is less than that of the other two Synoptic writers, though it is real enough and should not be underestimated. Mark's christology, in other words, is more sober in moving away from the historical Jesus. So we should not be surprised to find in his Gospel the most coherent continuation of Jesus' preaching about the kingdom of God, interpreted in the political key that is now familiar to my readers and that best accounts for the central core of Jesus' preaching. His preaching is religious, to be sure, but only in a political key can we get a clear understanding of most of his parables and debates.

What exactly is this *logical* continuation of Jesus' preaching? Here let me offer my working hypothesis regarding the oppressed on the one hand and Jesus' following and coworkers on the other. Insofar as the *first* group (the oppressed) is concerned, we already know that Jesus makes *no* demands on them. The kingdom is theirs because they are suffering under the world's existing structures. This does not mean that Jesus has nothing to say to them by way of exhortation or nothing to do for them by way of announcing what the kingdom will do on their behalf. But as we saw in the previous chapter, everything Jesus does for sinners and the poor is clearly different from the *radical conversion* he demands of their oppressors as a precondition for entering the kingdom.

Insofar as the *second* group (Jesus' disciples) is concerned, Jesus does make demands on them. The demands are not preconditions for entering the kingdom because in principle his disciples have already sided with the poor and accepted the ultimate consequences of that choice. Instead Jesus demands certain qualities from them, prophetic qualities that are part and parcel of Jesus' mission. They must display all the clear-sightedness, heroism, and commitment that prophetism implies and that was certainly required of Jesus himself because his mission entailed a conflict with selfish interests no less crucial for being disguised.

Let us begin, then, with Mark's version of the demands Jesus imposes on his disciples. We shall see that the other two Synoptics, despite their different christologies, must sometimes line up with Mark's version.

We have already noted the particular importance that Mark gives to theological controversies. Along with the parables, these theological debates embody Jesus' active opposition to the ideological and religious apparatus responsible for oppression within Israel.

It is typical of Mark to point out that Jesus repeatedly insisted that his disciples must *understand* those mechanisms; otherwise their function would not really be efficacious. In the middle of a debate about the interpretation of the (moral) law, the disciples do not grasp Jesus' argument. Accustomed though he is to their frequent inability to grasp his teachings, in this case Jesus seems to find it totally unacceptable: "Then are *you also* without understanding? Do you not see that . . . " (Matt. 7:18). In this case we have already been told that Jesus' argument was in the form of a parable (Mark 7:17). And what are the parables essentially, when viewed *as a whole* and not interpreted as disparate teachings of a moralizing sort? The parables, most of them polemical in nature, present a liberating conception of divine revelation (with its ontological and epistemological criteria) as opposed to a different conception of divine revelation that breeds and justifies oppression.

Thus Jesus is not concerned about his disciples' failing to understand *one* parable. He is bothered by the fact that they don't grasp the *general* (anti-ideological) theology underlying all the parables. That is why he reacts so strongly to their questioning in one situation: "Do you not understand *this* parable? How then will you understand *all* the parables?" (Mark 4:13). It is as if he were saying that he could not applaud them, even in a limited way, for understanding some of the parables. If, and only if, they understand *all* the parables will they also understand the opposition between his conception of divine revelation and that of the Pharisees and the religious authorities in Israel.

It is understanding this opposition solely as religious, and failing to submit it to a political key in order to decipher it, that accounts for the inability to understand the parables and Jesus' point in using them. Using fairly similar (but not identical) terms, the three Synoptics insert a passage on Jesus' purpose between the parable of the sower and the explanation that Jesus gives to his disciples alone:

And when he was alone, those who were about him with the twelve asked him concerning *the parables.* And he said to them: "To you has been given *the secret of the kingdom of God,* but for those outside everything is in parables; so that they may indeed see but not perceive, and may indeed hear but *not understand;* lest they should turn again, and be forgiven" [Mark: 4:10–12 and par.].[1]

It is not the extraordinary toughness of these parables[2] that has made exegesis difficult but the assumption that Jesus intended to *obscure* the content of his message *through the use of parables.* The *literary genre* itself suggests that it is highly unlikely that Jesus intended to do any such thing. The problem is, once again, that people have lost sight of the political key.

Joachim Jeremias rightly points out this fact about the parables: "The hearers find themselves in a familiar scene where everything is so clear and simple that a child can understand it; and so obvious that again and again those who hear cannot help saying 'Yes, that's how it is' " (Jeremias 1966, 10). Even granting a bit of exaggeration in that statement, we must ask ourselves: How is it that "those outside," Jesus' adversaries, would " see but not perceive . . . hear but not understand"?

It is right here that we must go back to the political key. Jesus *is not giving a religion class.* He is bringing out and unmasking a conflict that uses religion as a disguise. Precisely because the parables as a whole *are perfectly clear,* they stand as a tremendous, public, justified *insult,* a thousand times more forceful than any insult that might be seen in a theological debate. If you read the parables in terms of the polemical intent reconstructed by Jeremias, you will see that Jesus' adversaries, pitilessly described in them, possess all the wicked, screwed-up traits of a human mind wittingly or unwittingly dedicated to the domination and exploitation of other human beings.

There are parables that live in our memory by virtue of the negative trait featured in their very title: for example, the "foolish" rich man, the "stupid" virgins, the "murderous" tenants. If you attribute all those derogatory adjectives to Jesus' adversaries, you will readily appreciate how and why the parables were not likely to be heard and understood by those being attacked so blatantly in front of the common people, who were their victims.

Let me put it another way. The parables, so crystal clear and spoken before crowds, were not meant to convince and convert the opponents of the kingdom. Their purpose was to point up the wide chasm between two different, opposed value-worlds structured by equally opposed and irreconcilable premises of both an ontological and epistemological nature. They sensitize us precisely because they unmask and stress the conflict that gives the kingdom its power and its impact.[3] Discipleship under Jesus cannot be imagined if one does not have a basic, overall understanding of that root conflict. One must understand "the secrets of the kingdom," and such liberating understanding will not come from roots in the common people, or simplicity of heart, or the fact that one is poor. The common people, victims of the religious ideology that oppresses them, will not be able to teach the disciples of Jesus how to dismantle the religious apparatus that is oppressing them.

I am not making up anything. The secrets of the kingdom that must be understood by Jesus' disciples are needed in order to avoid the mistaken, opposite mentality. The *imperceptible but effective* nature of the latter is brought out clearly in the image of the leaven, here used in a pejorative sense. Indeed when viewed in a political key, leaven seems to be the most natural image for our modern concept of a distorting, oppressive *ideology.*

The disciples of Jesus, then will not automatically be able to guard against *the leaven of the Pharisees,*[4] that is, their mental outlook that encroaches upon the whole culture.

> And he gave them this warning: *"Open your eyes* and beware of the leaven of the Pharisees. . . ."* They were discussing with one another the fact that there was no bread. Realizing this, Jesus said to them: ". . . Do you *not perceive or understand?* Are your minds that dulled? *You have eyes, can't you see? You have ears, can't you hear . . .*" [Mark 8:15–18; Segundo text translated].

Despite the surface similarity between the *fact* noted here by Jesus and the *intention* he attributed to the language of his parables, there is a fundamental difference. His disciples are not in need of conversion. What they must do is "open their eyes." They must sharpen their dulled minds so that they will be able to resist the onslaughts of the opposite mentality, a mentality allegedly enjoying divine support and even being accepted and digested by its victims. So that his disciples may be able to effect this crucial penetration into the secrets of the kingdom, Jesus divides his parabolic teaching into two steps. First come the parables themselves; understood in terms of their polemical thrust, they should make clear and heighten the basic conflict. Then comes Jesus' explanation and interpretation of his *whole* parabolic teaching, which is offered to his disciples in private (see Mark 4:33–34). Jesus thus associates his disciples with the religio-political task of unmasking the mechanisms of ideological oppression, giving them an assignment as hazardous as his own.

When the sons of Zebedee ask Jesus for the two positions of greatest power in his kingdom under him, he replies: "Are you able to drink the cup that I drink?" (Mark 10:38). As if to say: Can you suffer what I am going to suffer? Then he summons the Twelve and informs them that whoever would be first must be the servant of all the rest, offering himself as example: "For the Son of man also came not to be served but to serve, and to *give his life as a ransom* [the price of liberation] *for many*" (Mark 10:45).

Now the very last section of that verse, which goes beyond the contrast between serving and being served , may be a postpaschal addition in the messianic tradition of the Servant of Yahweh. But it could also be a forecast of the logical denouement of the conflict unleashed by Jesus' preaching, because it follows upon Mark's version of the three passion predictions we studied earlier. The point here is that Jesus foresaw the same destiny of suffering for his disciples. They would drink the same cup, and that meant more than just serving.

We have already considered the fourth Beatitude in Q, which was addressed to the Christian community according to both Matthew and Luke. That Beatitude sees the similarity of destiny in terms of the fate reserved for *the prophets,* and that is what Jesus foresaw for his disciples. We find a version very close in Mark, who is followed by Luke. In his eschatological discourse Jesus makes this prediction: "You will be hated by all for my name's sake" (Mark 13:13; Luke 21:17).[5]

There we have the essentials [6] of the demands that Jesus makes on the group composed of *his disciples,* his coworkers in the proclamation of the kingdom. They follow logically from the conflict-ridden nature of that announcement, and they entail nothing less than complete assimilation to Jesus.

II

Having considered the adversaries and disciples of Jesus, we may now ask what demands Jesus makes on the third group: sinners and the poor. Using our basic political key and following the logic of everything said so far, we arrive at an answer that will seem strange and unaccustomed: *none.* If the poor were still subject to (moral or religious) conditions in order to enjoy the coming kingdom of God, that would mean the collapse of the original Beatitudes and their revelation of God. They could not say of the poor that the kingdom is theirs, precisely *because* of what they suffer from their inhuman situation. The God of Jesus is a good politician. God does not pass judgment on a human being who is not yet truly human. That is why God is coming with the kingdom: to restructure a society that impoverishes, marginalizes, and oppresses the vast majority of human beings, turning them into subhumans. God is coming, the *power* that God truly is, to conquer the strong one who holds the human being in its power, in order to restore to the human being its humanity (see Mark 3:27 and par., but especially Luke 11:22: "and divides his spoils").

Before anything else, therefore, the poor are the *object* of the kingdom. Only the kingdom can convert them into complete and total *subjects*. This clearly gives the lie to the (ideological) misinterpretation that says that the message of Jesus, because it is religious, must give priority to the conversion of individual hearts over the change of *structures*. Hence it clearly shows that we must use a political key in order to understand Jesus' message and his revelation of God to us.

Let us look at this more closely. According to Mark and the other evangelists, Jesus engages in two types of activity with respect to the poor as a group. His work is thaumaturgic and didactic as he paves the way for the arrival of the kingdom. It is the "doing" and "teaching" with which Luke sums up his ministry (Acts 1:1).

1. The "doing" or "works" of Jesus reported in the Gospels obviously center around the extraordinary deeds we call "miracles." Our word is a poor translation of the original Greek term used by the Synoptics, which means "powers." With Jesus, you see, the kingdom begins to have visible power at least. The manifestation of this power or force occupies a central place in Mark's Gospel especially, the most narrative of the Synoptic Gospels. The crowds are witnesses to, and objects of, Jesus' thaumaturgic and beneficent power.

I am not going to make any pronouncement here on the (metaphysical) possibility of miracles in the strict sense. That would only remove us still further from a culture where no distinction was made between the extraordinary and the miraculous. Two points do seem indubitable with respect to Jesus: he had extraordinary powers to alleviate evils and heal illnesses, and he used those powers especially for the poor and needy; moreover, he did so to announce to them in a creditable way the nearness or presence of the kingdom of God.

Remember the exhortation used by the Synoptics to sum up the preaching of Jesus: change your outlook and believe in the good news. The logical thing to assume about that statement was that "and" might well be replaced by some such phrase as "so that you may believe. . . ." To believe in the good news a person would first have to consider it *good*. Hence the most obvious sense of this change of outlook or *conversion* would be that a person sides with the poor, for whom the kingdom is good news in the fullest sense. That we have seen in the previous chapter.

But the poor themselves are also in need of a certain change of outlook or conversion so that they may *believe* in the good news, precisely because it is *so good,* so seemingly incredible, and so different from their accustomed situation. The kingdom does not need the poor to believe that it is coming, which raises a problem we shall consider at the end of this chapter. Nevertheless Jesus wants to announce its coming to them through signs; that is the import of his thaumaturgic activity.

Let us begin with the miracles that Jesus dispenses liberally, and mainly to the poor.[7] We have already had occasion to see that those miracles—and their specific relationship with the poor—constituted signs[8] of the proximity or presence of the kingdom. In them the kingdom is made manifest with power. Not surprisingly, then, what is true of the Beatitudes is also true of Jesus' miracles: they are not addressed to the possessors of specific subjective or moral qualities but to those in dire need, and precisely because they are in need.

In that sense we can say that far too much attention has been paid to a few narratives in which miracles are linked to the *faith* of their beneficiaries (see Mark 2:5; 5:34-36; 6:6; 9:23-24; 10:52; 11:22-24). What exactly is the nature of that faith and to what extent does it impose conditions on the miracles? That is a problem we shall consider later. The point here is that we find far more cases where the miracle, like the kingdom itself, comes to those who need it precisely because they need it and because God's love is essentially *compassionate.* In some instances compassion is mentioned (Mark 1:41; 6:34; 8:2) or there is a reference to doing good (Mark 3:4). But in most cases there is no explicit reason at all. The description of some ill is followed by an account of its cure. Indeed one passage suggests indiscriminate curing of those who touch Jesus' garment: "As many as touched it were made well" (Mark 6:56). This is even more obviously the case when the object of a miracle is a crowd, as in the case of the multiplication of the loaves narrated by Mark (6:30f.; 8:1f.).

In the same category of unconditioned miracles are all of Jesus' efforts against demons, his efforts to liberate the possessed. Clearly both possession (as a privation of freedom and personality) and its diabolic character rule out in the possessed person any faith, in the normal sense of the word, that might condition liberation. If anyone is truly the *object* of a miracle, it is a possessed person.

The case of persons possessed by the devil merits a few considerations before we proceed with our discussion of the unconditioned miracles of Jesus. It should not surprise us to see the designation "possessed" or "possessed by a devil" applied to sick people or those afflicted with some physical handicap such as deafness or muteness. In a society whose medical knowledge was rudimentary, the world of illness and handicaps was populated by malign spirits. There was only a vague distinction between being sick or handicapped on the one hand, and being possessed on the other.[9] In general, we can say that illnesses confined to the exterior (e.g., fever, leprosy, hemorrhaging) were recognized as such. Those somehow connected with the psyche tended to be regarded as diabolic possessions. That would include convulsions, mental disturbances, and other maladies that normally blocked the use of some capacity associated with the mind: that is, paralysis, muteness, and stuttering.[10]

The distinction is not always clearcut, as I said, but it is meaningful and highly important. We can see that, if we focus our attention on Jesus' struggle against the satanic or diabolical as recounted in the pages of Mark's Gospel. The language is particularly mythical in this connection, to be sure, but that does not give us the right to reject it. Instead we must interpret it.

In this process of interpretation we must once again get rid of the individualistic, moralizing key which prompts us to see diabolic power as the origin of the temptations that are posed to our free will so that we might break some law and offend God. The Synoptic *image* of the diabolical is different, and once again the key is sociopolitical. One of the most illustrative accounts in this connection is also one of the most mythical: the account of the possessed man of Gerasa (Mark 5:1-20).

Our present-day cultural tendency—be it anthropological, moral, or religious—would be to see the diabolical in the attitude of a person: for example, Jesus' adversaries.[11] The vast majority of the Synoptic texts, by contrast, apply that adjective to infrahuman situations where liberty and purpose are lacking.

Consider the description of the possessed Gerasene. *Before* his liberation by Jesus he is depicted as one "who lived among the tombs . . . no one could bind him any more, even with a chain . . . he was always crying out and bruising himself with stones."[12] *After* the cure or the expulsion of the demon, we find him "sitting there, clothed and in his right mind." He is planning a social destiny for himself. Jesus corrects him, to be sure, but nevertheless approves his fundamental intention.

There can be no doubt about it. This total struggle with a power that enslaves human beings and strips them of their humanity cannot be understood in a moralizing key: as an individual call to a free decision, to a conversion to faith, on the part of the "patient." Why? Because this person, precisely insofar as he is possessed, is suffering from a negative, inframoral quality. It is the political key that is operative here as elsewhere: Jesus makes *no* demands before curing and restoring the "spoils" of humanity to their legitimate, original owners. In so doing, he is carrying out his mission. He is announcing the proximity of the kingdom, which is addressed—without restrictions—to all the poor, all the victims of inhumanity. The difference between the kingdom of Satan and the kingdom of God is not that human beings sin more or sin less. It is that they freely *can sin* or not, when the kingdom of God restores their human condition to them.

It is true, as I already noted, that a few Markan passages *relate miracle to faith*. But there are two questions we must ask ourselves: What exactly is this relationship? To what attitude is Mark referring when he uses the word "faith"?

Insofar as the first question is concerned, we must be careful not to equate the relationship between faith and the outcome of *prayer* (see Mark 9:23–24) on the one hand and that between faith and a *miracle* on the other, even though both do implicitly or explicitly entail the element of petition. This distinction is based on a very important reason. The *only* prayer that Jesus teaches, the one that is *distinctively his* and that he promises will be totally efficacious, is the Our Father: *the prayer for the coming of the kingdom.*[13] Its infallibility does not depend on whether a human being says it or not, nor on the psychological force one invests in it. It stems from the infallibility of God's own *project* and the one who will realize it, the Holy Spirit.

By contrast, the miracles are not the *arrival* of the kingdom in any strict sense but rather the announcement and sign of its coming. As such, they do not have the amplitude of the kingdom itself. They are conditioned and limited by their sign-function and their signifying capability. Thus a miracle performed for someone whose ontological and epistemological premises are manifestly not *in accord* with the arrival of the kingdom would not have the correct signifying quality, however much the person may be in need of the miracle.

Keeping this important distinction in mind, we do well to note that in Mark's Gospel a miracle never seems to be *explicitly* conditioned by faith.

On the occasion of Jesus' visit to his home town of Nazareth, Mark records: "And he *could do no mighty work* there, except that he laid his hands upon a few sick people and healed them" (Mark 6:5) *and* "he marveled because of their unbelief" (Mark 6:6). Once again the latter "and" could be more than a connecting conjunction; it could signify a causal connection. But that is no more than an hypothesis. If there is no such causal reference intended here, then it is Matthew who will provide it. In his redaction it is the prudent Matthew who likes to establish a causal link between faith and miracle, just as he chose to link happiness and virtue in the Beatitudes. So his version reads: "And he did not do many mighty works there, *because of* their unbelief" (Matt. 13:58). No such explicit causal connection is offered by Mark, though the reader is free to introduce it.[14]

But even if we assume that Mark never explicitly conditions a miracle on the faith of the recipient, there are three cases where he certainly establishes a close, positive relationship between the two. The first is the case of the paralytic let down through the roof by his friends and set in front of Jesus. "And when Jesus saw *their* faith" (Mark 2:5), writes Mark, Jesus began by pardoning the sins of the paralytic and ended up curing him. The other two cases are also miracles, where Jesus addresses the recipients in these basic terms: "Go, *your faith has saved you*" (Mark 5:34, 36; 10:52; Segundo text translated).

If we consider that Jesus uses such a strong term, *salvation,* for the cure effected, we must conclude that in some preliminary or significant way the kingdom of God itself has arrived for the person in question. What exactly can this *faith* be, to which such power is attributed?

It is obvious that theology has turned this question into an atemporal matter, besides mixing it up with the problem of the efficacy of prayer. It has come up with two qualities which it thinks could have the same result today: (1) faith as a psychological conviction that a miracle is going to occur; (2) faith as theological belief in the messiahship or divinity of Jesus.

We get a very different impression, however, when we read Mark's account of such occasions, including those dealing with the liberation of possessed people. To him, it seems, *faith* is not such a precise and circumscribed thing. It is an existential reality of much greater amplitude (see Mark 9:38-39).

Remember that Jesus is trying to show the power of the kingdom through signs of its nearness or presence. Since they are *signs,* and signs *of the kingdom,* they really have to point up a coherence between the values of the coming kingdom and the values being *visibly* sought by those who approach Jesus and ask him for miracles. Thus the effort of the paralytic's *companions* (whether "their faith" includes him or not)[15] is enough for Jesus to see an occasion for a practical announcement of the kingdom through a display of "power." To this fundamental coherence of values Mark, or Jesus himself, gives the name "faith."

That may explain the Nazareth episode, if some connection is to be admitted between Jesus' refusal or inability to perform many miracles and the people's lack of faith. Perhaps the prevailing atmosphere of *envy* did not offer Jesus a propitious occasion, so that his works of mercy might be related in a meaningful way to the values of the kingdom. Like the banquet in the parable, the kingdom itself will include "good and bad" among its recipients because it is for those who are suffering. But the *signs* of the coming of the kingdom, in order to be understood as such, are more limited than the unfolding of the kingdom itself. The signs are conditioned by signifying qualities that, the kingdom itself, always in a political key, sets aside in its actual realization.

Now it is precisely the *signifying quality* of the miracles that leads us to grasp a crucial element in the relationship between Jesus the wonderworker and the poor: *the messianic secret.*

It is true from beginning to end that the kingdom of God has as its *object* the poor, marginalized masses of Israel. But that does not mean that Jesus would not take advantage of every available opportunity to turn them into conscious *subjects* insofar as that was possible, and insofar as people could or would like to be such.[16] The messianic secret is not so much concerned with some doubt or incoherence in Jesus' self-awareness.[17] It is mainly bound up with the task of consciousness-raising through miracles.

It has been noted that Jesus opposes the idea of being called "Messiah." He allows it only from his own disciples (or rather, the Twelve), and only in very special circumstances: the Galilean crisis. The miracles present a different problem. In most instances, even the most clear and obviously public ones are followed by a command not to divulge them (see Mark 1:40-45; 5:39, 43; 7:32-36; 8:25-26; 9:9). That goes far beyond any secret about his status as Messiah and requires a broader explanatory hypothesis. A similar attitude prevails with regard to possessed people, even though his status as Messiah may be divulged clearly: "They knew him" (Mark 1:34; 3:11-12). Here we might also add all those instances where Jesus finds himself obliged to put some distance, if only physical, between himself and human needs in order to be able to teach.

One cannot help but relate this "open secret" to the ambiguity of the signs of the kingdom. Here the ambiguity is not theological in nature, as it is in his polemics with the Pharisees. The signs of the kingdom are real benefits. There can be no doubt about them as such insofar as their recipients are concerned. It is something else that poses the difficulty here. In the euphoria of receiving them, it is much harder for people to perceive their quality as *signs,* as facts that point to a meaning which goes far beyond the benefit received.

Mark depicts Jesus besieged by countless throngs of people who need his beneficent power, whether any kingdom is coming or not. How is Jesus to give the fullest signifying power possible to benefits that are needed in and of themselves? How can he strip away the aspect of desperate yet superficial urgency so that his deeds announce something that is in the same vein but that goes much further? How can he create a distance between deed and person that will make room for thought and reflection?

Any reader of Mark's Gospel will notice Jesus' concern to evade the image of being a dispenser of miracles in his dealings with crowds of people. What is more, it does not matter to him whether he is regarded as the Messiah or not, so long as this identification is not premature and does not block awareness of what the messianic kingdom means as a radical change.

This should make clear the signifying and didactic value of Jesus' miracles vis-à-vis the multitudes, without in any way obscuring the compassion aroused in him by the most urgent human needs.

2. That brings us to the second activity of Jesus in relation to the multitudes: teaching, and specifically, teaching in *parables.*

As we just saw, through the approach rather narrowly defined as the "messianic secret," Jesus is trying to maintain the distance he needs in order to be able to teach.

At first glance the Gospel of Mark is a bit disconcerting in this respect, but in fact it is very logical. Our first impression is that Jesus rarely addresses his words to those who, according to Q, are "blessed" by the arrival of the kingdom. In most cases, the content of his remarks seems to be addressed to the other two groups, summoning adversaries to conversion and his followers to discipleship. In his polemics with the Pharisees, his disciples and the multitude may be present, but obviously his words are addressed to his adversaries (see, for example, Mark 3:1-6). In many instances Mark notes that Jesus is addressing his teachings to his disciples, as we saw in the previous section of this chapter.

Only on comparatively few occasions does Mark concretely depict Jesus teaching the multitude. But he does indicate in a general way that Jesus taught them "many things," or "as usual," or "at length." And though Mark does not say much about the *content* of this teaching, it is clear that Jesus' teaching activity consisted of parables "so far as they were able to understand" (Mark 4:33). In short, the very same clarity of the parables, which closed the eyes of his enemies because they bore ill will and were ashamed to be treated that way in front of the people, served to open the eyes of those who heard them without prejudice and who found them of interest because they discovered that they had been created and spoken in their defense (see Mark 4:14f. and par.).

When we recovered the intrinsically polemical character of most of the Synoptic parables, we were able to perceive what the multitude undoubtedly perceived in some more or less confused way: that is, Jesus' attack on the ideological mechanism that turned the religion of Yahweh into an instrument of oppression in Israel. But Jesus' teaching to the multitude included many other parables where the polemic is absent, toned down, or subordinated to other aims.

We have parables that invite people to the following of Jesus or discipleship: for example, *the lamp, the sower,* and *the pearl* (see Mark 4:1-23 and par.). Other parables, like the Beatitudes, seem to be designed to announce the proximity and certainty of the kingdom's arrival to the multitude of sinners, sick people, and marginalized: for example, the Markan parables of *the seed that grows by itself*[18] and *the mustard seed.* These parables announce the unconditional joy that is approaching those who are greatly in need of joy and hope.

These parables abound in the other Synoptics as well. Only here, as in the case of the polemical parables, we must rediscover where the original emphasis lay. Consider our customary explanation of the parable of *the weeds mixed in with the wheat* (Matt. 13:24-30, 36-43). We say it refers to the patience implied in the simultaneous presence of good and evil in historical events. But the eschatological nature of the context in which Jesus utters his teachings points in a different direction.[19] The weeds inextricably mixed in with the wheat explains what has been happening *up to now.* This is the moment of the kingdom, the moment when the ambiguity comes to an end. The weeds are going to be separated out once and for all. The disconcerting effects of the mixture are going to come to an end. Thus it is a parable of joy, as are the parable of *the net* and the Lukan parable of *the rich man and poor Lazarus* (Luke 16:19-31), to mention only two possible examples.

In the first two sections of this chapter we have been trying to sum up Jesus' attitude or approach to the last two groups who are defined by his message. We cannot minimize the fact that the shadow of the cross, which his disciples must carry "daily," has caused us to forget something just as important: Jesus was, and wanted to be, a sign of *joy* for the masses in Israel. From this person—whom his enemies called a glutton, a drunkard, and a friend and cohort of publicans and sinners—the masses learned that God was preparing something marvelous for them, something that matched or even exceeded the pain and suffering they had been forced to bear up to that point.

III

In the last two chapters we have been learning that a clearcut logic enables us to detect, distinguish, and correlate the attitudes that Jesus demands of the three groups defined by his message: adversaries, disciples, the multitude.

These same attitudes, demanded or hoped for, also shed more light on Jesus' conception of the coming of the kingdom and his own function with regard to it.

It is too simplistic to say that Jesus announces the kingdom and its coming. Why announce something that is going to happen anyway? The function of merely announcing a future event would make sense only in conjunction with God's will to offer a final summons to conversion to those who will find its arrival to be the worst possible news.

We could thus alter the gospel text slightly and give an even more logical rendition of Jesus' preaching, one closer to the impact of John the Baptist's message: *Believe in the bad news and have a change of outlook*. Notice that I used "bad" instead of "good" and reversed the order of believing and converting.

If you are announcing the kingdom in order to convert people who are going to be its victims rather than its beneficiaries, then the logical order would go something like this: (1) the time is fulfilled, proving that the kingdom is coming; (2) you must accept this fact, believe in it; (3) so you have a basic reason for changing your outlook and attitudes, for undergoing a conversion.

Strange as it may seem, however, that is not the order used by Jesus. The three Synoptics are unanimous on the point. Moreover, we have three important pieces of data that militate against that logic, which results from viewing Jesus' function as a proclamation aimed at converting people.

1. Insofar as a proclamation geared toward conversion in the face of the terrible thing to come is concerned, on several occasions Jesus attributes such a proclamation to John the Baptist and contrasts it with his own mission. The same passages also indicate that John's function has already come to an end, whereas Jesus is still carrying out his. It is also clear that John's function ended in failure. The children in the marketplace did not mourn over the "dirges" of John the Baptist, who "came neither eating nor drinking," as a prophet of approaching catastrophes (Matt. 11:16-19; Luke 7:31-34). The real sinners did not believe him and undergo conversion, whereas the publicans and prostitutes did (see Matt. 21:32; Luke 7:29-30).

2. In contrast to John, Jesus himself defines his proclamation as an announcement of joy to sinners and the poor. And he goes even further than that. He says that his parables (his main preaching instrument) are not designed to convert the adversaries of the kingdom; he states that in fact the parables are purposely designed to make conversion difficult. Such a purpose is hardly believable in terms of any standpoint except a political one, which essentially entails bringing real conflicts out into the open and accentuating them. Indeed such an intention seems so incredible that both Matthew and Luke, in their own different ways, try to tone down the crude harshness of Jesus' remark.

3. This point is more subtle. In his chief controversies with the Pharisees, the order of Jesus' demands runs directly counter to the logic of conversion mentioned above. They are to undergo a change of heart first, then believe in the good news. Jesus does not begin by proving that the kingdom is coming and that conversion is *therefore* necessary. He starts off by proving that the premises by which his enemies live, act, and interpret the Scriptures are false, that they must be changed *to benefit the human being*, whether the kingdom is near or not.[20] It is only when such a change has taken place that there will be any point in scrutinizing the signs of the times to see whether the *good* news of kingdom's arrival is correct or not. Only thus will someone be able to believe it.

If we take these three points into account, we can see that Jesus' activity cannot be reduced to the proclamation of a kingdom that is coming anyway, whether the announcement of it is recognized or not.

We get the impression that Jesus is doing *something more* than proclaiming a future event. He is *generating an historical conflict*. If that is visible in his whole relationship with his adversaries, it becomes even more clearcut in the demands he makes on a second group: his followers or disciples.

It is an undeniable fact that Jesus gathers disciples. And that fact gives the lie to simplistic conceptions of the coming of the kingdom. Apart from the aim of converting people *in extremis*, it is difficult to explain why Jesus should announce the kingdom that God is going to introduce in any case. But it is even harder to explain why the last prophet of an already imminent kingdom needs disciples, needs to amplify and multiply his work of announcing and denouncing.

With a touch of historical irony, some people say that Jesus announced the coming of the kingdom but what arrived was the church. To say that, however, is to evade the real issue here, to indulge in a simplistic accusation of posthumous infidelity. Why is it necessary or appropriate *for the kingdom* to be announced or prepared for by a group of prophets who are specifically destined to reinforce the conflict generated by Jesus, and to be hated as he was?

This problem takes on its full dimensions, however, when we consider Jesus' activity on behalf of sinners and the poor, particularly his work of consciousness-raising and of dismantling the ideological mechanisms of religio-political oppression. No one can pretend that this work is peripheral to Jesus' life, just a way of spending time and "doing good" until the kingdom decides to come.

In other words, the *totality* of Jesus' public life, in terms of what is most historically reliable, makes clear one thing: Jesus is seeking *to place historical causality in the service of the kingdom.* And not only does he invest his all as *perfectus homo* in that service; he invests his disciples' all as well.

In an earlier chapter I cited the opening words of Bultmann in his *Theology of the New Testament.* Prior to any exegetical investigation he asserts: "The dominant concept of Jesus' message is the *Reign of God.* . . . Reign of God is an eschatological concept. . . . The coming of God's reign is a miraculous event, which will be brought about by God alone without the help of men" (Bultmann 1951–55, 2:4).

Everything I have said up to this point should enable my readers to pass judgment on this issue,[21] which is essential for the next chapter. I will not conceal my own opinion, however. I think that one would have to erase practically the whole gospel message to arrive at such a definition of the coming of God's kingdom or reign. Everything we have seen so far shows Jesus, not only announcing its coming and preparing it in history, but also associating the group of his disciples with this historical causality.

CHAPTER X

The Arrival of the Kingdom

My readers undoubtedly have noticed that we are approaching a limit, now that we have differentiated the material in Jesus' proclamation that is addressed to each of the three groups generated by his presence and activity. That limit, which is also the aim of these chapters, consists in determining in a balanced, prudent way what we can know with most certainty about the history of the prepaschal Jesus.

We are not at a limit because it is not possible or legitimate to go much further in the field of *interpretation*. We certainly could go further in discovering its rich significance, particularly in the light of the paschal events. We are at a limit because we have come to the end of the most historically reliable data provided to us by the Synoptics.

But there is something else that affects all of that. If I ask what ultimately might go to make up the kingdom—or better, reign—of God, which Jesus came to announce and prepare, readers might think I am planning to go back and sum up everything I said in the previous chapters. To a certain extent that should be the case. The fact that God reigns can only mean that God's values have been fleshed out in reality. And Jesus pointed up what those values were in the most conflictive and radical way.

So what else is there to know? In a sense, *everything*. Because, to tell the truth, *the kingdom announced and prepared for did not arrive.*[1] That, at least, is the impression history gives us.

Those considered blessed by Jesus because of its coming continued in their miserable state, whereas the rich and the satisfied continued to triumph. The hungry begot and multiplied new generations of hungry people right down to our own day. Unless, of course, we are dealing with the sort of extraterrestrial happiness and satiety promised to the righteous in the theologies of the last (Greek) sapiential books or the Pharisees.

So just when we think we have fitted the historical data into a solid, logical framework, we come up against a series of questions that pose the issues all over again. Did Jesus announce the imminent coming of a kingdom that did not in fact arrive? Or did it come in some way that even he had not foreseen? And in either case, was there justification for the conflict that Jesus com-

150

bined with his proclamation of the kingdom, and that he played out and lost on the political plane? Did that conflict have merely symbolic value, or was it charged with an historical causality on which the arrival of the kingdom depended? And if the kingdom did arrive, what does that have to do with our human history and its objectives? Is the kingdom an eschatological reality, as is commonly said: that is, an ultimate reality signaling the end of time and history?

All these questions are possible and even legitimate. That is so, in part, because the term "kingdom of God" scarcely fits into any grammatical or stylistic mold. It is hard to find its equivalent in difficulty, aside from Paul's surprising and contradictory use of certain terms.

Matthew, more than any other Synoptic writer, cites Jesus using expressions related to the kingdom in these three forms: "the kingdom," "the kingdom of God," and "the kingdom of heaven." Sometimes the content suggests it is a dynamic reality (something that moves), and sometimes it appears to be a static reality (a place or even a thing).

But even when we opt for one of those lines and seek to carry it through to the end, we run into major obstacles. Suppose we consider the kingdom as a dynamic reality for a moment, as a reality that moves in space or time. Surely it makes a difference to know whether we are to locate its presence in the past, the present, or the future. But all three phases of time are used in reference to the kingdom!

It is even more difficult to make logical sense out of the images that present the kingdom as a place or static thing. At one point it seems certain that it is a space or realm where God passes judgment. But this gives way to the impression that it is a possession or inheritance: given to some, hidden from others, or snatched away violently by still others.

Then there is the abundant use of the term in parables, many of them beginning with a vague comparison or simile. But rather than actually comparing the kingdom to something specific, the expression used might better be translated as: "It is the case with . . . as with" (Jeremias 1966, 79–80). In these vague terms Jesus or the evangelist likens the kingdom to all sorts of processes in nature, person, or social life.

We have no choice, then, but to plunge into this semantic forest. The term is too central to leave it in its shadowy ambiguity. And it is not enough to point up its political origin and import, as we have been doing up to now.

As we enter this final stage in our quest for the historical Jesus, we cannot raise our hopes too high. It is not just that my efforts so far, in my opinion, have not succeeded in shaping a coherent whole out of all the elements involved in Jesus' expectations of the kingdom's realization. The fact is that even the early church was not able to do that in a univocal way, it seems. From the beginning, therefore, it preferred to replace the expression "kingdom of God" with others that were more precise, even if more abstract and less rich.

As I indicated at the start of this chapter, the problem is that we are on the razor's edge of the dividing line between history and theology. Few certain data about the prepaschal Jesus can help us here. The interpretations derived from what we know, or think we know, of the paschal events will have a decisive character in this area; it could not be otherwise. So it should be clear that this chapter stands astride two necessary and positive realities: the investigation of the history of Jesus of Nazareth and the creation of christologies (i.e., of interpretations of that history designed to serve the changing needs of the various early Christian churches).

I

A good way to start is to look at the beginnings. According to Matthew, it all starts with the *appearance* (Matt. 3:1,13) of two personages who, at first glance, bring the same message: "Change your outlook [undergo conversion], because *the kingdom of heaven is near*" (Matt. 3:2; 4:17; Segundo text translated). These two people are John the Baptist and Jesus.[2]

It is clear that Matthew is trying to stress that the two prophets are identical and hence that the kingdoms whose nearness they are announcing are also identical. Indeed he is the only Synoptic writer who carries the identification to that extreme.

But quite apart from the data provided by the other two Synoptics, even the treatment of the first Gospel shows us the two prophets diverging in their idea of what the nearness of the kingdom means in the concrete—perhaps increasingly as time progresses and circumstances change.

We have one indication of this in the *lifestyle* that each adopts to signify the message he is proclaiming, as Israelite prophets were wont to do. We noted that both Matthew and Luke summarize this divergence in succinct, pointed terms: "For John came *neither eating nor drinking*, and they say, 'He has a demon'; the Son of man came *eating and drinking*, and they say 'Behold, a glutton and a drunkard, a friend of tax collectors and sinners!' " (Matt. 11:18-19; Luke 7:33-34; see also Matt. 3:4).

Both Matthew and Luke let us see that this difference in lifestyle correlates with different content insofar as their explicit preaching about the approach of the kingdom is concerned. John the Baptist preaches the imminent appearance of the "wrath" of God, of a *judgment* that seemed suspended for the moment. The reality is far otherwise, according to John the Baptist:

> Even now the axe is laid to the root of the trees; every tree therefore that does not bear good fruit is cut down and thrown into the fire. . . . His winnowing fork is in his hand, and he will clear the threshing floor and gather his wheat into the granary, but the chaff he will burn with unquenchable fire [Matt. 3:10,12; Luke 3:9,17].

The austere tension evoked by this preaching is summed up by Luke, who notes that John's baptism was "a baptism *of repentance for the forgiveness of sins*" (Luke 3:3).

It is suggestive that Jesus' *lifestyle* dovetails with the first individualized words of his preaching in Matthew's version: "Blessed [happy] are the poor in spirit, for theirs is the kingdom of heaven" (Matt. 5:2). And this is followed by the promises of happiness that constitute the *joyous* start of the Sermon on the Mount.

Thus it is not surprising that in the preaching of Jesus, unlike that of the Baptist,[3] the announcement of the approach of the kingdom is the proclamation of a joyous thing, a piece of good news, an *evangelion*. On various occasions in the prepaschal life of Jesus, Matthew translates the expression he must have found in Q: "the goods news (gospel) of the kingdom" (Matt. 4:23; 9:35; 24:14; Luke 4:43).

Comparing these two beginnings, that of the Baptist and Jesus, we can already point up a feature that has probably not received enough attention. It is the Baptist who better embodies the apocalyptic ideas of his day. It is he who combines "the kingdom of God"—though actually it is doubtful that he really used that term—with a cosmic catastrophe and judgment (see Amos 5:18-20; Zeph. 1:14-2:3; Ezek. 22:24). Jesus, by contrast, effects a bold and suggestive transformation. He relates the day of Yahweh with the coming of Yahweh's kingdom and the resultant joy.

Even admitting that, some might argue that there is no real change in viewing the kingdom as a dynamic reality that is drawing near, imminent, and announced as such. But that is not true, strictly speaking, and a new effort of comparison will take us further.

The proximity of judgment and eschatological urgency leads the human being, as it should, to decisions and changes that are radical and hence simple as well. Matthew clearly alludes to this fact when he has John the Baptist remark ironically: "You brood of vipers! Who warned you to flee from the wrath to come?" (Matt. 3:7). In those last times many people in Israel did in fact make a move to seek pardon of their sins and in the quickest possible way. It is also obvious that John considered it possible for them to manage it.

This implies that "the fruits worthy of a change of outlook" have been simplified as much as possible. Such simplification is typical of any urgent situation. Thus Luke's version (unique among the Synoptics) of the Baptist's detailed preaching has a strong tinge of realism insofar as it presents John summarizing what the impending judgment requires of different social groups.

To the multitude of people he says: "He who has two coats, let him share with him who has none; and he who has food, let him do likewise" (Luke 3:11). To the publicans: "Collect no more than is appointed you" (Luke 3:13). To some soldiers: "Rob no one by violence or by false accusation, and be content with your wages" (Luke 3:14). It is as if each group were about to go through a check, strict indeed but not complicated. Each bears the mark of its group situation, and conversion has to do with the group's central sin. Nothing more.

Now if people want to talk about "eschatological urgency" with reference to Jesus, they must admit that Jesus is poles apart from the sort of simplification that goes with an urgent situation. According to Matthew, who is backed up by the convergent testimony of the other two Synoptics on this matter, Jesus not only makes the law more interior, subtle, and comprehensive (see Matt. 5:17-48; Luke 6:27-35) but also relativizes it. He forces people to interpret it in a way that is always complex, that takes into account intentions and circumstances (see Mark 7:1-23; Matt. 15:1-20).

Moreover, we have looked closely at the complex and profound teaching of Jesus in parables, which indicates who the real sinners in Israel are and what hermeneutic premises should be used to interpret the law. Anyone who does that must find it more and more improbable that Jesus conceived the imminent arrival of the kingdom in any way akin to that of the Baptist, in any way that stripped all meaning and importance away from the complex process required to manage historical mechanisms and change them over the long run.

Thus everything points us to a hypothesis that accords much better with the facts we know, even though we lack enough data to prove it directly. It is very probable that the two preachers of what was "near" used different terms to define it and that the expression "kingdom of God" is exclusive to Jesus.[4] It is more likely that John used a different image more connected to the theme of his preaching: for example, the classic phrases "the day" or "the day of Yahweh." This is all the more probable if we take seriously the hypothesis of Mowinckel that was discussed in the Introduction to Part Two: that the "royal" messianic expectations concerning the Son of David and the new kingdom to be founded by him are more political than eschatological, not only in origin but later development.

Despite all the *eschatologization* effected by long centuries of foreign domination and the sapiential literature, this origin remained alive and well in Jesus' day. The existence and activity of the Zealots proves it. We know that Jesus never joined up with them, but we are also aware of his message about the kingdom, the conflict it triggers with the religio-political authorities of Israel, and his defense of the poor and oppressed precisely as such. All those things posed a certain ambiguity—even in the eyes of his closest disciples—about the possible relationship between the Zealots and Jesus' followers: two groups looking for a kingdom, Yahweh's kingdom, and expecting Yahweh to establish it rather than to pronounce any apocalyptic judgment.[5]

But aside from these possible differences in expressions and the important distinctions noted in my hypothesis, it is clear that both John the Baptist and Jesus point to a *dynamic* reality. It is moving in time and, at the start of their preaching at least, it is *near* or at hand. Certainly it is the conception that Jesus has of the kingdom in the earliest stage of his ministry. The kingdom is drawing near, replete with the power of God behind it. One must be on the lookout: that is, give up false securities in the present order and be attentive to the radical transformation implied by the arrival of God's reign. And one must petition for its arrival in prayer (see Matt. 6:10).

What, then, are we to say when we find a passage in Q that says it has "already arrived" and a comment in Matthew suggesting it has taken place "before the time" (Matt. 8:29)?

We have seen that Jesus considered his miracles to be something more than signs, to be real manifestations of the very same power that was energizing the kingdom and bringing it to the land of Israel. On one occasion Jesus, taking the part for the whole as it were, goes so far as to say: "But if it is by the Spirit of God that I cast out demons [an inescapable conclusion, as we have seen], then the kingdom of God *has come* upon you" (Matt. 12:28; Luke 11:20).

But remember the objection of the demons themselves! They complain that Jesus is molesting or tormenting them "before the time" (Matt. 8:29). And the time in question is clearly the time of the arrival of God's kingdom. So we are forced to reach the following conclusion. On the one hand the partial presence of the power brought by the kingdom allows one to speak of the kingdom's presence whenever that power is manifested. On the other hand Jesus makes only limited use of that power. (Because he is a human being? Out of respect for the divine initiative? Because he is still acting within history?) He does not transform *everything*. So that, strictly speaking, defers the arrival of God's kingdom to a *future* time.

It is true that this future quality of the kingdom in Jesus' eyes is never expressed directly by a verb in the future tense. But it shows up in other images that clearly suggest a time other than the present.

The first Beatitude, for example, states that the kingdom belongs right now to the poor (in spirit, according to Matthew's christology). The Greek text used the present tense of the verb (*estin*), although the verb "be" was probably not in the original Aramaic. But when it comes to the rest of the Beatitudes, which attempt to spell out and concretize this possession, all the parallel verbs are in the *future* tense: they will possess the earth, will be consoled, and so on. And the same is true in Luke's briefer version.

Moreover, Matthew sometimes abandons dynamic images of the kingdom and depicts it as a place, or as a space of time in which things happen. But these things are in the future at the moment that the evangelist reports them from the lips of Jesus: "Whoever then relaxes one of the least of these commandments . . . *shall be called* least in the *kingdom* of heaven" (Matt. 5:19); "Many *will come* from east and west and sit at table . . . *in the kingdom* of heaven" (Matt. 8:11; Luke 13:28–29); "I tell you I *shall not drink* again of this fruit of the vine until that day when I drink it new with you in my Father's *kingdom*" (Matt. 26:29 and par.).

By way of conclusion, then, we can say this. It is certain that no image takes for granted the here-and-now presence of the kingdom in full and complete form on this earth, but all those that point toward the future conceive it as being near. Its nearness, however, does not assume an apocalyptic character that would rule out careful attention to the complex mechanisms of history.

It is not easy to reconcile these items of data, the most certain that we have. Let us see if other data might shed new light on the problem.

II

When we move to other uses of the expression, "kingdom of God," we do not seem to find more light, alas, but rather more obscurity.

As I already indicated, the first thing that surprises and disorients us is the shift in images from something dynamic to something *static*. The latter expressions, probably less primitive or original, are much more frequent in Matthew than are dynamic images or expression. The ratio is almost two to one.

The clearest and probably oldest image in this group—certified by the threefold tradition in any event—is that of "entering" (or reaching) the kingdom (see Matt. 5:20; 7:21; 18:3; 19:23, 24; 21:31; 23:13).[6]

It is as if the arrival of the kingdom, its imminent approach, had come to a standstill, to be replaced by a different dynamism: now it is the human being who moves towards the kingdom. But it is not easy to integrate those two dynamisms into a meaningful, coherent image.

Remember that the dynamics of the kingdom and its arrival are destined to transform the whole fabric of human relationships, to change the world for the benefit of those who are suffering in it. By contrast, the dynamic that prompts a person to seek entrance into the kingdom and wonder who can do that is of a more individualistic and moralizing sort. In that line the expression always seems to be used to define the minimum conditions required for admission into the kingdom. To be sure, that fits in perfectly with the moralistic key that seems to typify Matthew, of all the Synoptic writers. It would account for his version of the Beatitudes. Above all, it would explain his particular summary of the Sermon on the Mount: "For I tell you, unless *your righteousness* exceeds that of the scribes and Pharisees, *you will never enter the kingdom of heaven*" (Matt. 5:20).

But similar expressions show up in Mark, who is much more persistent in applying the political key, and in that key the only thing that makes obvious sense is that it is the kingdom that is coming. At most we might assume that the two dynamisms (of the coming kingdom and the people entering it) would converge in one activity, akin to that of taking a bus that is already running.[7] In that sense entering the kingdom that is coming, learning its secrets (Mark 4:11), would typify only *one* of the three groups we have examined: Jesus' disciples, who enter the kingdom as collaborators.

Unfortunately that is not the case. Mark uses the expression "enter the kingdom" six times, and every time it refers to minimum moral conditions for saving oneself and not being thrown into hell (Mark 9:47; 10:14–15, 23, 24, 25; 12:34).

In dealing with Mark, however, there is a hypothesis that should not be overlooked. It would bring together the two types of expressions about the kingdom of God in a fairly logical way.

Let us start with the original idea that it is the kingdom that comes. Then we can ask ourselves: Who will adapt themselves to it? Who will enter into

its dynamic and hence into the values and the happiness it brings? Who will
have to change their values if the kingdom is to incorporate them into its
dynamic?

Now, in the light of those questions, let us look at all the cases where Mark
writes about "entering the kingdom." We find that he is not talking about
minimum moral conditions at all. He is talking about the profound conversion demanded of the adversaries of the kingdom. Jesus is unveiling the
things that are profoundly opposed to the kingdom and its arrival: wealth,
the loss of child-like simplicity as a hermeneutic requisite, and the inability to
gauge correctly and fully between the absolute and the relative, an ability
which is the proper mark of human existence. Jesus is not doing here what we
see in Matthew's Gospel. He is not establishing the bases of a new righteousness, of some minimum morality compatible with the kingdom. If you will
forgive the anachronism, he is not talking about moral merits. Instead he is
denouncing the radical opposition to the kingdom and the opposition's
mechanisms. Those mechanisms could be called psychological or anthropological, if they did not all converge in a *political* reality: the oppression of the
multitudes in Israel.

In Mark, in short, it is still possible to subsume both static and dynamic
images under the term "kingdom of God," as well as the use of the expression "entering the kingdom." That is not true of Matthew, whose stress and
key are different.

The case of Luke is interesting in this connection. From a material point of
view, he is close to Matthew in his abundant use of expressions relating to the
kingdom. Yet that is not the impression we get from reading his treatment.
The term appears approximately fifteen times in his own distinct material
that is not paralleled in Mark or Matthew. But in only one instance does his
use clearly seem to diverge from the line we have noticed in Mark. It is when
Luke cites Jesus' remark about putting one's hand to the plow and then turning back: "No one who puts his hand to the plow and looks back is *fit for* the
kingdom of God" (Luke 9:62). In every other instance the import of the
expression can be explained in terms of his polemic with adversaries and,
above all, the dynamism of the kingdom itself.

Moreover, Luke stresses that the kingdom is "good news" (Luke 4:43),
that it is "near" (Luke 10:11; 21:31), that it is "not coming with signs to be
observed" (Luke 17:20), that people believed it "was to appear immediately" (Luke 19:11), and even that it has been given or has arrived (Luke
12:32; 17:21). And, of course, he also keeps picturing it as a future banquet
(Luke 13:28; 14:16; 22:29, 30). In Luke the dynamic line of Jesus is the same
as that of the kingdom. Where Matthew has Jesus saying that his disciples
have left everything "for my sake," Luke writes "for the sake of the
kingdom" (Luke 18:29).

That brings us to the material which Matthew shares with Luke, and which
probably came from Q. There is not too much of it, and it does not differ
noticeably from Mark's line. As we have already seen, the central Beatitudes
in their original form dovetail with the attitude and message of Jesus pre-

sented by Mark throughout his Gospel—even disregarding the Sermon on the Mount or its equivalent in Luke.

One point can and should be noted. Contrary to practically all the familiar apocalyptic perspectives, the coming of the kingdom does not evoke a merely *passive* hope (that may include enthusiasm, fear, or recourse to prayer). Human beings *collaborate* in its coming. Indeed that is the least we can say about the involvement demanded of them. This is evident from the oldest sources of the Synoptics (Mark and Q) right down to the specific data furnished by Matthew and Luke.

I think that everything presented in the previous chapters, and particularly in the last section of Chapter IX, makes clear that the preaching of Jesus is more than a mere *announcement*. This would include what he entrusted to his disciples. It does not just notify people of an event that is bound to take place anyway. It also is the setting in motion of mechanisms that will be *constitutive* of the actual reign of God. Moreover, the antiquity of the expressions about "entering," both in Mark and in Q, points up the decisive nature of the option that is being proposed to human beings. They are being informed of the ontological and epistemological premises that are indispensable if one is to associate oneself with the dynamism of the kingdom.[8] Some sections of Q, as if accentuating this line of thought, seem to depict the presence of the kingdom as a *object* of human activity.

When Jesus differentiates the time period preceding the Baptist (which may or may not include the latter) from his own, he says that "now the good news of the kingdom of God is beginning to be announced, and *everyone is making efforts* to enter it" (Segundo text translated). One may even prefer the even stronger version of Matthew, which has given rise to so much comment: "From the days of John the Baptist until now the kingdom of heaven has suffered violence, and *men of violence take it by force*" (Matt. 11:12; Luke 16:16). No matter what theological reasons one may have, it is difficult to strip this ancient *logion* of the sense that the kingdom is somehow an *object* of human effort in history.

We find confirmation of this in Jesus' warning not to be preoccupied with one's own necessities in life. This is the reason he gives: "Instead, *seek* his kingdom, and these things shall be yours as well" (Luke 12:31; Matt. 6:33). One could hardly seek something if the initiative behind it belongs exclusively to God. The conclusion seems to be inevitable: there is a causal connection, however small and secondary, between the establishment of the kingdom and human activity directed toward it.

That is not the case, of course, if one shares Matthew's conclusion that the connection is established by *merit*. Indeed we can see the theological cast of his editing work because Matthew adds "*and his righteousness*," by which he means the new interpretation of the moral law taught by Jesus in accordance with his gospel.

But Luke's *logion*, which is undoubtedly the earlier version, goes further. Consider, for a moment, the connection in Matthew between the righteousness of the kingdom of God and the fact that God gives everyone what is needed (which is what the use of the passive here means). If we set aside historical causality, this can only mean a miraculous recompense given to people who were looking for something other than what they finally received. Now let us disregard Matthew's moralistic key, as Luke did, and consider the only key that fits Luke's version, the very key we found to be verified in the preceding chapters. We find that the meaning becomes extraordinarily simple. Why did we not think of it before? To obtain the kingdom is to see to it that everyone has the dose of humanity they need to be human beings—just as flowers and birds have their proper doses in the vegetable or animal kingdom. So we are not dealing with a reward for morality, much less for laxity. We are dealing with an essential, intrinsic constituent of the kingdom: namely, that *all* have their principal human needs solved. Even if they may not be thinking about it explicitly, those who seek the kingdom are watching out for their own needs understood in terms of this global context.

Thus it is *from within* historical causality that human beings collaborate with the kingdom. That is why a radical displacement of energy is entailed. If the kingdom were only a divine judgment accompanied by cosmic catastrophe, if it only called for simple, significant conversions as did the preaching of John the Baptist, there would be no sense to what Jesus demands that people do *for* the kingdom. If people want to assimilate themselves to his mission, he says, they must open up and make themselves totally available. In other words, they must leave behind house, wife, brother, parents, and children (Luke 18:29).[9]

The difference from the Baptist is already obvious, if we are to believe Luke's version of the Baptist's preaching to various groups as cited earlier. But it becomes even more obvious when we see that people are promised a hundredfold in return for this sacrifice in "this time," even before eternal life "in the age to come" (Luke 18:30 and par.). This only confirms our interpretation of the things promised "as well" to those who first seek the kingdom and thus give it priority over their own self-interests (Luke 12:31).

It certainly is exegetically tempting to apply this interpretation to the response that Jesus makes in an eschatological context and that only Luke records: "The kingdom of God is *not coming with signs to be observed*" (Luke 17:20). This could allude to the suddenness and unexpectedness of an apocalypse, but Luke clearly gives it a different meaning. First, he associates the coming of the kingdom with the *present*: "For behold, the kingdom of God *is in the midst of you*" (Luke 17:21). Perhaps this means that now, as a result of Jesus' revelation of the secrets of the kingdom, we can begin to have a conscious convergence between the efforts of human beings and the efforts of God in the building of a kingdom that is spread out over the course of history.

Second, there is the other reason Jesus gives in answer to the Pharisees' question about the coming of the kingdom. He makes clear that its coming is completely contrary to any process of *simplification*, though not to partisanship or bias. People will not be able to say: "Lo, here it is! or there!" (Luke 17:21). Why? It is not because of the universality of the apocalypse as opposed to the partiality of the kingdom evident now (see Matt. 24:23, 26–27); it is not because of the danger of false messiahs arising (see Luke 9:49–50). Rather, it is because the kingdom of God is *already* present and at work *without drawing attention to itself*. The impossibility of seeing it now, according to Luke, is due to the *complex* and in-depth nature of the way it is operating. This points us to the dense fabric of historical causality, poles apart from the simplicity of apocalypses. And it also means that the decisive issue is not exhausted once one has pinpointed Jesus as the true Messiah amid so many false ones (see Matt. 12:32; Luke 12:10).

To sum up this overview: we find that it is only Matthew who puts us off the track with regard to the kingdom in his editing work or his own distinctive materials.

Willy-nilly, he too bears witness to the twofold dynamism of the kingdom, as we have seen. But he personally prefers to picture it in static and largely *reified* terms. In a moralizing vision such as his, it is logical that everything viewed as the extrinsic *result* of a line of moral conduct would appear, apart from that, as a reward or punishment. It is also logical that the *criteria* at the root of action would show up as something external and pre-existent to one's actions. In Matthew, then, the kingdom is not only a reward to be given or denied (see also Matt. 21:43; 25:34; etc.). It is also seen as the realm where the criteria for acting in accordance with the new righteousness preached by Jesus (see, for example, Matt. 13:41–43; 18:1–4) hold sway in all their immutable ideality.[10]

Matthew's distinctive material, then, seems to form a strange block that hardly fits in with the rest of the data provided by the Synoptics. Perhaps my investigation has succeeded in doing two things with regard to that material. The first thing is to reduce the number of elements in it that do not dovetail with the general line—complicated but intelligible—that we have discovered in Mark, Q, and Luke's distinctive material.

The second thing is more profound. It has to do with the irreducible material that still remains in Matthew's material or his editing. How do we explain it? One explanation is the peculiar nature of his christological ideas and their tieup with morality, as we have seen. But there must be something else as well. The fact is that no single key, rooted in one area of a human life, can account for all a person's ideas and actions—particularly when that life is rich and deep. Politicians have their ideas about art and religion, and they deal with those areas too. Psychologists know that alongside the variety of individual problems there are economic and political mechanisms that affect all the members of a group or class.

Here I have been using a political key to explain the prepaschal Jesus. But I am not thereby suggesting that the religious should be relegated to a secondary plane, if there indeed is such a thing as an exclusively religious plane (see Volume I). Still less am I suggesting that *everything* about Jesus can be explained by the political key. All I am saying here is that the political key is the best code for deciphering his destiny and teaching as a whole.

If we look at a particular saying of Jesus, we can sometimes see the political context that frames and partially explains it, but we can also see other content that is not exhausted by that context. Take his injunction to become as little children in order to enter the kingdom.[11] Reading it on its own terms, and even more in conjunction with other teachings, we must be aware of the political context surrounding it. But that context does not exhaust the teaching. There is a crucial mainspring underlying the morality taught by Jesus: we must see and feel ourselves to be children in the Father's eyes, and only on the basis of that premise should we try to interpret the law revealed by God the creator.

We can assume that Jesus often presented moral teachings that cannot be reduced to a political frame even though they may not have been dissociated from his effort to trigger a political conflict. Take, for example, his preaching about acting gratuitously: turning the other cheek and so on (see Matt. 5:38–48; Luke 6:27–35).[12]

These moral judgments by Jesus, like his political activities, were designed to reveal the Father. There seems to be no doubt that Matthew, more concerned than the other Synoptics in the divine origin and criteria of these moral teachings, chose to subsume them under the originally political expression, "kingdom of God" (see, for example, Matt. 5:20). Instead of simply using the word "God" to designate the Absolute behind them, he chose to use the term hallowed by Jesus: *the kingdom*. This would explain the peculiarly Matthean nucleus of expressions about the kingdom that we have not been able to account for.

III

Now that we have put some order into the material, let us get back to the issue posed at the very start of this chapter: Did Jesus expect the arrival of the kingdom of God "with power" during his lifetime?

The general answer of present-day exegetes is: yes. Let us look at the reasons behind this answer and see how legitimate they are. The fact is that the issue is wrapped in more than a little obscurity.

The weightiest arguments in favor of an affirmative answer are two things we find in the triple Synoptic tradition. Both refer to the time of the kingdom's arrival, though they may use such terms as "the end" or "the coming of the Son of man."

The first is a *logion* of Jesus that the three Synoptics place at a point in time near Jesus' first prediction of his passion. In all likelihood that would be after the Galilean crisis and before his final preaching in Jerusalem. According to Mark, Jesus is supposed to have said: "Truly, I say to you, there are some standing here who will not taste death before they see that the kingdom of God has come with power" (Mark 9:1 and par.).[13]

The second, on the other hand, is a little "apocalypse" that the three Synoptics place in Jesus' final preaching in Jerusalem, just before his passion. Our present-day Bibles label it as an "eschatological discourse." It is more sober in Mark, more florid in Matthew and Luke.

It seems to begin with the disconcerted question of the disciples after Jesus predicted the destruction of Jerusalem (see Mark 13:1–4 and par.). Accustomed to prophetic ways, they ask for "the signs" that will herald those events. This evokes a long discourse, which begins in Mark with the formula: "And Jesus began to say to them. . . ." He tells them the signs. But signs of the *local* tragedy are followed by signs of a cosmic tragedy affecting the sun, moon, and stars. And that is to be followed by "the Son of man coming in clouds with great power and glory" (Mark 13:26 and par.).[14] Then the evangelists add a puzzling paradox. On the one hand, "of that day or that hour no one knows, not even the angels in heaven nor the Son, but only the Father" (Mark 13:32 and par.).[15] On the other hand the time is so close that Jesus can say the same thing he has already said about the arrival of the kingdom: "Truly, I say to you, this generation will not pass away before all these things take place" (Mark 13:30 and par.).

To these two passages I must add a third, which is not common to all three Synoptics. Luke omits it, in line with his general tendency to leave out disrespectful things. It is the *cry* of surprise and confusion with which Jesus dies on the cross: "My God, my God, why hast thou forsaken me?" (Mark 15:34; Matt. 27:46). This exclamation seems to prove that events did not turn out as Jesus expected.

But what exactly is the force of this line of argument proving that Jesus was mistaken in predicting or foreseeing the *immediate* arrival and fulfillment of the kingdom of God "with power"? Let us take a closer look at the way the case is argued.

To begin with, its force depends on the fact that it is separated from the rest of the data. Then it becomes all the more probable insofar as people effect a Copernican revolution and turn it into *the key to everything else.* If we are going to stick to anything in the historical reconstruction of Jesus of Nazareth, you see, it has to be to the data that is clearly prepaschal, that cannot derive from or be confirmed by the paschal events. If Jesus made a mistake, the data that record and reveal this mistake must, historically speaking, be the surest.

In other words, the kingdom did not arrive "with power" during the lifetime of the generation that heard Jesus prophesy its arrival. So we should start to reconstruct the historical facts about Jesus of Nazareth around this certainty of his that was clearly and cruelly belied by events. Thus the inner logic of his message, for example, must be viewed as less certain because we do not know to what extent it might have been influenced, even unwittingly, by the paschal events.

If this hypothesis becomes more likely insofar as we separate these items from the rest, that is even truer if we go on to show that the latter can be explained as a consequence of Jesus' mistake about the future—in short, if we show that the rest of the data makes even clearer sense if we assume that it is suffused with the eschatological urgency central to the hypothesis in question.[16]

Now I certainly am not going to go back over everything presented so far in terms of this new key. My presentation itself should prove that I do not find it satisfactory. But it is worth the trouble to reexamine the core of this argument: its starting point. Several points merit particular attention.

1. If we did not have the sayings of Jesus just discussed—his *logion* about "this generation" and the "eschatological discourse"—it would never occur to us to introduce them into the gospel. It is not just that the rest of the material is far from being chaotic without them. There is also the fact that they seem to be an erratic block much more akin to the line of the Baptist than to that of Jesus.[17]

Even opponents recognize that their importance lies in the fact that Jesus *makes a mistake* in them. I might also add that they dovetail, even more than with the Baptist's line, with the classical eschatological expectations of books and wise men (where today's exegetes will seek them), and that they do not dovetail with the originality of Jesus of Nazareth, which could not possibly have been invented by his disciples. If there was a mistake, it is much more credible that it was a mistake made by his disciples and evangelists, that it was they who succumbed to the classical eschatological perspectives in trying to interpret the sayings of Jesus—not Jesus himself, to whom we are indebted for a complex, subtle message that is incompatible with such perspectives.

2. Let us take a further step and consider the application of the prepaschal criterion to this material. The assumption of the hypothesis under discussion goes like this: living after the paschal events, the evangelists would not have recorded a mistake of Jesus, clearly discernible as such, unless they felt obligated to do so by some inescapable prepaschal fact or reality.

But this argument ceases to have any force if we assume that Jesus did not make a mistake. Let us ask ourselves: How do we know *today* that the kingdom did not arrive, that the disciples of Jesus did not see him in the clouds of heaven with power and glory, and that they therefore *felt obliged* to record his *mistake*?

That assumption is to a large extent bound up with a literary ambiguity. In the rest of the New Testament authors, you see, the two terms that would enable us to *verify* whether Jesus made a mistake or not disappear for all practical purposes: that is, "kingdom of God" and "Son of Man." Those are the two terms in Jesus' questionable predictions about the near future.

But let us adopt a different assumption. Suppose that with different terms, and even before *the redaction of the Synoptic Gospels*, the first Christian communities expressed their conviction that the predictions of Jesus, or at least their substantive core, had been fulfilled. Then the argument of the opposite hypothesis is turned against its proponents. Instead of a mistake *recognized as such* being the key prepaschal datum, Jesus' prediction, fulfilled at Easter, becomes a prophecy *ex eventu*: a typically postpaschal datum.

Now look at Paul's introduction to his Letter to the Romans, written approximately ten years before the actual redaction of the Synoptics. Paul writes that Jesus was "constituted Son of God *with power* . . . *by his resurrection from the dead*" (Rom. 1:4; Segundo text translated).[18] Thus it is only after the resurrection that the salvific mission of Jesus, which Paul identifies with justification, can be fully realized and reach all the real (not just physical) children of Abraham. For it is the resurrection that constitutes the gift of the Spirit, that is, of God's *power* (see Rom. 4:25 and cf. Matt. 12:28). Everything suggests that in different terminology more suited to his addressees, Paul is saying that with Jesus' resurrection *the kingdom of God has already arrived with power.*[19]

Jesus' mistake, evident in his cry from the cross, would be reduced to his thinking that the power to realize and solidify the kingdom much more would come from God *before his death*. He may have thought that death would not interrupt the process, at least not until much later. Like all of us, Jesus (*perfectus homo*) went to his death without figuring that it would entail no more than two or three days in a tomb.

But another justifiable question might be raised here, even if one is willing to grant that the arrival of the kingdom with power and the vision of the Son of Man in glory were postpaschal data placed on the lips of the prepaschal Jesus as prophecies. Do we not still have to explain why people introduced into those prophecies *elements that turned them into mistakes*: for example, the end of the world with its accompanying cosmic catastrophe?

Here we do indeed reach one of the limits of our knowledge about Jesus of Nazareth. *No matter what hypothesis we may adopt,* we must admit that the evangelists depict him as being mistaken about the end of the world and the cosmic catastrophes that would precede it.[20] The gospel testimony and the most implacable logic force us to choose between one of three possibilities insofar as the origin of this mistake is concerned. It was committed by Jesus himself or by the evangelists in recording his teachings or by the early church, which confused different warnings and made a mistake in situating the criterion of verification.[21]

Once the problem is posed in that way, I must call the attention of my readers to a *limit* that is necessarily imposed on any *historical* quest such as the one we have been undertaking. A methodological consideration must be noted and respected. Faced with the problem just posed, a christology can furnish solutions that are not solutions at all on the plane where we have been conducting our search so far: the history of Jesus.

From that history we know that the redactors of the Synoptic Gospels understood that Jesus, at one point in his life at least, predicted cosmic catastrophes culminating in the end of the world as being no further than a generation away. We also know that early Christian communities thought the same thing. Various members of the church in Thessalonia, for example, stopped working for that very reason (see 2 Thess. 2:1–3, 12).

It is not the proper task of this history to excuse Jesus for this error or to assert without reliable data that its origin lies in some misunderstanding of the disciples or evangelists.[22] A christology can certainly speculate on the limited or unlimited nature of Jesus' knowledge of the future,[23] but history cannot. History can only verify the reliablility of the data that attribute to him a prediction which in fact was not fulfilled.

The important thing here is to make a clear distinction, at least in principle and in terms of the elaboration of a hypothesis, between two very different possibilities or hypotheses: (1) Jesus lived, worked, and taught with a sense of complete and total eschatological urgency, foreseeing imminent eschatological catastrophes and the end of time.[24] (2) Jesus vainly expected the irruption in power of God's kingdom on earth during the span of his earthly life.

The first hypothesis would invalidate everything I have said so far, making it totally illogical.[25] But as opposed to the second hypothesis, it has *only one datum* to back it up: the eschatological discourse. Against it are a host of undeniable and important facts and structures, which contradict it. The second hypothesis must admit that Jesus waited in vain during his lifetime for the breakthrough of God's kingdom with power. But it confirms the fact that his community gradually came to realize that the breakthrough did take place, despite appearances to the contrary, with Jesus' resurrection from the dead. That would give rise to Paul's christological elaboration and development from his Letters to the Thessalonians to his Letter to the Romans.

I would like to call the attention of my readers to one further point regarding the boundary between *history* and *christology*. A big mistake seems to give a person, in this case Jesus, a certain dominion over history as a whole— not *in spite of* being cosmic but precisely because *it is* cosmic in proportions. It places him beyond history. So interpretation, freed from history, can fly off in all directions.

The situation is very different when we apply to Jesus a radically historical key such as the political one we have been using. The person in question takes on more solidity and consistency, to be sure. But now his roots in history seem to prevent him from jumping easily to other times, contexts, and cultures.

Jesus had a concrete, historical, human destiny. He "worked with human hands" (*GS*: 22) in the construction of the kingdom, as Vatican II put it in a somewhat different but not unrelated context. The means which Jesus used to reveal the Father to us in and through the concrete proximity of God's kingdom bear the stamp of history and its irreversibility. In short, they bear the stamp of any and every "ideology," as I defined that term in Volume I.

By the same token, to the extent that Jesus sinks his teeth into our history in that way he acquires a past and a future. He is bound up with a tradition, and he obligates us to make a creative effort whenever we want to speak of him, or be faithful to him, in a new context. Historical experiences prior to his time are not rendered useless, nor can we simply adopt his experiences by way of simple imitation or analogy.

This creative effort—its conditions, successes, and failures at times—is what I shall be dealing with in Volumes III, IV, and V. I hope the whole process will be fairly clear to my readers when I am finished.

APPENDIX I

The Resurrected Jesus

A point raised earlier takes on decisive importance here. In the preceding chapters I have been talking about Jesus, not as if he had not died (we have seen the conflict that led to his death), but as if he had not risen from the dead.

In the Introduction of Part Two of this volume I tried to suggest the import of this omission and the reasons for it. My aim was to arrange and verify the most historically reliable data about Jesus of Nazareth, so I shifted *postpaschal* data from the domain of history to that of faith's interpretation of Jesus and events. I was not thereby attempting to pass judgment on the veracity of such data. But simple logic compels us to say that those data may represent a retrojection of Jesus' resurrection to earlier events. And even if they are not distorting, they hardly accord with the canons of history.

Does that mean that Jesus' resurrection does not constitute a "historical fact"?

Before we try to answer that question, we must proceed in orderly fashion and make clear that Jesus' resurrection certainly did constitute a verifiable fact in *the history of the nascent church*. It may seem to be a subtle distinction, but it underlines something that is very clear. No matter how we may characterize the *datum* of Jesus' resurrection (as truth or illusion, objective experience or subjective mistake), we can scientifically prove with the documents at hand that the *experiences* constitutive of that *datum* were historically decisive for interpreting Jesus and thereby defining the meaning, function, and structure of the early Christian church.

Those data may not be historically verifiable with respect to Jesus himself, as we shall see in this appendix. Nevertheless they are central constituents of the historical church. To use a different example, we can consider the data offered by such ancient historians as Herodotus and Titus Livius. From a scholarly point of view those data may not be reliable or trustworthy. Nevertheless we can appreciate the role, certainly a *historical* role, that the data furnished by those authors played in the formation of Greek or Roman culture.

The resurrection, then, is not a gap left unfilled at the conclusion of the previous chapters on the historical Jesus.[1] Indeed, as early as the Introduction to Part Two, I said something about the historical influence of the paschal experiences in prompting people to relate the messianic expectations of Israel to Jesus. I also noted another point that will be considered more fully in Appendix II: the change in stress and content of the early postpaschal preaching of the apostles as opposed to Jesus' own preaching.

Viewed from this standpoint, the paschal experiences represent a crucial step that can be traced historically. To use the terminology I discussed in Volume I, they are the connecting link between the *anthropological faith* of Jesus' disciples (closely bound up with Jesus' values) and *religious faith,* which situates Jesus himself within a chain of witnesses both before and after him. On the one hand the chain goes back to take in the whole Old Testament. On the other hand it goes forward to include the later followers of Jesus. Because Jesus' resurrection cannot possibly be scientifically verified, his later followers and disciples become decisive witnesses to a tradition in which one can place absolute trust.

Here we have the bridgehead or springboard from which christologies will launch forth to capture the meaning of history in all its variability.

I

If a people wish to enter the domain having to do with the significance of Jesus of Nazareth, the domain of christologies, they will have to trust that Jesus' disciples are sincere when they assure us that they are really certain they saw Jesus after his death, filled with new life, and that they felt obliged to draw important consequences from those experiences in order to interpret him.

The creative christologies to which I am alluding here would not have had the ability or energy to take off from the historical Jesus into the future if they had not been convinced that the statement, "Jesus rose from the dead," was *just as true* as the statement, "Jesus died on the cross" (even though the truth of the former statement differs from that of the latter insofar as its scientific verifiability is concerned). Paul himself makes the point explicitly (see 1 Cor. 15:17).

As soon as we note this logic and take the corresponding course, we run into an *odd fact* that is also *suspicious* in the eyes of many. In narrating the disciples' experiences with the risen Jesus, the Synoptics do not seem to change the literary genre they used to recount their experiences with the prepaschal Jesus. It is as if we were on the same plane of realities, as if anyone who chanced upon these scenes could have witnessed and *verified* the same thing.[2]

Our surprise grows when we see that John's Gospel shares this attitude of the Synoptics. The author of the fourth Gospel knew how to create new literary genres combining symbolism, philosophy, and theology in order to recount the activities of the prepaschal Jesus. But he *goes back* to the literary genre of the Synoptics (or one very similar) where we would least expect him to: in narrating the appearances of the resurrected Jesus.

We do well to reflect a bit on this problem, which is really the only one still confronting us after the specifications already set forth.[3] That is certainly the case once we realize that we cannot directly verify the resurrection of Jesus,[4] that we can only ascertain the veracity of the witnesses in a more or less negative way.

The situation changes if we take a closer and more careful look at the paschal narratives that *seem to be just like* the prepaschal ones. In a series of consecutive circles, as it were, we will come to see the profound difference between the two sets of narratives and its connection with their narrative content.

Even leaving aside the additions to these accounts that are recognized by exegetes (Mark 16:9–20; John 21), we see clearly that the accounts have lost their synoptic character, and this in connection with content of such crucial importance. It is no longer possible for us to get two or three superimposed pictures of one and the same scene, with their similarities and differences.

The only point on which the evangelists agree synoptically is, interestingly enough, the last element that might justifiably be called prepaschal and historical: the discovery of *the empty tomb* by the three women after the Sabbath was over. From there on they disagree on everything: where, when, and to whom the risen one appears; what he says to them; what they believe they know about him; and when he withdraws once and for all from their presence. All this material is scattered and disconnected to a degree that seems improbable to anyone who knows how freely a writer like Matthew, for example, dealt with his material.

According to Mark, for example, Galilee is the place for his disciples to go if they want to see the risen Jesus. According to Matthew, it is the place where they see him once, for the first and last time. In Luke, Galilee is only a memento of Jesus' initial preaching; the appearances of the risen Jesus take place only in Jerusalem or its environs (e.g., Emmaus). The same is true in John's Gospel, although an appendix tacked on to the fourth Gospel adds one appearance in Galilee that is totally different from the rest.

What does all that suggest? That here there is no general consensus such as there was for the facts that took place before Jesus' death, even though this seems to violate all the laws of memory? It would be premature for us to draw conclusions from this one element. But it is a matter of the utmost importance that should have been engraved on their memory more than other events. The fact that it is impossible for the evangelists to be synoptic on this matter must have something to do with the subject treated in their accounts.

Moving to a second circle, we can focus on the content of the teachings that Jesus addressed to his disciples during these appearances. Here again we find the same trait of disconnectedness. Luke, to be sure, does briefly summarize the theme of all Jesus' paschal messages by saying that he spoke of "the kingdom of God" (Acts 1:3). But there is no new announcement, no important correction, and no reaffirmation of basic principles. We get the impression that the words attributed to Jesus do not seem to suggest any new teaching here, something that could be set down objectively. Instead they seem to point to a new level of *comprehension* achieved by his disciples with regard to things that they already knew and that somehow had to do with their own status and mission.

Luke, for example, alludes to a crucial teaching yet leaves us completely in the dark about its concrete content. He tells us only this: "Then he opened their minds *to understand the scriptures*, and said to them, 'Thus it is written that the Christ should suffer and on the third day rise from the dead' " (Luke 24:45–46; see 24:6). The same holds true for what was learned by the disciples on the road to Emmaus: "And beginning with Moses and all the prophets, he interpreted to them in *all the scriptures* the things concerning himself" (Luke 24:27).

If we are to believe John, the risen Jesus communicated two things to his disciples. The first, when he tells them: "Receive the Holy Spirit. If you forgive the sins of any, they are forgiven; if you retain the sins of any, they are retained" (John 20:22–23). The second, in response to the proof demanded by Thomas and his little faith: "Have you believed because you have seen me? *Blessed are those who have not seen and yet believe*" (John 20:28).

Insofar as the first item is concerned, it seems obvious that John is consciously following, almost word for word, a *logion* that Matthew attributes to the prepaschal Jesus (see Matt. 18:18). In shifting the context to the postpaschal period, John seems to be suggesting that only then did they realize that what had seemed to be a prerogative of Jesus (see Matt. 9:6 and par.) was actually a structural reality of the kingdom itself that somehow was to be turned into an ongoing historical mechanism.

Insofar as the second item is concerned, it clearly contains one element that could be applied to all the paschal teachings of Jesus: an allusion to a future implication or meaning. The primacy of believers unable to verify directly this decisive datum of their faith points toward the postapostolic community, shedding light on its situation (already a reality when the fourth Gospel is being written), its value, and the factors conditioning it.

Much the same thing can be said about the teachings of the risen Jesus sketched in the apocryphal appendices: the crucial importance of faith and baptism (Mark 16:15–18), or people's respective functions in the nascent church (John 21:15–23).

Even sticking to Matthew and Luke, we find that an understanding of the church's mission arrived at *long after Easter* by the early Christian community has been turned into a teaching of the risen Jesus. We learn of the universality of a message that Jesus himself, in his prepaschal preaching, restricted to Israel (see Matt. 10:5; 15:24): "Go therefore and make disciples of all nations [the pagan peoples], baptizing them in the name of the Father and of the Son and of the Holy Spirit" (Matt. 28:19; Luke 24:47).

With respect to these paschal teachings of Jesus, then, we are led to conclude that the experience behind them is an understanding of Jesus and the following of Jesus which takes place later on the psychological and historical levels, but which finds its logical origin in the reality of the risen one. So although the literary genre of the narration *seems to be* the same, its laws have radically changed by virtue of its content.

Now let us move to a third circle. In *all* the appearances that are narrated in detail we find one point of the utmost importance that is incredibly underrated or minimized by some christologies.[5] It is *the difficulty people have in recognizing Jesus* in the risen figure and the procedures used by Jesus to effect this recognition.

We invariably find that the new way in which Jesus lives and acts does not permit people to recognize him, materially speaking, *at first sight*. In one case (the disciples on the road to Emmaus) Luke offers a miraculous explanation for this failure to recognize Jesus: "Their eyes were kept from recognizing him" (Luke 24:16); note that Mark 16:12 says that "he appeared in another form to two of them." On another occasion, however, Luke attributes the failure to psychological factors having to do with the disciples themselves (see Luke 24:37, 41). Matthew is content to say this about the disciples who encounter the risen Jesus: "And when they saw him, they worshiped him; but some doubted" (Matt. 28:17). With regard to the same appearances, John points up odd circumstances that could have affected their ability to recognize Jesus: "The doors were shut" (John 20:19, 26). In other instances, however, he offers no reason at all for the failure to recognize Jesus. Take the curious case of Mary Magdalene, who confuses him with the gardener but recognizes him when he utters her name (see John 20:11f.).

On *every* occasion, however, the bridge between the risen Jesus and the prepaschal Jesus is built in an indirect way. There is some reminiscence of Jesus as he was, some characteristic of him that remains or reappears despite the transformation he has undergone: another miraculous catch of fish, the pronunciation of one's name, the breaking of bread, the wounds received on the cross, and so on.

It is clear that we are faced with an intentional literary procedure designed to break down a realistic reading of the narrative. The antinomy or contradiction (Jesus being the same yet unrecognizable) signals a radical difference between their prepaschal experiences and their postpaschal experiences.

Finally, there is another important datum, usually implicit but surfacing explicitly at times, that will provide our last turn of the circle: Jesus' appearances confirm the *existing faith* of the witnesses; they are not a *valid* proof *independent of that already existing faith*.

I just said that this datum sometimes surfaces explicitly to a certain extent. I am talking about the sort of thing that crops up in the verification made by Thomas (John 20:29). Just when it would seem that these paschal happenings would or should shift the disciples from believing to seeing and verifying, we are surprised to find that the use of the word "believe" (or related words such as "doubt") is proportionately greater than it was in accounts of the events that took place before Jesus' death.

It is as if Jesus' original exhortation ("have a change of outlook and believe in the good news") is still reverberating, though admittedly on a new level. The resurrected Jesus appears only to those who believed in his original exhortation and have stuck with the values he represented, however weak may have been their understanding of his major ideas and however vacillating may have been their faith when confronted with the scandal of the cross. I repeat: the risen Jesus appears *only to them*.

Here we have an important datum. Despite the apologetic use of the resurrection from the very start of Christian preaching, his disciples cannot cite one single appearance of the risen Jesus to anyone outside their own group, the people who were with him even before the paschal events. That formidable event did not have one single *impartial* witness.

The sober fact is all the more interesting insofar as Jesus himself seemed to take a big step down the road of apologetics at one point. Exasperated by the pretensions of the religious authorities to pass judgment on him in God's name, he himself appeals to future verification: "You will see the Son of man seated at the right hand of Power, and coming with the clouds of heaven" (Mark 14:62 and par.).

How easy it would have been, at least for a christology "from above" like that of John, to narrate the fulfillment of this prophecy by Jesus! But none of the evangelists do that. If we try to find an *objective* reason why things happened the way they are actually narrated to us, we find a profound reason in the nature of the divine *economy* at work here. If people have self-justifying values that are directly opposed to those of Jesus, they will not be convinced even if someone "should rise from the dead" (Luke 16:31).

Thus the apologetic use of Jesus' resurrection in universal, verifiable terms is ruled out by what the gospel narratives tell us: the pursuit of the same values that Jesus held dear is an indispensable prerequisite for being able to "see" and recognize the risen one.

Thus the very concept of *verification* must be opened up to allow for two different meanings. On the one hand the gospel narratives do not allow us to talk about any *scientific* verification. By very definition such verification can be universalized; one need only reproduce the same external conditions of observation and make sure that the very same elements are at work. On the other hand it is obvious that the paschal narratives do claim to be a verification of something. Specifically, the course of events, quite apart from the will of the disciples themselves, enables them to verify how right it was to adhere to the very same values that structured the life and death of Jesus of Nazareth.

So we come back to our initial question: Is the resurrection of Jesus a *historical* fact? If by "fact" we mean something that can be verified in the scientific sense just described above, then the answer must be no. And this is true, not just in fact, but *in principle*. There are many items of data, distant in time or space, which do not allow us to make any direct verification in fact, but which do possess all the essential requisites for scientific verification. That is not the case here.

What is more, our study of the literary genre of the gospel accounts of the risen Jesus in this chapter has brought out another noteworthy point. The authors of those accounts offer us reliable indications that they clearly perceived the question, which is not as modern as the term "scientific" might suggest with reference to the other type of verification. In the case of the gospel accounts of the prepaschal Jesus, for example, there is a certain degree of practical unverifiability, given the temporal and cultural distance that separates us from them, and that was already beginning to separate the evangelists themselves from the facts they were narrating. But in principle those accounts are essentially verifiable in the usual sense. Such is not the case with the paschal events. Whether we trust the gospel accounts of them or not, we see that the accounts as written down bear all the marks of a different type of *verifiability*, the second type described above.

One thing we can say for sure is that those accounts do purport to be authentic *data*, not merely lyrical expressions of affection or subjective impressions. When the disciples say that they are *witnesses* to the fact that Jesus rose from the dead (or that God resurrected Jesus), as we find them saying in the preaching of Peter (see Acts 1:32; 3:15; 5:32) and his companions, they are not simply trying to say that they love Jesus or that they remember him the way he was when alive or that he still lives in their memory. What exactly, then, is the content of such seemingly odd and unique forms of expression, which seem to be both unverifiable and yet verified?

II

This question is an essential one for any and every christology ever formulated, be it in the past, present, or future. To answer it, we must go back to a central point discussed in Volume I: *transcendent data*.

There we saw that in every human life whether the human being realizes it or not, a body of *data beyond* (i.e., transcending) any and all verifiable experience takes root. It has to do with the possibility of impressing on reality a certain set of values we plan to make our own.

This process is different from, but not alien to, another process we engage in as human beings. Faced with different witnesses to what a satisfying life is, in making our own decision we choose those witnesses who seem to be capable of offering us a greater happiness by the adoption of their values. Our choice has to be made through the medium of witnesses because no human being can personally experience in advance the possible happiness or goal that awaits him or her at the finish of one road in life, much less of all the possible roads in life. One's choice entails a wager on certain values as those that will bring happiness and success in life, and to that wager I gave the name "faith." And here it has a basically anthropological or human sense rather than a specifically religious sense.

Confronting every human being at the other end of the spectrum is the domain of *objective* reality: reality as it is, as opposed to the set of values that guides us in deciding what reality ought to be or what we want it to be. To say that human knowledge of this second domain is objective is not to say that it is true or even disinterested. All cognition is, and will always be, in the service of some *efficacy*: the realization of certain values. "Objectivity" here alludes to the shift in course that cognition must make in order to achieve efficacy. It must allow for the communicability of data and the universality of its *verification*. To achieve the greatest effectiveness possible, one must stick to a type of verification that is possible for everyone, hence even for those who give a different meaning to their lives and structure life around a different set of values. Only by paying this price, for the sake of efficacy, can human beings communicate and accumulate knowledge.

But between these two realms (faith and efficacy), so clearly opposed in principle, there is always and necessarily another zone where they intermingle as complementary. This is the zone of *ultimate or transcendent data* about reality and what it can offer us. They are *data* because they do not deal with what ought to be (values) but rather with what is: with reality and its more remote possibilities or probabilities. But they are also *ultimate* in two senses: (1) because they have to do with the limits of reality and hence could be verified only if reality as a whole presented itself at one and the same time; (2) because they appeal to a kind of eschatological verification. By that I mean that they are the foundation for an existential bet or wager made by every human being, which could be phrased as follows: "*In the end* you will see that I was right." This is eschatology as an essential and integral component of every human life. As is the case with every wager, the future is set up as the criterion.

As I noted in Volume I, some may claim that only those with a gift for words—orators, teachers, writers, poets—can give explicit form to such transcendent data. For most people those data will remain implicit, even though they may be solid and operative. A large dose of symbolism will always be needed to transmit them in a meaningful way that does not strip them of their characteristic transcendence.

Here let me offer an example that might seem to have no connection whatsoever with the resurrection accounts we are studying. In *Swann's Way* Marcel Proust has his narrator reflecting on a musical phrase by Vinteuil as an example of the enduring effect of works of arts and certain conceptions on our lives:

> Perhaps it is not-being that is the true state, and all our dream of life is without existence; but, if so, we feel that it must be that these phrases of music, these conceptions which exist in relation to our dream, are nothing either. We shall perish, but *we have for our hostages these divine captives who shall follow and share our fate. And death in their company is something less bitter, less inglorious, perhaps even less certain* [Proust 1970, 268–69; my italics].

This is obviously a line of argument, so we ask ourselves what exactly its logical mechanism is. How does it work?

First of all, if it makes sense to think like that, then the implication is that the author of this line of thought has first chosen and then gone on to cultivate certain specific values. The beauty of a musical phrase, after all, is not a datum that can be scientifically verified. It assumes that one has given certain values priority over other values and has educated one's taste accordingly. That process of education would entail effort, and hence *faith*, as I described it above. Something else also depends on the values-structure that one has chosen: the fact that a certain degree—not objective—of such beauty can be regarded as possessing the "divine" quality that is basic to the force of the argument.

Second, through these esthetic experiences in the musical realm the author finds reasons to imagine the limits of objective reality in a certain way. Those experiences lead him to conclude that the return to not-being is "less certain." To put it in other words, which might well not have found approval with the author even though I think they are equivalent: he concludes that some sort of immortality, transmigration, resurrection, or whatever you might want to call it, is more likely than not-being.

Third, his argument generalizes and transcends "verifiable" human experiences with hostages. It implicitly presupposes the existence of "something" outside of ourselves and coextensive with the whole reality that would be lost if those human creations were to disappear with us. Ultimately that something is always conceived as "someone" because no computer is capable of appreciating values unless it has been programmed to do that by someone who establishes the values.

Fourth, the argument gives way to a curious short circuit. It appeals to a verification precisely at the point where the real conditions for verification cease. It admits that as long as we are alive, the wager is precisely that: a wager. Only when we no longer have life—this life in which scientific verifications are possible—will we know whether we have made a good wager, whether what we considered more certain was really so.

To be sure, there is good reason to fear that logical positivists would demolish this sort of argument and say it is meaningless. But I would maintain that they, despite their negation, must still enter the same borderline, transcendent, eschatological zone to structure their own human lives. They must do so, even if only to systematically diminish the boundaries of reality vis-à-vis the realization of the ought-to-be that is established by values—without being able to verify that diminution, of course.[6] I would further maintain that they will always make some wager against the apparent limits of reality, even if it be done completely unwittingly or by way of doubts. They will always sacrifice something to that which cannot be verified in a scientific way. They will always take "hostages," even though they may claim to the outside world that those hostages have value only for themselves as individuals.[7]

Now what relationship does the category of *transcendent data* and its workings have with the gospel accounts of Jesus' resurrection? The connection is crystal clear. We can say without fear of mistake that all the literary precautions adopted by the evangelists, which we have been examining in this appendix, are designed to distinguish this transcendent datum from the other historical data presented in the prepaschal accounts.

With the resurrection of Jesus we come to a borderline. We cross a threshold into the ultimate. But that ultimate is not an abstract category. It is the concrete datum embodying the response of total reality to the question of the ultimate fate of the values taught and practiced by Jesus; it is the final treatment that Someone gives to the "hostages" that Jesus kept in his limited, ideological human existence faced with death, and did so in a historical, verifiable way.

But there is obviously one big difference between the argument of Proust in our example and the resurrection accounts. Proust's narrator admits that he *does not yet know* the outcome of his wager; the apostles, after the paschal events, *claim they do know it.* Proust's narrator postulates a datum; Jesus' disciples believe they have seen it, that they are *witnesses* to it. As I see it, two major considerations must be brought in at this point.

1. The wager contained in the values taught and practiced by Jesus would make sense and have perfect existential logic even if the resurrection had not taken place. In that case the logic would be exactly the same as that in Proust's argument. The wager in Jesus' life, his "hostages," would be waiting for the eschatological conditions of verification, as is the case in the life of all other human beings. That would in no way disqualify or discredit Jesus of Nazareth, not even from the religious point of view. He would be in the same situation as all the great figures who spoke on behalf of Yahweh and introduced the transcendent data that mark the history and tradition of Israel. Like the patriarchs, Moses, and the prophets, Jesus would have been left waiting for divine verification. But that does not mean that the data on ultimate reality brought by him would be less deserving of faith, any more than their data would be.[8]

According to the evangelists, however, things did not turn out that way. They tell us that the disciples had an opportunity to peep into the ultimate and there *verify*, in the risen Jesus, a basic transcendent datum. The ultimate in the midst of history: that may seem to be an antinomy or outright contradiction. It brings me to my second major consideration.

2. The disciples simultaneously live and do not live the *ultimate* realities with respect to Jesus. They simultaneously live in history and in the eschatological realm (even if only tangentially and by way of scattered sparks). This is brought home to us clearly by the peculiar characteristics of the literary genre used in the gospel accounts, as we have seen them in Section I of this appendix.[9]

The narratives of Jesus' appearances are not historical: not because they are false but because they are *more than historical.* They belong to the eschatological plane, the plane where the meaning of history is judged and verified.

Thus they relate experiences of an anticipated eschatology, and it is as such that we must interpret and judge them.

Paradoxical as it may seem, it is profoundly true that the accounts of the risen Jesus' appearances are much *less mythical*, in the strict sense of the word, than the accounts of (e.g.) miracles in the prepaschal life of Jesus. In fact, they are not mythical at all.

Remember that the miracles aspire to be a totally objective sign open to verification by any observer.[10] That would include his adversaries, of course. And the verification itself lies in proving that only some sort of supernatural causality can account for the happening in question (see Mark 3:27 and par.).

Now one of the basic elements in the definition of "mythical" is the injection of some metahistorical causality based on transcendent powers into the course of ordinary historical causality (which is always verifiable, in principle). Miracles, then, interrupt the course of historical events that science can relate to natural causes. So whenever we are confronted with this double causality, we are confronted with the "mythical" in the purest sense of the word.

But notice what the resurrection accounts do, as we have analyzed them. Even though they seem to embody the most sensational miracle in the history of Jesus, they do not, strictly speaking, recount any miracle at all! The presence of the eschatological is there, without any need to replace or break through any natural law.

In the account of the multiplication of the loaves, the arithmetical difference between the five loaves at the start and the full baskets at the end, after all have eaten their fill, is offered as verification to all that some supernatural power has intervened. In the case of the risen Jesus, however, the impartial spectator cannot perceive or detect a thing, not one single thing![11] And the transformation in the disciples, even if it is considered sudden and radical, can still be explained perfectly well as the achievement of a deeper level in their faith in Jesus of Nazareth, who died on the cross.[12]

To go back to our Proust example about "divine captives" that make our return to not-being "less certain," it is as if we were to read on his next page that these same hostages made such a return *impossible*. No reader would conclude that the narrator or author had been present at a miracle in the interval. We would simply say that he had become more optimistic. Within the limits of ordinary, verifiable human experiences he may have had more opportunities to see how his chosen values forced themselves upon him, thus becoming truly effective hostages within the process of ordinary historical causality.

That is why I said that eschatological reality touched the historical existence of Jesus' disciples *tangentially*, giving them a chance to experience the *outcome* of the wager embodied in Jesus' values. The word "tangentially" is not meant to suggest any diminution of meaning or importance. It simply refers to the imperceptible and unverifiable way in which eschatology crept into their actual history. Once their experiences with the risen Jesus took place and opened up a meaning to them, they discovered that this meaning was already present and expected in what they knew before. There is no perceptible break in continuity.[13]

That brings me to a final consideration, which readers may disregard here if they wish. It should make more sense by the time I have finished my treatment in Volume V, but I will mention it here for those who are interested.

The impact of Jesus' resurrection on the realm of human meaningfulness is one of *redundancy*, to use a crucial element in the scientific system of Gregory Bateson (see Volume I). To a certain extent the world of meaning, like the physical world, is a *quantum* world. The meaningfulness of things does not advance inch by inch with each new datum that is added.[14] What happens in the world of nature by chance, also happens in the world of human language purposively (be it ordinary or artistic language). Comprehension advances, thanks to accentuations, accumulations, repetitions—that is, redundancies—that rise as waves to assault some new threshold of meaning.

Suppose, by way of example, we look at the zoological evolution of the primates. If we scrutinize the process carefully, we will see only infinitely small and gradual changes in cranial capacity, thumb displacement, and spinal adaptation to walking upright. Then suddenly we find ourselves before a new world of meaning, a world that calls for new cognitive approaches. The old sciences (mathematics, physics, chemistry, biology) can still see their laws at work in the new being, to be sure. But one has the unmistakable sensation that a *threshold* has been crossed. We face something incommensurably different from the tiny changes noted before, which those very sciences enable us to detect and measure. Once we have passed that threshold—and here is where *redundancy* comes in—it seems that the single elements do not continue to develop on their own. Instead they seem to join up in some unforeseen journey towards new goals. New "shortcuts," such as psychology and sociology, are now needed for us to comprehend in an *economical* way the behavior of a being we feel compelled to call *new*.[15]

Thus every threshold may be viewed as a gift, as an accentuation of gift, novelty, purposiveness. Redundancy in the realm of meaning, then, presents itself to us as a free gift, as *grace*, as an opening to meaning.

This is what happens with the resurrection. It is an invasion of the ultimate, the eschatological, into history. It is not some second line of causality that would replace or annul historical causality, any more than psychology or sociology are when they are needed to explain the human being. Rather, within an infinitely small change in the line of historical causality, it is the irruption of a new world of meaning that is offered to human existence.[16]

APPENDIX II

More on the Political Key

The death and resurrection of Jesus force us to go back and consider for one last time the appropriateness, if not the legitimacy, of applying a political key to the historical data on Jesus.

I will not abuse the patience of my readers by reiterating my justification for the use of that key. Nor will I rehearse the reasons why its use in no way seems to contradict the undeniable fact that Jesus' life and message embody a religious revelation, that is, testimony about God. But if we take the political key seriously, and if we think Jesus himself took it seriously in comprehending his own mission, we cannot help but ask ourselves whether such an interpretation can really do justice to the final facts of his life, hence to *all* the facts.[1]

Our political (or better, religio-political) key seems to collapse in the face of two *overall* realities: (1) At no time in his life, much less near its end, does Jesus seem to be interested in making any use of the political power that his message and activity have created on behalf of the poor of Israel. (2) In the Synoptic Gospels, even after the paschal events, the community of Jesus' disciples bears clear witness to the (political) conflict stirred up by their master, yet that community apparently makes no effort to reproduce the same conflict in its own mission.

In reality this whole book, not just this appendix, attempts to respond to those two realities as well as possible. Here I simply want to clear away some obstacles and pave the way for my long-term consideration of the issues.

I

Readers who have followed my presentation of the historical data on Jesus so far will not, I hope, share Bultmann's view that his destiny and the death that ended it were absurd. The political key, which we have applied to his life, his message, and the conflict triggered by them, clearly shows great coherence and significance. We could say that Jesus had the friends he logically deserved to have, and the same would hold true for his enemies, his followers,

178

and even neutral spectators. But as I have suggested earlier, there comes a point, equally logical, when the political key seems to give out, when some other type of interpretation seems needed to account for the facts.[2]

Perhaps we are so used to the all too familiar ending of Jesus' life—death and resurrection—that we take it for granted and leave no room for any question to arise in our minds. But the question itself is inescapable, and it did arise in the minds of his disciples. From the gospel accounts themselves we learn that the conflict provoked by Jesus reached a point where the forces on the two sides seemed about equally balanced. Each side feared or foresaw the victory of its adversary.

In the Lukan tradition, the disciples on the road to Emmaus tell the stranger that they "had hoped that he was the one to redeem Israel." Their hope was not based on fanciful dreams or illusions. It was based on the power that Jesus had often displayed in deed and word before "all the people" (Luke 24:18-21). Remember that Jesus often felt compassion for the multitude. Seeing them as "sheep without a shepherd" (Mark 6:34 and par.), he used his power to feed them. But why did he not use that very same power to give them a more stable and structured solution than one meal in the desert? And then there comes the time when Jesus' adversaries shrewdly surmise that it is the right moment to go on the attack. It turns out that Jesus, who had been so astute and perceptive in detecting and managing the threads of the conflict, has made *no preparations whatsoever* for the predictable outcome or devised any tactic to make sure that he could go one with his work of consciousness-raising.[3]

One hypothesis suggests that he left everything in the hands of a higher causality operating wholly on its own. I have already discussed why this hypothesis is unsatisfactory, why it does not tally with his message or his actions. But if we start with the assumption that Jesus was fully and completely human (*perfectus homo*), interested in history and its laws of causality, then we confront an enigma. So let us consider some of the ways people try to get around that enigma.

We can set aside one subterfuge right away because it obviously runs counter to the gospel texts: that is, the claim that the term "kingdom of God" refers to an ultramundane reality that transcends all the categories and conflicts dividing human beings in the course of history.[4] We basically know that Jesus did not pass through the history of Israel in that tangential way, and everything said so far in this book offers convincing proof of that fact. It is not in terms of some other world but in terms of his insertion in this world and his own people that we must question Jesus' consistency insofar as he seems indifferent to the possibility of utilizing the power he has acquired in defense of the poor.

There is a second hypothesis that I also regard as escapist (see Chapter X, Section III). It claims that Jesus saw himself as nothing more than the proclaimer or prophet of a kingdom that God alone, without any human help, was about to inaugurate on earth, in Israel specifically. Although this view does not oblige us, in principle, to give up the political key in order to understand Jesus' proclamation, it would explain why Jesus limited himself to proclaiming a new society and avoided taking concrete steps toward its political realization. The power and the moment to do that would remain in God's hands alone. Jesus mistakenly foresaw the miraculous arrival of the kingdom from above as imminent. Its delay forced Jesus first, and then his disciples, to look for interpretations that fitted the facts and to find a mission that would fill the interval.

This hypothesis contains certain theological presuppositions about God's relationship with history.[5] They do not run counter to the idea of proclaiming the kingdom in a political key, but they do oppose the idea of anyone's trying to realize the kingdom by way of politics or any other form of historical causality. That would include Jesus. It was perfectly logical for him to use politically weighted terms and images to prepare people's minds for the coming reality, but the real-life, mortal conflict of powers generated by Jesus was a mistake in two senses. It was a theoretical mistake for him to have situated this divine intervention in terms of a single generation (see Mark 13:30 and par.), when it was to take centuries or millennia. He also made the practical mistake of accentuating a political conflict that was only meant to serve a symbolic function; as a result, the eyes of many were closed and the proclaimer of the kingdom was put to death.

According to this second hypothesis, then, we need not reject the political key a priori insofar as the proclamation of the kingdom is concerned. But we must reject it, or worse, consider it a mistake on Jesus' part, in trying to understand Jesus' activity. Perhaps the evangelists made a mistake in carrying it to such extremes, or perhaps Jesus himself forgot that his function was that of a mere announcer and tried to force the gates of history to open up for the arrival of the kingdom. In the case of Jesus, however, the mistake was not carried through to its ultimate consequences. Although he provoked the conflict, he gave it up as misguided when he realized that God's power kept its independence and was not going along with him (see Matt. 15:34).

That is the price—too high a price, in my opinion—which the second hypothesis must pay to explain both facets of one and the same phenomenon: (1) that Jesus proclaimed the kingdom in terms of political power; but (2) that there was no cause and effect relationship at all between the political causality in the concrete history of Jesus of Nazareth and the introduction of God's kingdom into the world, not even under the higher causality of God.[6]

I prefer a third hypothesis. It seems to be more faithful to the certain data we possess, it does not multiply alleged errors, and at the same time it stops before the mystery of a human destiny, which must always be chosen in the face of an unknown future and death.

In order to spell out this hypothesis, I would like to begin with an alternative one which I regard as extreme and unrealistic. Within the basic context of the political key, the alternative hypothesis says that we must choose either *structural change* (without the prior conversion of individual minds and hearts) or the *mental conversion of individual persons* (prior to all structural change). What does this mean in the case of Jesus? Jesus, we are told, bore witness to the view that an external change of sociopolitical structures is worthless unless people's hearts have been won over first. What is more, a change in structures must go hand in hand with a change in outlook among the majority of the people at least. Otherwise the use of political power becomes an act of violence, no matter what forms of coercion may be used.[7]

Formulated in those extreme terms, the alternative is not human because it does not take into account the energy-limitations within which all human action, be it individual or collective, must operate. For that very reason it is usually nothing more than a conservative ideological trap, closely related to the alleged "death of ideologies."[8] A real human being will always take a position closer to one alternative on the spectrum. That is the only thing that a planning process can calculate and choose.

Moreover, we have already had ample opportunity to see that the crude either/or alternative (structural change *or* personal conversion) was alien to the idea of the kingdom of God preached by Jesus. This is certainly clear in the case of the Beatitudes at least, when we read them in their original tenor and note the *woes* that follow them.

That brings us back to our subject here: Jesus' unpreparedness to tackle the power struggle that would take place in Jerusalem and thereby help the poor. It proves, I think, that to some extent Jesus sacrificed the urgent need for structural change to the radicalness of such change. But if he did make that sacrifice, it was only *to a certain extent*. Jesus could not and did not completely evade the urgency involved, which is part and parcel of living only to die. So neither could he ensure once and for all that the transformation proposed by him would be irreversible.

Let me give an example here. The urgency of Jesus, the fact that he does not have limitless amounts of time at his disposal, is palpable in the way he presents his adversaries. The brutal clarity of the parables blinds them, stereotypes them, and discredits them—forever, one might say. But it is precisely in that wholesale condemnation, that urgent desire to effect something "forever," that the danger of historical reversibility lies. In countless ways it is obvious that the Christian church has felt itself guilty of that radical condemnation in some obscure but unmistakable way and has felt it to be unjust. It is not "Christian" to treat anyone that way. Using that ploy, the new "scribes" and "Pharisees" have taken over the Christian law and used it to oppress humanity once again, but now no one feels he or she has the right to identify and attack those new oppressors with the very words of Jesus. Fortunately, no one has to use that sort of invective anymore, if for no other reason than that such oppression no longer occurs after Jesus! . . .

But even when we do strip the argument and its alternative of its extreme and unrealistic aspects, we do find an element in it that is worth considering in connection with the strange political end of Jesus.

Applying a political key to his life and message, as I have been doing so far, does not mean presenting him as a person waiting for the very first opportunity to exercise political power. We debase the political function and the key it signifies when we reduce it to the ambition to exercise power, even if we grant that the person or group in question would know more or less what to do with that power if they got it.

I have indicated the importance Jesus placed on dismantling the ideologico-religious apparatus that served, however unwittingly, to oppress the multitude in Israel. That is why he gave this ideological fight a central place in his own mission and that of his disciples. That does not at all mean that we must reject the political key, still less that Jesus was indifferent to power. It simply indicates that Jesus occupies a certain place in the political spectrum ranging from the rapid use of power to long-range consciousness-raising. We undoubtedly find traces of urgency in Jesus. But when we interpret his activity in a political key, it would seem that it is aiming much more at some sort of *long-term* efficacy.

But what, after all, is the long term in politics? Is it not the effort to radicalize from within, prolong, and make irreversible a process of transformation that sooner or later will need *power* to displace *the powerful*?

Having reached this point, we stop before the mystery of a person. Because he was perfectly human, we cannot assume he had something improper for human nature: knowledge of the future that would do away with the risk of any and every option.

Perhaps he thought he had much more time ahead of him to carry on his long-term policy of consciousness-raising on behalf of the poor and the kingdom. Perhaps he was counting on some powerful intervention of the kingdom itself to ensure that period of time. It is even more likely that he was surprised by the crucial moment that brought him to his death and by the silence of God. We just do not know for sure. But that does not invalidate the overall key to his ministry, forcing us to replace it with another.

II

We run into our second obstacle when we try to verify indirectly our interpretation of Jesus' history by making use of data situated *after* the paschal events.

For the prepaschal events we have used a political key and followed it through to the final stage of the conflict, when Jesus unexpectedly desists. Our key is not free of prejudice, of course, since no key is, but we have seen that the historical material fit logically and coherently into that interpretive mold.

Well, those materials come to us from the community formed by Jesus' followers. If our interpretation is correct, it is so because it dovetails with the voluntary or involuntary testimony of Jesus' disciples. No historical approach to the figure of Jesus can prescind from the first community. So would it not be logical to assume that the early Christian communities must have given themselves a mission parallel to that of Jesus? Is it too much to expect that the data we possess from those communities would somehow confirm our interpretation of Jesus, reproducing in community form his message, his activity, and the key for interpreting both?

To be sure, between the "historical Jesus" and the "historical church" lie the paschal experiences and their impact on the disciples. We have already seen, however, that those experiences do not wipe out recollection of Jesus' prepaschal traits. Decades later, they are recorded in the Synoptics, which echo the postpaschal catechesis of the Christian communities. So could we not assume that if we had data on those communities akin to the data recorded about Jesus, we would see a certain parallelism or similarity between the two sets of data?

Now it is one of the Synoptic writers (Luke) who, along with Paul, furnishes us with the data we can know today about the origins of the church. And there is no doubt that the expected parallelism is not there, at least at first glance. Luke, who gives us countless bits of testimony about Jesus' life and message that fit effortlessly into a political key, depicts a Christian community expressing itself in a very different key from the very start. Moreover, for centuries that community will not generate any political conflict because it has shouldered the cause of sinners and the poor.[9] Whether we apply a political key or not, in other words, the many conflicts in the primitive Christian church recorded by Luke bear no similarity whatsoever to the conflict that was generated by Jesus of Nazareth and recorded by that same Luke.

Let me offer one little example here. Suppose we took the attacks made on the Christian church in the first century or even later. Then suppose we tried to find the reason for them in one of the most derogatory accusations made against Jesus himself and reported by Luke: that he was "a glutton, a boozer, a friend of tax collectors and sinners." Such an effort would be futile and silly. That reason does not fit the facts with respect to the early church.

Many people, no doubt, would be tempted to conclude from this observation that my interpretation of Jesus is erroneous and that we should go back and correct it. But how are we to explain the fact that it is *the very same Luke* who gives very different reasons for the two conflicts? No work of correction can really bring the two sets of data into harmony.

In my opinion, we have very sound reasons for assuming that between the prepaschal Jesus and the postpaschal Christian church lies a more significant hiatus than is normally thought, whether we judge that hiatus in positive or negative terms. Let me present some of the reasons for this opinion.

1. Jesus could not simply be copied. Assuming his mission in very different circumstances entailed an arduous task of creation that was effected only slowly and with varying degrees of success.

Just consider this important fact. From the data at our disposal we know that none of the three Synoptic Gospels in its final form was addressed to Christian communities *located in Palestine*, that is, in the same context where Jesus' own life and message unfolded. Mark and Luke address themselves to converted pagans. Matthew, it seems, is writing for a community of Jewish Christians, but because he is probably writing after the destruction of Jerusalem, he is writing to people living in the diaspora—probably in Syria, and perhaps Antioch specifically. Their milieu, in any case, is much more strongly impregnated with Greek culture and sociopolitically dependent on Rome than was the theocratically structured milieu in which Jesus lived in Israel.

When Q, the originally Palestinian source of Matthew and Luke, reports Jesus saying "blessed are the poor," we know that he was thinking of the poor of *Israel*. It is not that he was positively excluding the pagan poor. It is simply that his own spontaneous thinking was framed in the categories of his own people's religious tradition. The coming kingdom is the kingdom that God promised to Israel through the prophets. There would be no sense in announcing to the pagan poor the arrival of a kingdom that they had never heard about. Jesus feels an urgent need and obligation to help the poor. That logically points to the poverty he can see with his own eyes. It also points to adversaries who are right around him and who are using the religion of Israel to depict people's situation of poverty as deserved and justified.

We today find it easy to move from the poor of Israel to the poor (*period!*), or the poor of the world, if you will. It is a simple matter of addition or multiplication for us. But if we want to talk about the historical church as we talk about the historical Jesus, then the clearest and most certain datum is that it never occurred to anyone in Jesus' entourage to envision such an extension of the term, even after the paschal events. They had no suitable concepts with which to do that, and none were provided by the historical message that Jesus preached in the context of Palestine.[10] It was certain unforeseen events, initially associated in some vague way with the power of the Spirit and manifestations of it outside the Jewish milieu, that led to the first great crisis in the nascent church: the possibility of incorporating (converted) pagans into the Christian community and the preconditions for such incorporation. I will come back to this point later.

Another fact may be of more direct interest here. It has to do with New Testament documents addressed to Jews in the diaspora, which became their real-life context after the destruction of Jerusalem. Even those documents (e.g., Matthew's Gospel and the Letter to the Hebrews) had to give up the political key of Jesus' message, and for a very sound and simple reason. Outside the Palestine and its sociopolitical context, the orthodox Jewish religion and the ongoing interpretation of its law by the scribes no longer constituted the ideological mechanism of oppression that Jesus had concretely attacked in its proper context.[11] Take Matthew, for example. Whenever his redactional work is visible to us, we see him replacing the political key of Jesus' message and approach with a religio-moral key that could better be appreciated by his audience outside Palestine. This does not mean that every substitution or replacement of key is innocent or effective. That all depends on the intelligence and creativity of the person doing it.

2. Even *in Palestine itself*, between the time of Jesus' death and the destruction of Jerusalem, we do not find anything similar to the conflictive proclamation of the kingdom uttered by Jesus of Nazareth. Something must have happened, as early as Easter, that explains this change.

One very important point must be made before I go any further. The whole issue at stake here goes far beyond the abandonment of the political key evident in Jesus' preaching. If we can believe the Acts of the Apostles, the preaching of the nascent church in Jerusalem, a few days after the paschal events, *is not similar to the preaching of Jesus at all.*

It is said that Jesus preached the coming of the kingdom and what actually arrived was the church. If we eliminate a certain element of exaggeration, this statement may help us to understand the change. For several reasons the discourses of Peter (Acts 2:14f.; 3:11f.; 4:8f.) and Stephen (Acts 7:2f.) will serve as suitable examples here. They fit into the Jerusalem context, and they were supposedly given shortly after Pentecost, when the words of Jesus' own preaching still echoed in the the ears of those present.

It is not just that the political key has disappeared, to surface again many years later in the Synoptics. It is that the new preaching focuses on something completely different. Peter and Stephen preach about Jesus as the Messiah. Whereas Jesus never preached about himself at all, much less about himself as the Messiah, this seems to be the basic content of the church's preaching after Easter.

Here we have the second reason why we cannot look to the early Christian community for any confirmation of the political key used in Jesus' own preaching. That paschal experiences had too much of an impact on the nascent church for us to expect that it would simply pick up the prepaschal themes of Jesus.

At first the cross seemed to be the most radical lie that history could give to the pretensions of a small community deprived of its leader and defender. By the same token, the experiences of the risen Jesus constituted the most powerful confirmation that reality could offer a seemingly defeated and disrupted community. Here was a decisive article (*stantis aut cadentis ecclesiae*) if there ever was one in history. And whether we approve or disapprove, it was only natural that it would center the attention and preaching of the Christian community on a point other than the one that was central for Jesus himself. Now, after the death of Jesus on the cross and his apparent abandonment by God, the self-justification of the community gathered around him by means of the Easter event becomes a matter of crucial urgency. We sense that we are in touch with something authentically historical when we hear words like these: "Jesus, whom you delivered up and denied . . . whom God raised from the dead. To this we are witnesses" (Acts 3:13, 15; see 2:22–24; 4:10; 5:30; 7:51–52, 56).

Faced with the fact of the resurrection, the disciples shift emphases. The key word of Jesus' prepaschal preaching, "conversion," no longer has to do with understanding and pursuing his thoroughgoing criticism of an oppressive religious ideology; now it has to do with believing that Jesus is the Messiah (Acts 2:38).[12] Now "salvation" in "the name of Jesus" takes the place of the "year of grace," that is, the realization on earth of the values of the kingdom that will transform the plight of the poorest and most exploited members of Israelite society (see Acts 2:47; 4:10–12).

This new emphasis displaces the political key of Jesus in the concrete post-paschal activity of his disciples, if not in their memory. Whether we approve or not, we can at least understand the surprising differences between the preaching of Jesus and that of the early Christian church. It is not that the message of Jesus was *lost*; the Gospels themselves are the best proof that it was not. But the fact is that we can get to it only *indirectly*.

3. The two factors discussed above help to explain why we cannot find support in the early church for the hypothesis that has guided our study of the historical Jesus. There is a third factor to consider, this one being more positive and helpful to us. But it too helps us appreciate how much rethinking has to be done in order to re-create the actual content of Jesus' message faithfully in different circumstances.

The New Testament churches cling tenaciously, if somewhat obscurely, to a central idea in Jesus' message. It is a blasphemous practice, they feel, for any community invoking the God of Jesus to tolerate *indigence*, at least within its confines (see 1 Cor. 11:17–34; James 2:2–9).

Along the same lines, there is no reason for minimizing the importance of the inner structure of the first Jerusalem community as reported by Luke:

> And all who believed were together and had all things in common; and they sold their possessions and goods and distributed them to all, as any had need [Acts 2:44–45].

> Now the company of those who believed were of one heart and soul, and no one said that any of the things which he possessed was his own, but they had everything in common. . . . *There was not a needy person among them,* for as many as were possessors of lands or houses sold them, and brought the proceeds of what was sold and laid it at the apostles' feet; and distribution was made to each as any had need [Acts 4:32, 34–35].

This selling and distributing of goods in accordance with people's needs may seem simplistic and naive today, given the modern development of capitalism, but it did not fail to give rise to problems. It is clear that the early Christian community did not want to give up those practices and focus exclusively on the preaching of "salvation." Remember that it tried to create a balance between the two tasks and to divide up responsibility for them when they seemed to conflict as a unified assignment. Thus the *apostles* were entrusted with the task of proclaiming the message of Jesus (or Jesus himself), and *deacons* were to see to it that the Christian community actually exemplified before the world what Jesus had preached (see Acts 2:47; 4:33).

We should not underestimate or minimize the political as well as religious tenor of all this in the context of Palestine and Jerusalem, particularly in a time and place in which it was not common practice. We must also remember that a community does not ordinarily conceive its mission or function as a mere extension or multiplication of its founder's work with additional personnel,[13] particularly when the founder is a very creative person who cannot be imitated readily. A community has its own way of imitating and following its founder; it does not simply mint his original image indefinitely.

We can also detect traces of Jesus' political key in the church after it was carried beyond Palestine by Paul's preaching and ceased to be structured as a community holding economic assets in common. The surrounding society was a slave-holding society, and the insignificant Christian community could not change that external fact. But even though the conflictive power of Jesus' initial message might not be there, there was a real political tenor to the formation of a community in which such status differences were radically abolished insofar as the internal functioning of the community itself was concerned. Paul proclaims the principle in theory (see Gal. 3:28; 1 Cor. 12:13) and demands that it be put into practice as well, in Jesus' name (see Philemon).

We must not delude ourselves, however. In the last analysis our third factor brings us to the same conclusion we reached in the case of the first two factors. The political key, so central for understanding the message of Jesus of Nazareth himself, does not reappear *as such* in the early Jerusalem church or in the later Christian churches located closer to the center of the Roman Empire. Moreover, the evidence we have seen so far confirms what we might have expected in any case. Although new keys such as those of Paul and John would give unexpectedly creative dimensions to the message of Jesus, the Christian community would not always live on those heights. It would often succumb to the temptations of facility and repetitiveness, confused and dazzled by more external realities and problems.

One historical datum confirms this tendency. In the face of its postpaschal success, the church would begin to show great concern for its own expansion and hence for the minimal preconditions for baptism: that is, the sign of initiation into the new ecclesial community (see, for example, Acts 8:5f.; 8:36; 10:45–11:17). This tendency would snowball when it became normal for pagans to believe in Jesus and seek admission into the community. What was to be demanded of them *as a minimum*? Incredible as it may seem by comparison with what we find in the Gospels, this question would give rise to the first big crisis in the early church, creating divisions and promoting the first authoritative communal response at the gathering known as the "Council of Jerusalem" (see Acts 15).

This example should make clear that the keys must be continually recreated in order to bar the way to a trivializing of the message. Faced with an unexpected question from the pagan world, the Christian community's answer in no way resembled Jesus' own message as such. It decided to tell pagans "to abstain from the pollutions of idols and from unchastity and from what is strangled and from blood" (Acts 15:20, 29; see Paul's distinct version in Gal. 2:1-10).[14]

To sum up: it is the internal coherence of the material provided by the Synoptics, as filtered through the criteria of historical trustworthiness, that should decide what key we use to understand the prepaschal Jesus. Even with the limitations noted in Section I of this appendix, and even without the slippery verifications noted in Section II, I think that the political key used throughout this volume remains the most adequate one for an historical approach to the words and deeds of Jesus of Nazareth. Christologies will have to start from there.

Notes

Chapter I: The "Gospel of the Cross" and Its Key

1. I would not deny, of course, that Boff's work considered here is a christology. It is only a partial christology because it focuses almost exclusively on the passion. That does not detract from its positive value insofar as it provides many elements opening christology up to an authentic, contemporary way of talking about Jesus of Nazareth. The passage cited in my text is a good example. Moreover, the "partiality" or "incompleteness" of Boff's gospel—focusing solely on the cross—is no greater than that of other writings in the New Testament itself. The Letter to the Hebrews, for example, analyzes only Jesus' relationship with the definitive cultic dispensation.

2. Kasper seems to arrive at practically the very same scheme when he writes: "The question of man's purpose in life cannot be answered from within his own history but only eschatologically. Implicitly, therefore, in all the fundamental processes of his life, man is driven by the problem of life and its ultimate purpose. The answer will not be found until the end of history. For the moment all man can do is to listen to and look at history and try to find signs in which that end is portrayed or even anticipated. Those signs will always be ambiguous within history; they will only become clear in the light of faith's perception of that end of history, just as conversely that perception must constantly make sure of its own validity in the light of history. Only if the problem is seen in this comprehensive perspective can the testimonies of the early Church and of the later church tradition be understood meaningfully" (Kasper 1976, 136).

It would seem that Kasper should end up with the very scheme that I do. Why does he not? Because in fact he does not accept the self-validating character of the premises, i.e., their necessary character as a wager. I think he tries to validate them by a reasoning process with an empirical base, thereby converting the *premises* into *conclusions*. But it is precisely their self-validating character that makes faith necessary: i.e., taking the risk of sharing in the values of another without demanding signs from heaven. It is symptomatic, I think, that Kasper moves from this formulation to the "sign from heaven" (the resurrection), rather than to the "signs of the times" (the concrete activity of Jesus) as we would expect him to do after his above remarks.

3. See note 11, Chap. III, below.

4. Of course it would be senseless to oppose biblical citations in a theological work. My point here is to differentiate the literal use of the Bible in a process of theological reasoning from the same sort of literal use when one is trying to get across a significant message by creating a new, contemporary, preponderantly iconic language for it.

5. Even before Marx referred to (the Christian) religion as the opium of the people, Balzac had put in a word. A more cynical but also broader observer of the details of

human society, Balzac put the following words in the mouth of one of his female characters: "As you can see, Armand, it is religion that keeps united the conservative principles which enable the rich to live tranquilly" (Balzac 1866a). Even granting the possible superficiality of the remark, or its particular context, we can easily show how dangerous use of the word "God" can be when we cannot give it more concrete and precise content than polite society or culture gives it.

6. I often disagree with the general orientation and specific content of Hans Urs von Balthasar's theology. But here I must admit how right he is in complaining about two gaps in current theology. Perhaps my remarks in Chapter I are making the same complaint in a different way. One complaint is that theology has not sufficiently derived theological profit from the moral experiences of the *saints*. Like the stained-glass windows of old cathedrals, he says, the saints often are like a closer, more up-to-date Bible (Balthasar 1948, 15; see also idem, 1957). His second complaint is that theology, in its thought processes, has not paid sufficient attention to *beauty*, which is of the utmost importance when we are dealing with meaning (idem 1965).

Chapter II: Antichristology?

1. I find it almost unbelievable that, even after Vatican II, this elementary, logical conclusion has not been drawn by theologians so closely identified with the council and of such stature as Hans Küng, for example. The false univocality of the word "God" clearly cannot withstand the criticism made of it by Vatican II. Yet that false univocality permits Küng to get away with the following statements: "The price paid by atheism for its denial is obvious. It is exposed to the danger of an ultimate lack of reason, of support, of purpose; to possible futility, worthlessness, emptiness of reality as a whole. If he becomes aware of it, the atheist is also exposed quite personally to the danger of an ultimate abandonment, menace, and decay, resulting in doubt, fear, even despair. All this is true of course only if atheism is quite serious and not an intellectual pose, snobbish caprice, or thoughtless superficiality." Is all this true without any regard for whether the God being presented is authentic or inauthentic? The question does not seem to bother Küng at all. He goes on to speak of belief in God: "The price received by belief in God for its yes is likewise obvious. Since I confidently decide for a primal reason instead of groundlessness, for a primal support instead of unsupportedness, for a primal goal instead of aimlessness, I have now reason to recognize a unity of the reality of world and man despite all disruption, a meaning despite all meaninglessness, a value despite all worthlessness" (Küng 1976, 75-76).

This exemplifies, I think, the latent danger in the shift to metaphysics that I brought up in Volume I with regard to Pannenberg and, above all, Tracy. And it holds true despite the precautions voiced by Tracy or by Schubert Ogden, who guides Tracy's thought on this point (Ogden 1977, chap. 1).

2. There are christological works from Latin America, to be sure. Praiseworthy as it is, however, Jon Sobrino's *Christology at the Crossroads* (1978) might have been more aptly subtitled, "A European Approach for Latin Americans." I think Leonardo Boff's *Jesus Christ Liberator* (1978) suffers from the fact that it was his first work completed after his theological studies in Europe. Even though it does not relate explicitly to Latin America, the method and approach of José Comblin's *Jesus of Nazareth* (1976) does give evidence of the author's personal involvement with our continent. And I would say that the work most truly representative of a Latin American christology is Boff's later work, *Pasión de Cristo* (1981), which I cited at the beginning of Chapter I in this volume.

3. "Its teaching [another synonym for *logy*] about Jesus Christ lies at the heart of every Christian theology" (Pannenberg 1977, 19). This is the opening sentence of his Introduction.

4. Both christologies "from above" (dealing with such categories as messiahship and divinity) and those "from below" (approaching those categories from concrete history) respond to one question: *What* (or who) is Jesus? It is a question that Jesus himself rejected and that blocks access to him.

5. See Pannenberg (1977, 33f.) for his descriptions of christologies "from above."

6. The "messianic secret" that Jesus keeps, especially in Mark's Gospel, is nothing else but this. And exegesis of the messianic titles that Jesus allegedly attributed to himself during his ministry tends to forget one important fact. When it comes to the title "Son of Man," the only one that probably did appear in Jesus' own talk, exegesis tends to overlook the fact that even when the evangelists rightly or wrongly identify that figure with the "I" of Jesus, they make it clear that it did not constitute a messianic title for them, at least at the start. See pp. 52ff., above.

7. "Many feel it would be premature to undertake the elaboration of a christology right now. The classic Catholic syntheses . . . are based on a prescientific exegesis that felt secure in its possession of the faith within the general milieu known as Christendom. Hence they do not allow present-day believers to express their faith in Jesus in a reflective way" (Duquoc 1972, 2:1).

8. That is why I agree with the opening remarks of José Comblin in his *Jesus of Nazareth:* "In this book we intend to meditate on the human—simply human—life of Jesus Christ. We want to examine again this Jesus of Nazareth just as the disciples knew him and understood him—or did not understand him—when they walked with him in the rough valleys of Galilee, roaming the villages of Israel, when they did not yet know him as Lord and Son of God" (Comblin 1976, 1).

9. Those human witnesses, in turn, are witnesses to themselves because Jesus found them already interested in what his human life demonstrated and attested. Hence some christologies begin their task in a very strange way, it seems to me. How do they see their task? Here is Pannenberg, for example: "This involves what we as Christians have to say about Jesus in contrast to what one who is definitely a non-Christian or who provisionally abstains from a final, personal decision might say about Jesus. . . . The distinctiveness of the Christological way of speaking about Jesus resides in its theological character" (Pannenberg 1977, 19). Unlike Comblin, Pannenberg does not seem to realize that the most realistic way to approach Jesus, the way that matches the approach of his first witnesses, is today the way of the people "who provisionally abstain from a final, personal decision" until they see what Jesus says and does, and what the significance of that human being might be. To choose Pannenberg's starting point is to be forced, however unwittingly, into a christology "from above," even though one may claim to be doing a christology "from below" as Pannenberg does. Thus Pannenberg actually undertakes the very type of christology he claims to be rejecting.

10. I think that this fact, but not its methodological consequences, is perceived by Pannenberg when he writes: "Something of the particular intellectual situation of the respective witnesses, of the questions that moved their times and to which they answered with their confession of Christ, also always adheres to the New Testament accounts of Jesus. This is the basis for the diversity of the New Testament witnesses to Jesus, which is not to be overlooked. Because the New Testament testimony to Christ so clearly bears the stamp of the particular contemporary problematic of the witnesses, one cannot simply equate Jesus himself with the apostles' witness to him, as

Kähler expressed it in his formula about 'the whole Biblical Christ' " (ibid., 23).

11. That is why I find Machovec̆'s attitude curious and illogical. He is bold enough to approach Jesus from a Marxist position and ask: "Why are you speaking to me?" But then it is as if he goes on to say: "Keep talking to me because I am enormously interested in what you have to say. It does revive my spirit, as St. Augustine put it. But I know that I cannot believe in you!" But is not any acceptance of the existential testimony of another person an irreplaceable, in some way, belief in that person? Is Machovec̆ not playing loose with words here?

12. This sets up the educational chain of "learning to learn" that I discussed in Volume I. And it is the only way that the human being Jesus, within his own historical coordinates, can foster rather than undermine our own specific human creativity.

13. See Leonardo Boff: "One consequence . . . is that a reading situated outside the immediate interest of the New Testament accounts should precede any preliminary critical work. It must constantly notice the scope of the New Testament interpretation and the historical reality of the events narrated. It must ask honestly to what extent they are projections of a prior theological interpretation and to what extent they are events that really took place in the way they are interpreted. And we too must constantly ask ourselves to what extent our own interest forces the texts to say more than they do say, to what extent we project more than we actually have. In the New Testament accounts, fact and interpretation form an homogeneous unity. It is what we possess today as a literary text. In terms of our own interest, which differs from the New Testament interest, we must try to separate the fact from the interpretation given by the early church and recorded by the evangelists. Only thus is room created for our own reading, which also seeks to be theological. We thus put ourselves, without further pretensions, in the same situation as the evangelists. Like them, we proceed to a theological interpretation of the Lord's passion. The attitude of faith is the very same; only the *Sitz im Leben* ('life-situation') differs" (Boff 1981, 297).

Chapter III: Jesus in the Grip of Theology

1. On the *Diatessaron*, its author, its career, and opposition to it, see Léon-Dufour (1963, 57–61).

2. A little further on Pannenberg adds: "We repeat, Kähler is correct in these statements, insofar as he protests against setting the figure and message of Jesus in opposition to the apostolic preaching in such a way that no sort of continuity between the two would exist any longer. However, it does not follow from the rejection of such false antitheses either (1) that the effects of the person Jesus are to be found only in the apostolic preaching or (2) that what is 'truly historic' about Jesus is only his 'personal effect.' This effect radiated outward into definite and, already in early Christianity, varied historical situations. Therefore, something of the particular intellectual situation of the prospective witness, of the questions that moved their times and to which they answered with their confession of Christ, also always adheres to the New Testament accounts of Jesus. . . . Because the New Testament testimony to Christ so clearly bears the stamp of the particular contemporary problematic of the witnesses, one cannot simply equate Jesus himself with the apostles' witness to him. . ." (Pannenberg 1977, 22–23).

3. Precisely because of this problem, we find the following title and subheading in Chapter 2 of Pannenberg's work: "Christology and Soteriology. The confession of

faith in Jesus is not to be separated from Jesus' significance for us. The soteriological interest cannot, however, be the principle of Christological doctrine" (ibid., 38).

Translator's note: The word "principle" in the English translation of Pannenberg's work might better have been translated "starting point."

4. What Hans Küng says about something else would apply to our topic as well: "In the last five hundred years—to go no further back—no solemn doctrinal statement has been issued by Rome on the critical question of what Christianity really means, what the Christian message really implies. . ." (Küng 1976, 88). Insofar as christology itself is concerned, the observation would basically apply to the last ten centuries or so (see Rahner and Thüsing 1975, 75-79). Either the formulas of Chalcedon have simply been repeated, or else, on a few specific occasions (Abelard in the Middle Ages, A. Günther and A. Rosmini in more-recent times), errors have been condemned in declarations that could scarcely be called solemn or extraordinary. Everything suggests that after Chalcedon the multiplicity of conceptions about Christ ceased to preoccupy the authorities of the Catholic church.

5. A bit further on Kasper explains: "Hans Urs von Balthasar has been prominent in pointing out the immanent danger of all these approaches. The problem in his view is that in them Jesus Christ is set in a predetermined scheme of reference, and that the eventual result of the consequent cosmological, anthropological, or world historical diminution of faith is a mere philosophy or ideology" (Kasper 1976, 18).

6. Pardon me for a humorous aside. In his "Open Letter to José Míguez Bonino," Jürgen Moltmann actually addresses Latin American theology as such and explicitly criticizes Gustavo Gutiérrez, Hugo Assmann, and myself as well. After acknowledging indigenous elements in African, Japanese, and Black American theologies, he acidly remarks that the only distinctive thing about Latin American theology seems to be its recourse to Marx and Engels—who, of course, were German.

Who would believe such a remark after reading what so many important German theologians have to say about avoiding ideology! One would think they are doing theology in the Amazon Jungle! By contrast, Leonardo Boff starts off his partial christology with a few words that deserve to be taken far more seriously than Moltmann's remark does: "No text and no investigation, however objective it may seek and pose to be, can fail to be structured around some horizon of interest. To know is always to interpret. The hermeneutic structure of all knowledge and science means that the subject—with his or her models, paradigms, and categories—always enters into the composition of the experience of the object, meditated by a language. The subject is not a pure reason; he or she is immersed in history, in a sociopolitical context, and is motivated by personal and group interests. Hence a purely disinterested cognition free of ideology does not exist" (Boff 1981, 11).

7. Hence it should not surprise us that Pannenberg's alleged christology "from below" starts right off looking upward to "signs from heaven." Here is his subtitle thesis for Chapter 3, where he begins his christological work: "Jesus' unity with God was not yet established by the claim implied in his pre-Easter appearance, but only by his resurrection from the dead" (Pannenberg 1977, 53). Thus the pre-Easter institution of discipleship was apparently only a *pretext* invented to lead a few people, for mistaken reasons, to the unique decisive event wherein Jesus won their authentic interest.

Translator's note: Segundo's Spanish edition of Pannenberg has *actuación* ("activity") where the English edition has "appearance."

8. And of art as well. See Bateson, *Steps to an Ecology of Mind* (1972), especially

the chapter entitled "Style, Grace and Information in Primitive Art," pp. 128-52. In that chapter Bateson offers an analysis of Balinese painting (pp. 147f.).

9. It hardly needs to be said that an overall judgment of Bultmann is made all the more difficult by the fact that all sorts of different debates have swirled around him, not all of them related to one another. They have dealt with the historicity of Jesus, demythologization, the philosophical (or anthropological) preunderstanding required for the interpretation of biblical revelation, and so forth. For our purposes here it is both unnecessary and impossible to deal with all those issues. So I have restricted myself to those points that must be brought up to situate my own effort here and make it comprehensible.

10. It seems obvious that Bultmann's demythologization goes only half way. First of all, this is because Bultmann cannot, strictly speaking, talk about a "theology" of the New Testament because the idea of a divine revelation in Jesus Christ is itself *mythical*. Jesus would be, at best, "the especially impressive manifestation of a possibility man has of being an authentic human being" (Kasper 1976, 45). What, then, would it mean to have faith in him? Would it mean something akin to what I explained in Volume I and will explain further here in Volume II? See the whole section that Kasper (ibid., 43-48) devotes to this issue.

11. As Hans Küng seems to think: "Theology can never be content to be graciously tolerated within a field where conclusions are notably inexact and lacking in binding force, as if 'religious truth' were similar to 'poetic truth' " (Küng 1976, 87). His statement proves again how theology has unwittingly been moving farther and farther away from the eminently poetic fonts of its knowledge; the Bible, patristics, and the church tradition of the saints and mystics.

12. Note my earlier comments on the futile efforts to eliminate ideology by resorting to sober *common sense* (Pannenberg) or *receptivity*. The latter was the great argument which Karl Barth raised—in vain—against Rudolf Bultmann.

13. In Protestant sectors these objections, quite logically, were not unconnected with various objections to natural theology.

14. A clear example of this point is Jesus' own use of the political term "kingdom." Precisely because it held interest for people, it lent itself to all sorts of prejudices and preconceptions. Jesus could have easily avoided misunderstandings by creating a new word, one without concrete resonances for his listeners, and then gradually filling it with the precise meaning he had in mind—except that he would have found himself all alone long before that process was finished!

15. I have already noted my refusal to eliminate mythical language or to downplay the historical aspect of Jesus of Nazareth. In *The Liberation of Theology* (Chap. I) I also criticized Bultmann's neglect of the ideological element that necessarily comes into play in the hermeneutic circle. The latter process goes like this: preunderstanding, interpretation, new preunderstanding, etc. The task I am trying to explain and set up here is described as one of *deconstruction* by Leonardo Boff. We must deconstruct or dismantle a language that is no longer ours: "My reflections here center around a labor of deconstruction. Three common representations of Christ's salvific activity will be subjected to critical analysis: his saving work as sacrifice, redemption, and satisfaction. And I am talking about deconstruction, not destruction. The three cited models are theological constructions designed to comprehend the salvific significance of Jesus Christ within a particular time and cultural space. To deconstruct means to see the building in terms of its construction plan and redo the construction process, pointing up the temporal nature and possible obsolescence of the representational

material while, at the same time, revealing the permanent value of its import and intent. . . . Critical analysis is meant in a positive sense here: that is, the ability to discern the value, scope, and limitation of a given affirmation'' (Boff 1981, 109–10).

16. Rahner's essay under discussion here is part of a collaborative effort with W. Thüsing originally published as *Christologie—Systematisch und Exegetisch* (Freiburg-im-Breisgau: Herder, 1972). Rahner deals with "transcendental" considerations in the first part. Thüsing offers exegetical considerations in the second part. It is Rahner's presentation that interests me here (Rahner and Thüsing 1975, 21–80).

Translator's note: All citations here are from the Spanish edition used by Segundo. I cannot find the material and thesis cited by Segundo in the English-language edition of the Rahner-Thüsing work: *A New Christology* (New York: Seabury, 1980).

17. As used currently in philosophy, the term "idealism" is the opposite of *realism*, which is used in varying senses with a more or less naive cast. Realism basically places time among the a posteriori data. As I tried to make clear in Volume I (Chapter IX), Kant is an idealist only in the sense that historical materialism gives to that word.

18. Rahner and Thüsing 1975, thesis 8b, p. 25 (my italics). The parenthetical remark is Rahner's. The why and wherefore of this assertion is explicated in thesis 6: "The bases in human existence that make *possible* such a unique relationship with another human being must find clear and articulate expression in a 'transcendental christology' '' (p. 22).

19. Ibid., thesis 10, p. 25. All the italics are mine, except for the word "mutual."

20. Ibid., thesis 8a.

21. The word "religion" as used by Tracy in *Blessed Rage for Order* would be another example of the emptiness I am discussing here. See Volume I, Chapter II, Section II of this work.

22. Rahner and Thüsing, thesis 12, p. 26.

23. That *Being and Time* was in the nature of a "transcendental" anthropology (in the service of an ontology) became clear and explicit in Heidegger's second period. At that point he was writing *Kant and the Problem of Metaphysics*, which deals with the ontological import of Kant's "transcendental imagination." But there were clear indications of this fact in Heidegger's examination of human existence in *Being and Time* itself. Thus he differentiates authenticity and inauthenticity but points out that he is not making any value judgment. One does not interest him more than the other because he is exploring the basic existentialist (*existenzial*) structures that make *both* possible: i.e., the structures of a transcendental cognition or epistemology (see Heidegger 1962, section 34, 35, 38, etc.).

24. See notes 23 and 26, above and below.

25. Rahner and Thüsing, thesis 11, p. 26.

26. Readers familiar with Heidegger may recall his treatment of moral conscience, for example. He describes it as a voice one experiences or hears sporadically. Since it is sporadic, however, we must say that there is a definite equivalence between *heeding* and *not heeding* that voice insofar as human existence is concerned. In other words, hearing and not hearing oneself called or summoned are equally real. The being of the human persona must be the ground of both one and the other, since we are dealing with two "factic" possibilities of *Dasein* ("being there": Heidegger's word for human existence). This reduction of the ontic to something factic, this comprehension of the ontic as something merely ontic, opens up the possibility of our going deeper to find the *fundamental* ground, the ontological. In the case of moral conscience, Heidegger finds that ground in the experience of being at fault or guilty or in debt.

That is the basis of the voice of conscience (paying heed to that fault or guilt) and of uneasiness of conscience (not paying heed to it). Thus the fundamental ontological structure of conscience, its existentialist structure, is revealed in *both* one form and the other.

27. Rahner and Thüsing, thesis 9, p. 25.

Introduction: A "History" of Jesus?

1. The criterion for finding a replacement for Judas in the ranks of the Twelve—not for the sake of some potential "apostolic succession" in the future but probably in memory of the Master and as a number symbolizing the twelve tribes (or the totality) of Yahweh's Israel—is that the person must have accompanied Jesus from his baptism (by John) to "the day when he was taken up from us" (Acts 1:22), clearly an allusion to Jesus' ascension (see Acts 1:11). I wrote "to his passion" (inclusively) because the subsequent period takes in the experiences relating to Jesus' resurrection. While those experiences are on a level that is certainly real, that level is not "historical" in the modern scientific sense we ordinarily imply. As we shall see in due course, Jesus' resurrection is not empirically verifiable as something which, independent of faith, could constitute a historically valid proof for all. Thus the *period* of the appearances of the Risen One vary for each New Testament author: probably one day for John; forty days (see Acts 1:3) for Luke, or even longer if we are to include in them the apparition to Stephen (see Acts 6:15 and 7:55); months or years (perhaps three years) if we, like Paul, count his Damascus experience among them (see 1 Cor. 15:8).

2. See Mark 6:52; 9:10, 32. On two occasions John separates what the Twelve understood *before* the paschal events from what they understand *after* them (see John 2:21-22; 12:16). We do not know if this is a literary device or a desire for historical fidelity.

3. Those dealing with the destruction of Jerusalem, for example. If we realize that in all likelihood at least two of the Synoptic Gospels (Matthew and Luke) were redacted *after* its destruction by the Romans in the year 70, we feel more sure about a vague exclamation by Jesus, such as the one recorded by Matthew and Luke (and probably part of Q, their common sourse): "O Jerusalem, Jerusalem, killing the prophets and stoning those who are sent to you! . . . Behold, your house is forsaken and desolate" (Matt. 23:37-38; Luke 13:34-35). And we feel far less sure about the details of this "desolateness" added by Luke: "For the days shall come upon you, when your enemies will cast up a bank about you and surround you, and hem you in on every side, and dash you to the ground, you and your children within you, and they will not leave one stone upon another in you" (Luke 19:43-44). Here we have a clear reference to a siege, though the details are still rather vague insofar as they stem from direct knowledge of events that took place only a short time earlier. Moreover, it is possible that we are dealing with a circular argument here. The assumption that Matthew and Luke (not Mark, who records that Jesus' only prediction about the temple was that one stone would not be left upon another [Mark 13:2] were redacted after the events depends largely on taking their references to the concrete destruction of Jerusalem as prophecies after the event. Furthermore, there is no compelling reason to reject the possibility that Jesus himself prophesied the siege and destruction of the holy city. Hence the criterion under discussion is only a gauge of historical *trustworthiness*.

4. On Jesus' predictions of his passion see Chapter VI, Section III; on his predictions of the coming of the kingdom, be it imminent or not, see Chapter X.

5. See, for example, André Myre, "Développement d'un instantané christologique" (1977): "The Bible and Judaism offer neither one simple or unique definition of the eschatological prophet nor a coherent description of his mission. In the domain of eschatology the words serve to convey a tension rather than to offer a precise presentation of what God's future will be. Hence we should not be surprised by the fluidity of the expressions used. It can be explained by the diversity of the various contemporary Jewish circles, by the various chronological stages of such conceptions, and by their mutual contamination. But however vague and complicated it all may be, we can glimpse the reality. At the time of Jesus we do find an eschatological hope in Judaism which concerns a prophet who is to come, and who will play a role in the end days. Some think that this prophet himself will establish the new eon. Some think he will be the precursor of the Messiah. And others think he will accompany the latter when he comes." See my commentary on the tradition of the eschatological prophet in this Introduction, p. 57f.

6. The outcome seems to be that the discovery of this line remained a central element *within* the Christian community but not for *outside* consumption. In Jewish circles at least, the focus was on basing Jesus' messiahship on the fact of his resurrection, and citations from the Old Testament refer to that. There is a general reference to suffering: "But what God foretold by the mouth of all the prophets, that his Christ should *suffer*. . ." (Acts 3:18). Unlike the prophecies dealing with resurrection, however, those dealing with suffering are not stated or put down in writing. The main reason for this is probably the absence of a tradition centered around a suffering and executed Messiah. But the fact that the Christian community was already thinking about the Servant of Yahweh in this line of argumentation shows up implicitly in one theological element of importance: "This Jesus, delivered up according to the definite *plan* and foreknowledge *of God, you crucified and killed* . . ." (Acts 2:23). A distinction is thus made between the death of Jesus as a redemptive plan (as it appears in the suffering servant poems) and the death of Jesus as the outcome of a conflict of human interests.

7. Particularly by Paul, as we shall see in Volume III. And also by the Letter to the Hebrews, where Jesus is presented as both high priest and propitiatory victim.

8. Léon-Dufour may not always be consistent with this affirmation. Nevertheless it is unavoidable if, as most exegetes admit, Jesus never declared himself to be the Messiah, at least before the passion episodes and his appearance before the Sanhedrin.

9. Moreover, in Aramaic the expression means something even simpler: "a man" or "this man." So it is very unlikely that the mere use of this expression would make people think of the personage in Daniel, unless other details of the prophecy were added: his coming on the clouds of heaven, etc.

10. This hypothesis seems to take insufficient account of one thing. Though Jesus may not have preached his messiahship openly, even his prepaschal *claims of power* point up the impossibility of his subordination to some future Son of Man. See, for example, Pannenberg 1977, Chap. 3, esp. 63–66.

11. Nueva Biblia Española, heading "hombre" in the New Testament "Vocabulario Bíblico Teológico," p. 1924. On the original sense of this expression, so translated into Greek, see also J. Jeremias 1971, 1:260f.

12. Mowinckel's classic work is reviewed in detail by J. Coppens in the article entitled "Les origines du messianisme" (1954).

13. This ambiguity probably occasioned the two great crises in Jesus' ministry,

insofar as we can reconstruct it: the Galilean crisis (particularly if it followed the multiplication of the loaves, as John 6 seems to indicate) and the Jerusalem crisis, which began with his triumphant entry and ended on the cross.

14. "The details that follow reflect a state of affairs not known until the days of Solomon and after; this satire implies extensive experience" (JB, note e on 1 Sam. 8:11). The use of "until" represents a correction as far as the chronological starting point for this division of labor is concerned. The latter intensifies and is increasingly justified in ideological terms right down to Jesus' time. It is important and enlightening to note the explicit political reservations of Samuel and to compare them with the religious reasons and justifications that Jesus attacks (see Chap. VIII in this volume). On the politico-religious rejection of the monarchy in Samuel, see Rad 1962, 1:58–59.

15. The manuscripts indicate that they were added to the original text. This confirms even more clearly how the needs of the Christian community prevailed over the literal sense given to the parable by Jesus.

16. The maxim, "Many are called, but few are chosen," might have a connection with the "narrow gate" (Matt. 7:13–14; see the version in Luke 13:23f.). If so, it would have even less connection with this parable. In Matthew the "narrow gate" implies the need for greater effort, which is directly contrary to the teaching of the parable.

17. Reinhold Niebuhr's work under discussion is a brilliant analysis of Christian anthropology and is truly ecumenical in spirit. But it seems obvious to me that his image of Jesus as rejecting all historical power does not derive from a particular reading of the Gospels so much as from certain theological presuppositions that are adopted more or less unconsciously: e.g., the principle of *soli Deo gloria*.

18. The criticism offered by Sartre regarding evaluations of Valéry or Flaubert would apply even more forcefully here. See Volume I, Chapter VII, p. 193.

19. Besides complicated theological explanations, it has been alleged that with these words Jesus is alluding to the whole content of Psalm 22, which ends with thanks for God's saving aid. But that hypothesis presupposes too much sophistication in a dying victim of crucifixion (and in readers of the gospel); and it hardly dovetails with the nature of a *cry*, which is how Matthew clearly depicts it.

20. See J. Jeremias 1971, 1:1–41: "How Reliable Is the Tradition of the Sayings of Jesus?" I might add that Jeremias, based on his knowledge of Aramaic, is quite optimistic about the possibility of recognizing the very words (*ipsissima vox*) of Jesus in the Synoptics.

21. In Part One ("Presuppositions and Motifs of New Testament Theology"), Section I, he states: "The coming of God's Reign is a miraculous event, which will be brought about by God alone without the help of men" (R. Bultmann 1951–55, 1:4).

22. My effort here is not one of biblical exegesis. Hence in the following chapters I will use the criteria set forth in this Introduction without alluding specifically to them. I shall base my comments on the historical and exegetical data that seem more certain to me without burdenng my readers with disquisitions and proofs that are alien to the aim of this book. My only purpose in this Introduction was to give readers a general overview of the scientific basis for everything that follows in this volume.

Chapter V: Jesus and the Political Dimension

1. These traps and clichés are not avoided by people who do not go in for cultural criticism as a specific intellectual task. So it should not surprise readers to find allu-

sions to Pope John Paul II's Opening Address at the Puebla Conference in the following pages (January 28, 1979). Here is what the pope says in section I, 4, for example: "Now today we find in many places a phenomenon that is not new. We find 're-readings' of the Gospel that are the product of theoretical speculations rather than of authentic meditation on the word of God and a genuine evangelical commitment. They cause confusion insofar as they depart from the central criteria of the Church's faith, and people have the temerity to pass them on as catechesis to Christian communities. In some cases people are silent about Christ's divinity, or else they indulge in types of interpretation that are at variance with the Church's faith. Christ is alleged to be only a 'prophet,' a proclaimer of God's Kingdom and love, but not the true Son of God. Hence he allegedly is not the center and object of the gospel message itself. In other cases people purport to depict Jesus as a political activist, as a fighter against Roman domination and the authorities, and even as someone involved in the class struggle. This conception of Christ as a political figure, a revolutionary, as the subversive from Nazareth, does not tally with the Church's catechesis. Confusing the insidious pretext of Jesus' accusers with the attitude of Jesus himself—which was very different—people claim that the cause of his death was the result of a political conflict; they say nothing about the Lord's willing self-surrender or even his awareness of his redemptive mission. The Gospels show clearly that for Jesus anything that would alter his mission as the Servant of Yahweh was a temptation (Matt. 4:8; Luke 4:5). He does not accept the position of those who mixed the things of God with merely political attitudes (Matt. 22:21; Mark 12:17, John 18:36). He unequivocally rejects recourse to violence. He opens his message of conversion to all, and he does not exclude even the publicans. The perspective of his mission goes much deeper. It has to do with complete and integral salvation through a love that brings transformation, peace, pardon, and reconciliation" (Eagleson and Scharper 1979, 59–60).

2. In Volume II of his truly weighty and ecumenical study of Christian anthropology, *The Nature and Destiny of Man,* Reinhold Niebuhr makes clear how the various postmedieval divisions of Christianity represents the rediscovery, not always well balanced, of elements of the gospel message that had gotten lost in the earlier amalgam.

3. And here European theology goes to extremes hardly compatible with good faith or at least with what one might expect from intellectuals aware of the ideological danger that ever lurks in the instruments they use.

4. Many other well-known conflicts of the prophets in the same specifically political vein could be mentioned, such as the clash between Nathan and David over Uriah (see 2 Sam. 12:1f.).

5. The political decision can be mistaken. Regarding the acceptance of the oracles of the prophets into the canon of Scripture, H. Cazelles has this to say: "We must note one curious fact about this political activity of the prophets. It normally ends in political failure. Nevertheless the disciples of the prophets gathered together their oracles and recognized their validity as divine 'word' " (Cazelles 1971, 512).

6. Sharp proof of the church's uneasy position on this matter can be provided by Section 42 of *Gaudium et spes (GS),* which is certainly one of the most progressive texts of Vatican II. The section begins with the problem of knowing to what extent the church can serve the cause of *the union of the whole human family.* Significantly, the first statement to follow the posing of the issue is reductivist with regard to potential conflictivity: "Christ, to be sure, gave his Church no proper mission in the political, social, or economic order. The purpose which he set before it is of a religious nature. But out of this religious mission itself come a function, a light, and an energy that can

serve to structure and consolidate the human community according to divine law. Moreover, where circumstances of time and place make it necessary, the mission of the Church can—or better, ought to—initiate efforts on behalf of all human beings." It is hard to see how the church, in line with its proper mission, can have an officially authorized social doctrine if its mission is not social. But let us set that issue aside and ask: Is there anything more *proper* to the church than its *faith?* Well, this is what *GS 11* has to say in about faith's *mission:* "Faith throws a new light on everything, manifests God's design for the *whole* vocation of the human beings, and thus directs the mind to *solutions that are fully human"* (my italics). Where? Obviously in historical reality with its many different planes, whether they be individual, political, social, or economic. But how can that be done without causing division? That is why we find little inclination on the part of the church or the conciliar text to become concrete on those planes. The conciliar paragraph cited above, for example, uses the word "can" twice before it is compelled, by its own logic, to correct itself and say "ought to." Further on, in *GS* 42, again in connection with the union of the human family, we read: "By virtue of its mission and nature, the Church is bound to no particular form of human culture, nor to any political, economic, or social system. Hence by its very universality the Church can be a very close bond between diverse human communities and nations. . . ." Each word is carefully weighed, of course, and the statement is essentially unassailable. But the overall context inevitably suggests that there are no crucial conflicts between those systems, where "solutions that are fully human" might be at stake, where it might be necessary to make a choice and accept suffering, so that in fact the church does not have the facile unifying universality claimed for it.

7. This gave rise to the theory of the two swords, the two kingdoms, or the two planes in theological thinking. It should be noted that Augustine's theory of the *two cities* does not dovetail with this approach to defining or delimiting the areas of competence. Even though his theory might tend to confusedly equate the "city of God" with the church, it basically represents a prophetic reaction, in God's name, against the reason of state.

8. In many cases even this exception does not exist, except for the very naive. When the church thinks it can affect the political realm—and who would not want it so?—through the economic or social arena, it does so; and on rare occasions it even says so. At the start of this century in Uruguay, for example, the church confronted a political process of secularization. So three religious unions were created: the Economic Union, the Social Union, and the Civic (i.e., political) Union. The function of the Social Union was described in the following terms: "It is necessary to have a very clear idea of the true essence of the Social Union. It is not a religious institution, even though its slogan . . . is to defend the principles of Christian social justice. Our Social Union in Uruguay will be what the *Volksverein* ['People's Union'] is in Germany, as described by its director, Dr. Otto John: 'The *Volksverein* for Germany is a social league . . . dedicated to the economic and intellectual uplifting of the *Catholic* people *so as to create, indirectly, the preconditions for improving the religious situation*' " (Rius-Perea Report, 1911, in accordance with the directives of the third Catholic Congress).

Chapter VI: The Central Proclamation of Jesus

1. When Matthew uses the expression "kingdom of heaven" instead of "kingdom of God," exegetes unanimously agree that he is using a circumlocution, in accordance

with Hebrew practice, to avoid using the sacred name of *God.* This expression of respect, therefore, has nothing to do with some fulfillment of the kingdom "in heaven": i.e., after death. For the Jews of that day the expression "kingdom of heaven" did not have the purely religious and extraterrestrial connotation that it has *mistakenly* acquired for many present-day Christians.

2. A similar occasion mentioned in John's Gospel is worth noting (see John 6:15). Jesus flees from those who would make him king, but he does not seem to try to dispel their existing, ongoing misconstrual of his own function in the kingdom.

3. For the moment I am setting aside the fourth Beatitude (and the fourth "woe!"). Even though it is part of the (final) redaction of the Q source, it embodies a church problem and hence it is unlikely that it goes back directly to Jesus. Even if it did go back to Jesus, it must have derived from a different context. It was added to the Beatitudes in the redactional work of Matthew and Luke, who subordinated the first three Beatitudes to the needs of their respective churches. This may have led them naturally to add this Beatitude about persecution and the way to react to it.

4. The economic status of the ordinary publican in Galilee is a moot question. But Jesus' poor take in those who are suffering and marginalized, as we see in the second and third Beatitudes; that would certainly include the publicans. So we are not surprised to find them included among the "scandalous" friends of Jesus to whom the kingdom of God is promised (see Matt. 21:31).

5. In Israel the Pharisee was an ideologically dominant force whatever may have been the average economic situation of his group. The latter reality is hard to determine on the basis of the data at our disposal.

6. To facilitate the "synoptic" perception of the reader, I am presenting in three parallel columns the three versions of the three predictions. Almost totally identical expressions are italicized.

Mark (Peter's confession)	Matthew (P's confession)	Luke (P's confession)
(1) 8:31f.	(1) 16:21f.	(1) 9:22f.
The Son of man	He	The Son of man
must	*must*	*must*
suffer many things	*suffer many things*	*suffer many things*
and be rejected		and be rejected
by *the elders,*	from *the elders,*	by *the elders,*
the chief priests,	*the chief priests,*	*the chief priests,*
and the scribes,	*and the scribes,*	*and the scribes,*
and be killed, and	*and be killed, and*	*and be killed, and*
after three days	on the third day	on the third day
rise again.	*be raised.*	*be raised.*
(2) 9:31f.	(2) 17:22f.	(2) 9:44f.
The Son of man	*The Son of man*	*The Son of man*
will be delivered	*is to be delivered*	*is to be delivered*
into the hands	*into the hands*	*into the hands*
of men,	*of men,*	*of men.*
and they will kill him,	and they will kill him,	
and after three days	and on the third day	
he will rise.	he will be raised.	

(3) 10:33f.	(3) 20:18f.	(3) 18:31f.
Behold, we are	*Behold, we are*	*Behold, we are*
going up to Jerusalem	*going up to Jerusalem*	*going up to Jerusalem*
and the Son of man	*and the Son of man*	*and...the Son of man*
will be delivered	*will be delivered*	*...will be delivered*
to the chief priests	to the chief priests	
and the scribes,	and the scribes,	
and they will	and they will	
condemn him to death,	condemn him to death,	
and deliver him	and deliver him	
to the Gentiles	*to the Gentiles*	*to the Gentiles*
and they will		
mock him	to be mocked	will be mocked
		and shamefully treated
and spit upon him		and spit upon
and scourge him	and scourged	they will scourge him
and kill him	and crucified	and kill him
and after three days	and on the third day	and on the third day
he will rise.	*he will be raised.*	*he will rise.*

7. Against the antiquity of these predictions see the linguistic argument offered by Jeremias (1971, 1:277). Insofar as the central nucleus is concerned, he casts doubt only on the verb "must" (*dei*) of the first prediction, claiming it is of Hellenistic rather than Aramaic coinage. But Jeremias considers that these predictions of his passion made by Jesus are historical for the most part (1:278f.), and he admits the great antiquity of the second prediction (1:281).

8. Furthermore, Jesus' predictions of his violent death also appear in prepaschal contexts: e.g., Mark 12:8 and par; Matt. 23:37-39, etc. (see ibid., 282-83).

9. Küng goes on to say: "A Christological interest must be allowed for everywhere in the Gospels, but historical skepticism can become uncritical. No supernatural knowledge was required to recognize the *danger of a violent end*, only a sober view of reality. His radical message raised doubts about the pious self-reliance of individuals and of society and about the traditional religious system as a whole, and created opposition from the very beginning. Consequently Jesus was bound to expect serious conflicts and violent reactions on the part of the religious and perhaps also the political authorities, particularly at the center of power" (Küng 1976, 320).

For a different opinion see Pannenberg (1977, 245f.), where exegetical reasons appear to give way to theological ones. Whether one agrees with Küng or not, one must realize that we are not dealing here with two separate spheres: (1) the (Jewish) religious sphere and (2) the (Roman) political sphere, each with its own respective authorities and interests. The four Gospels agree that Jesus never constituted a political problem for the Romans and that the Romans recognized this fact. The *political* sphere which experienced the dangerous consequences of Jesus' message could only be the one dominated by the *religious* authorities of Israel.

10. On this key point Pannenberg is content to write: "The reproach of blasphemy (Mark 14:64) through the claim of an authority properly belonging only to God was probably the real reason why the Jewish authorities took action against Jesus, regardless of what the pretexts may have been in detail in the indictment itself" (ibid., 252).

Kasper adds an important point that I italicized: "*More difficult* than why Jesus was condemned by Pilate is the question of *what led to the condemnation by the Sanhedrin*. In the trial before the Council (Mark 14:53-65, and par.), two elements seem to have been important: the messiah issue, which was important to the accusation before Pilate, and Jesus' saying about the destruction of the Temple. The second was designed to secure the conviction of Jesus as a false prophet and blasphemer, for which the penalty was death (see Lev. 24:16; Deut. 13:4-6; 18:20; Jer. 14:14-15; 28:15-17)" (Kasper 1976, 113-14).

Hans Küng goes even further by starting off his section on this question with these words: "It has constantly been a source of amazement that the Gospel accounts of the trial cite so little to explain the motivation behind the condemnation of Jesus of Nazareth to death" (Küng 1976, 291).

11. It should not surprise people that this warning was given by Pharisees (if we can credit Mark 3:6). Contrary to literary simplifications, the Pharisees were not a monolithic group. On the other hand the warning could also have been a trap to nullify Jesus, either by getting him to go into hiding or by making him head for Jerusalem where the Pharisees had more powerful and self-serving allies than the Herodians of Galilee.

12. The accusation that the religious preoccupation of the Pharisees was a mere facade for ambition and their desire for prestige (see Matt. 23:4) could be a postpaschal interpretation based on Jewish resistance to the early church. In any case, it should not be viewed as a blanket negation of their sincerity. With the exception of the Essenes, who fled from the world, no group in Israel took the Yahwist faith and its attendant obligations (as they saw them) more seriously. This is something shared by the Pharisees and Jesus that does not rule out, but rather explains, the harshness of the polemics Jesus engages in with them. Some have tried to see an even closer relationship between Jesus and the Pharisees, suggesting that Jesus was a heretical Pharisee, as it were. In a course given in South Africa, J. Pawlikowski asserted: "My research has led me to conclude that Jesus participated theologically and politically in the general movement of the Pharisees." More specifically he claimed that "there is not the slightest doubt that Pharisaic conceptions of the oral Torah, rabbinism, and the synagogue played a significant role in the formation of Jesus' self-identity." Pawlikowski's view seems to lose its footing, however, when he tries to situate the Pharisaic movement in continuity with the prophetic movement, as one that defends the poor. Thus, depsite his explicit reference to the political dimension, Pawlikowski shows a lack of ideological suspicion. It is certainly true that the Pharisees acknowledged the revelatory value of the prophets, and of the social prescriptions of the law. But what use did they make of the law as such—with regard to the sabbath rest, for example? Pawlikowski's vaunted Copernican revolution, it seems to me, falls into the trap of focusing on isolated declarations and overlooking the overall ideological impact of Pharisaic theology (see Pawlikowski 1977).

13. References to notes in the Jerusalem Bible (JB) are given according to the scriptural verse to which the note refers, since page references may differ in different editions.

14. Moreover, on one occasion (according to Mark and Matthew) the Pharisees got together with the Herodians in Jerusalem to set a politico-religious trap for Jesus: what to do about tribute to Caesar (Mark 12:13; Matt. 22:16).

15. The abundant use (fourteen times) of the terms "hypocrisy" and "hypocrites" to describe the Pharisees is typical of the Matthaean tradition. Only twice does Mark attribute hypocrisy to the listeners of Jesus, and only once does it apply to the Phari-

sees. And it is worth noting that this application comes with reference to the trap laid for Jesus by the *Pharisees and Herodians together* regarding tribute to Caesar (Mark 12:15). The only other attribution of hypocrisy in Mark's Gospel and parallel passages has to do with the question of why Jesus speaks in parables. There hypocrisy is attributed to the people of Israel, as a theological explanation for their being replaced as the people of God with a mission proper and exclusive to them (see Mark 7:6 and par.).

16. The evangelists often use the term "high priests" in the plural, in referring to them as members of the Sanhedrin. It seems quite certain that they are referring not only to past holders of that function but also to representatives of the great priestly families who have had some high priest in their family tree. As a group, they clearly constituted the most conspicuous members of what we today would call the clergy class.

17. See Jeremias 1971, 1:143. He maintains that the quest for prestige was particularly evident among the scribes (p. 144). As opposed to the confusing data of Matthew 23:5, this is supported by the data in Luke 20:46 and Mark 12:38. It is more likely that it was a characteristic of both groups, which were not mutually exclusive in any case. Note also that the Markan and Lukan versions tells us that the scribes, with their clerical *status* (and not the Pharisees as such) combined ambitions for prestige with economic oppression of the destitute.

18. The evangelists obviously have no sympathy for the Pharisees, but they seem to despise the Sadducees even more because of their religious superficiality and cynical opportunism. Something of this attitude is evident in the question they pose to Jesus about the resurrection of the body.

19. One might object that the question makes no sense if the prediction is authentic. To solve the problem, we need only consider the specific prediction of *death* as postpaschal, as an explicit or implicit sequel to the sufferings involved in being "delivered into the hands of men." Note that the second prediction, considered by some as the most authentic one, stops in Luke's version at that point and does not add anything about death (see note 6, above). And there are other explanations that point up the compatibility between the prediction and Jesus' cry from the cross.

20. Starting at this point, exegetes can debate whether Jesus did or did not foresee God's victorious intervention to liberate him: i.e., his death and resurrection. Although present in the three versions, the predictions about these two events could be postpaschal. But it is very hard to deny that Jesus foresaw his own death in the face of such obviously prepaschal testimony as his parable about the murderous stewards of the vineyard.

Chapter VII: The Proximity of the Kingdom

1. The break between the Jewish religion and the Christian religion, so obvious today, did not exist at all for some New Testament writings. Take Matthew, for example. To that evangelist it is clear that Jesus stood in the best prophetic tradition of the Jewish religion, correcting deviations from it. Notice how Matthew's version of the mending parable differs from Luke's. The latter does not want an old garment mended with a new patch because the solidity of the new patch intensifies rather than solves the problem of keeping the old garment in shape (see Luke 5:36f. and Matt. 9:16f.).

2. In my exegesis of the Beatitudes I follow the classic work by J. Dupont (1954, esp. Vol. III) and its further extension and deeper exploration by André Myre (1977).

3. We have already had occasion to see that the Gospels add many morals to the parables of Jesus that Jesus himself did not give them. But that may well be considered less serious than the liberty they take with something as basic and crucial as the Sermon on the Mount.

4. Another sign of this forced unification is the use of "you" for both the Beatitudes and the woes. The use of "you" in the former is explained grammatically by the fact that Jesus is looking right at his disciples (be it a small group or the multitude that Luke sees as on the road to discipleship). This "you" becomes a verbal *artifice* when it comes to the woes because the object of the latter are not present from what we can gather. At the end of the woes, Luke, aware of the artificiality, tries to get things back on track. They were directed to third persons not present, so he has Jesus say: "But I say *to you that hear me . . .*" (Luke 6:27).

5. This is the sense that the word "righteousness" takes on more and more, particularly with the wisdom literature in the Bible. In his book, *Marx and the Bible,* José Porfirio Miranda attempted exegetically to prove that in the Bible "righteousness" invariably had a sociopolitical thrust. His effort was very clarifying insofar as the earliest stages of the Old Testament were concerned. But his argument is forced, in my opinion, when he comes to the sapiential literature and New Testament works that focus on this theme: e.g., Matthew's Gospel and Paul's Epistles.

The great value of Miranda's work, in my opinion, is that he strips the older texts on "righteousness" of the spiritualizing sense they later acquired (after the political panorama of Israel had disappeared). And he also does a fine job of showing that an underlying sociopolitical dimension *always* persists in the term, even when it comes to be used as a synonym for "holiness," "wisdom," or "the spiritual life."

6. I have already noted my agreement with Hans Küng on this point. But it does not stop Küng from claiming that Jesus transcends both the left and the right, as if both viewed the poor in the same way. It also does not stop him from making the bald statement that "neither in the West nor in the East, neither in scientific theory nor in political practice, has a different economic and social system been developed which could remove the defects of capitalism without producing other and worse evils" (Küng 1976, 46).

7. As we shall see, Jesus does not ignore the Old Testament tradition of the pious, humble "remnant" of Israel: the true Israel, the poor of Yahweh, as presented in such texts as Isaiah 4:3 and Zephaniah 3:11-13. But his preaching, particularly the Beatitudes, is addressed to the vast majority of poor and marginalized people. For the "remnant"—i.e., his followers in the building of the kingdom—Jesus has other exigencies and responsibilities (see, for example, Luke 12:32).

8. We know that this "year of favor from the Lord" constituted a *utopia*, for which Leviticus 25 tried to spell out a *topos*, a "political" locus, by turning it into legislation: "And you shall hallow the fiftieth year, and proclaim liberty throughout the land to all its inhabitants [v. 10]. . . . In this year of jubilee each of you shall return to his property [v. 13]. . . . The land shall not be sold in perpetuity, for the land is mine [v. 23]. . . . And if your brother becomes poor beside you, and sells himself to you, you shall not make him serve as a slave: he shall be with you as a hired servant and as a sojourner. He shall serve with you until the year of the jubilee; then he shall go out from you, and he and his children with him, and go back to his own family, and return

to the possessions of his fathers [vv. 39–41]." It should be noted that in all these dispositions Leviticus makes no distinction between those who had to sell their land, themselves, or their family, as a result of laziness or moral defects, and those who had accumulated land and possessions through toil and perseverance. In the jubilee year all are restored to equality of opportunity; from time to time, at least, that is necessary if all the members of a society are to be fully human beings.

9. We obviously also have a different image of poverty today, particularly of extreme poverty that goes hand in hand with beggary. The difference may be more quantitative than qualitative. People who are totally poor do exist in our societies, but they are inclined to keep themselves in isolation and hiding. We do know beggars and sick people who are totally without care, but in many countries people find it hard to imagine a society in which such people would constitute the average.

10. The young *rich* man of Mark 10:17–25 and Luke 18:25, and the rich people throwing money into the temple treasury of Mark 12:41 and Luke 21:1. Luke makes a point of not saying that the rich put in *large sums*.

11. See John Chrysostom, for example: "In the beginning God did not make some poor and others rich, nor at the moment of creation did God provide many treasures to some and not to others. Instead he left the same earth to all so that they might cultivate it. Hence no one can become rich without injustice" (Chrysostom 4:12). See also the *Pseudo-Clementines*: "All things in this world were to have been for the common use of human beings. But one person unjustly called this his, and another that his, thus giving rise to division between mortals." According to St. Ambrose, "Avarice divided up property rights" (Ambrose 8:n. 2).

12. Already in the parable of the rich man and poor Lazarus we read that when the two died, the rich man "saw Abraham far off and Lazarus *in his bosom*" (Luke 16:23). Now the "bosom of Abraham" does not designate the "limbo of the right-eous," as it came to do in later theology. It is an allusion to the custom of eating in a reclining position. In that posture Lazarus is seen with Abraham at the eschatological banquet, a synonym for the kingdom of God (see also Matt. 8:11). The fact that this takes place after death rather than now on earth undoubtedly fits in with Luke's idea of the prolongation of eschatological hope and the start of a theology that links the eschatological with what happens *after death*.

13. Here the Greek particle *de* is used, which generally has an adversative connota-tion. But its range of use is wide for connecting in Greek two phrases of opposite meaning. It is even correct—and in accordance with the only possible meaning—to translate it by *then* or *therefore* as recent Spanish translations like *La Biblia de Jerusa-lén* and *Nueva Biblia Española* do. Anyhow, this would be the implicit sense even if it were translated more literally by "now . . . though."

14. We know that the parables are not allegories in which each detail is to be inter-preted symbolically. Nevertheless we still encounter a difficulty here that is also evi-dent in the Beatitudes and other passages (Luke 1:53, for example). Why does the kingdom simply invert or reverse—so it seems—the groups that are to suffer and have joy, instead of eliminating suffering completely? Some might object that Jesus ac-tually absolutizes the class struggle and carries it into eschatology, whereas Marx is more "Christian" insofar as he looks for a classless society. Remember, however, that the kingdom is not equivalent to our heaven. For a more primitive outlook than ours, justice in a world of *necessity* (ananke) *and suffering* would come down to an equitable distribution of needs and pains. On the "conversion" discussed by the rich man and Abraham, see the next chapter.

15. "We are faced with the question of whether Jesus himself used the form of 'beatitudes.' It is not easy to reach any certain answer in this area. I would propose the following hypothesis. Jesus certainly made an effort to bring more happiness to a whole group of disadvantaged people deprived of rights: publicans, prostitutes, women, children, the sick, etc. He may have engaged in a long process of catechesis with them, in which he stressed the following: *you are lucky* (sick people, publicans, etc.) because God is on the verge of doing wonders with you. Christian tradition recorded this important aspect of Jesus' catechesis and then expressed it in brief, stereotyped formulas, inspired by their form and content in the Old Testament" (Myre 1977, 82).

16. Maintaining his supposition that the Beatitudes do not reflect the very words of Jesus (see note 15, above), Myre correctly writes: "There is no evangelical narrative that shows Jesus in the midst of 'poor people.' As we shall see, the vocabulary used to designate the people with whom Jesus was particularly present is less general than the vocabulary for 'poverty.' In that sense use of the word 'the poor' may well be more characteristic of Christian vocabulary than of Jesus. It is a general, typical, classic way of pinpointing those whom Jesus favored. So there is 'something of Jesus' in it, but on a deep rather than a superficial level" (ibid., 78). On the other hand if we assume, as does J. Jeremias, that the Beatitudes really were uttered by Jesus, then pretty much the same thing would apply to the term "the poor." Except that instead of being *less general*, it would be even more general. It would take in not only *all* the poor (frequented by Jesus or not) but also all those marginalized as sinners by the ruling religious ideology in Israel.

17. In this connection J. Dupont cites J. Bonsirven: "In the first century this derogatory term is applied to a part of the population: the ignorant as opposed to rabbis and their disciples, and people with an inferior piety or a facile, negligent moral life. This is the sense of Hillel's maxim (around 20 B.C.E.): the ignorant person does not fear sin and the *'am-ha'arez* is not pious (*hasid*)." Dupont goes on to say: "In the absence of proof to the contrary, the *'ammey-ha 'arez* are considered impure. Hence a pious Jew would avoid having any relations with them. In Jesus' day the 'people of the land' are made up of the pariahs of a society whose hierarchy is based essentially on religious criteria rather than wealth or political power. Represented by the Pharisees and the doctors of the law, the religious elite stands in opposition to the mass of people. The latter do not know the law well and have little concern for its prescriptions, especially those prescriptions dealing with ritual purity" (Dupont 1954, 3:431–32). On this subject see Section II of Chapter VI, above.

18. Jeremias (1971, 1:117) thinks that we have here a Semitic expression that connotes *exclusion* from the kingdom for those who come after or behind, as is the case in the parable of the foolish virgins. If that is the case, then my argument would be even stronger.

19. It should be kept in mind that the relationship between sin and poverty was more the fruit of direct (legalistic) observation than of theological theories. But the latter did come into the picture too, and as an ideology absorbed by the poor themselves, if we give credence to such passages as John 9:2. At first glance it might seem anachronistic that people would have equated sin and misfortune after the brilliant refutation of such a theology in the Book of Job. But Job's case was never viewed as a general principle, but rather as an exception. Centuries after the Christian message had appeared on the scene, Jesuits debated Voltaire as to whether the Lisbon earthquake should be interpreted as divine punishment for sins that must have been com-

mitted. Ideological use of this theology of divine retribution in social history has been, and still is, not only blatant but dreadful.

20. The passage under study makes clear that Jesus regards *eternal life* and the *kingdom of God* (or, of heaven) as synonyms. Both are expressions of eschatological well-being. With regard to the latter term, I have already noted two things that must be kept in mind. Reference to the kingdom "of God" or "of heaven" has nothing to do with an extraterrestrial reality. As the *Our Father* puts it: "Thy will be done *on earth* as it is in heaven." Second, in the New Testament era, use of the expression "kingdom of God" was dropped. It was replaced by such terms as "eternal life." Whereas Matthew clearly prefers the former term (36 to 3), John shows an opposite preference (17 to 2).

21. It is interesting to see that Luke formulates the question about the chief commandment in the same way: "What shall I *do* to inherit eternal life?" (Luke 10:25–28). If we assume some sort of Lukan dependence on Paul, as many exegetes do, and if we consider the fact that the third Gospel was written some years after Romans and Galatians, it becomes increasingly difficult to say that Luke's Jesus is so blatantly unaware of the so-called Pauline secret: i.e., justification by faith alone without the works (of the law). On this whole matter see Volume III.

22. Even if we admit that "eternal life" and "inheriting the kingdom" are synonymous, the difference could have been intentional insofar as the latter expression has an individualistic and legalistic vision of eschatological reality replacing a more political one in which riches are scrutinized in terms of a social task that must be carried out.

23. *Compassion* and *fidelity* are Yahweh's distinctive characteristics from the Mosaic revelation in the Yahwist version (Exod. 34:6) to the Prologue of John's Gospel. The latter translates them as "grace" and "truth" (John 1:14).

Chapter VIII: The Demands of the Kingdom: Conversion and Hermeneutics

1. I will stay with this number, which of course is based on definitions that can never be applied rigorously, even though I think that what Jeremias calls the parable of *the wedding garment* is nothing else but the finale to Matthew's parable of *the banquet*. I will indicate why in the course of this chapter. On the other hand I consider to be a parable what Jeremias calls the comparison of *the salt*. Here the number of parables in the Synoptics merely serves to point up statistically the importance of the polemical element in the parabolic teaching of Jesus.

2. C. H. Dodd (*The Parables of the Kingdom*) and J. Jeremias (*The Parables of Jesus*) have made significant contributions to our understanding of what the parables originally meant. My observations in this chapter are based on their work, particularly on that of Jeremias. Unfortunately, the apoliticism of Jeremias prevents him from drawing the theological conclusions that flow from the careful exegesis he has made.

Translator's Note: Segundo's references to Jeremias's work on the parables are cited with reference to the English edition entitled *Rediscovering the Parables*. It is an abridged version of his earlier work, *The Parables of Jesus*, in which some of the more abstruse linguistic discussions are omitted. But it contains the substance of the earlier work, and all the points brought up by Segundo.

3. Here, as in the parable of the rich man and Lazarus, Luke replaced the arrival of God's kingdom with the death of the individual. I have already noted the reason for this. If we restore what the likely original tenor was, then we find an even more logical

and forceful expression of the view that the arrival of the kingdom upsets all calculations based on the assumption that it will merely continue and extend the recompense afforded by wealth before its arrival (see Luke 6:21 and 16:25).

4. Hence I see no need to identify these "friends" with angels or intercessors, as Jeremias proposes to do.

5. It seems that members of the people of the land could not have enjoyed any such confidence. Here John may be more accurate when he posits the security of the authorities in the fact that "we are *disciples of Moses*" (John 9:28). This false security seems to be intimately bound up with possessing the official authority to interpret the law of Moses. We see this in a phrase of Matthew's Gospel noted earlier. When the wicked servant of the parable is unexpectedly expelled, he is put "with the hypocrites" (Matt. 24:51). This label is characteristically applied to the religious authorities in Matthew's Gospel, setting them off from the rest of the multitude in Israel, even though the latter might be able to claim that its members are "children of Abraham."

6. What some exegetes call "pastoral prudence" is an editorial feature of Matthew's work. Consider the fourth Beatitude (in the arrangement of Luke and Q), which is addressed to Christians against whom "all kinds of evil" are being uttered. To rule out laxism and make sure no one considers it a mistake, Matthew adds "falsely" (Matt. 5:11). Otherwise he would feel that the Beatitude would be meaningless.

7. Luke introduces these three parables in their proper polemical context: "*Now the tax collectors and sinners* were all drawing near to hear him. And the Pharisees and the scribes murmured, saying, 'This man receives sinners and eats with them' " (Luke 15:1-2).

8. According to this tradition, the context is the very same one that gives rise to Luke's three parables of joy: "And the scribes of the Pharisees, when they saw that he was eating with sinners and tax collectors, said to his disciples, 'Why does he eat with tax collectors and sinners?' " (Matt. 2:16 and par.). But Luke, prompted perhaps by a certain moralizing logic, or by the image of the physician, has Jesus utter a call "to repentance" (Luke 5:32). In all likelihood it originally was a call to joy. In this case Matthew, who is more prone to that type of prudent specification, omits it. Hence it must not have been there. We shall come back to this point.

9. It is here, right after the parable, that Jesus is accused of being "a glutton and a drunkard." This charge is then extended to the disciples of Jesus who, unlike those of John the Baptist, do not fast (see Mark 2:18 and par.). Jesus' response alludes to the joy of his presence, associated with the proximity of the kingdom.

10. In considering the consequences of the vineyard owner's not doing that, we do well to recall a point brought up by Jeremias. A denarius per day constituted what we might call "a subsistence wage." It was "only an amount necessary to support life." Thus the supposed "justice" or "fairness" demanded by the workers of the first hour would have the wage divided up according to the number of hours worked. This would mean dividing the workers and their respective families into two basic groups, whatever the failings of the workers of the last hour might have been. One group of workers would have the bare necessities of life; the other would not (Jeremias 1966, 28).

11. Jeremias makes an interesting observation about this appellation: "In all three places in the New Testament where this address occurs (Matt. 20:13; 22:12; 26:50), the person addressed is in the wrong" (ibid., 109).

12. The three Synoptics differ in the number and concrete fate of these servants.

Those who interpret the parable allegorically have seen the servants as Old Testament prophets. See ibid., 57.

13. I have already noted that in John's Gospel the Jewish authorities oppose Jesus with their certainty of being "disciples of Moses." Then they add: "We know that God has spoken to Moses, but as for this man, we do not know where he comes from" (John 9:29). But we might well ask: *How did they know* what they claimed to know? And were they applying to Jesus the same premises that led their forefathers to discern a divine revelation in Moses?

14. In writing of the first and second law, and of the old and new Israel, I am aware that we are forcing the thought of the Synoptics for the sake of clarity. That certainly is true in the case of Matthew at any rate. For him there is only *one* law. By revealing its hermeneutic key, Jesus brings it to fulfillment. The same must be said of Israel. It continues to be the people of Yahweh, in completeness and universality, thanks to Jesus.

15. The most well-known objection to interpreting this parable as an image of a *universal* judgment (not only in space but even more importantly in time) derives from the judge's use of the term "brother" (Greek *adelphos*). This term is characteristically used to designate members of the Christian community, though it might be noted that here the judge talks about "my brethren" (Matt. 25:40). Hence some see this parable as a parallel to Matthew 10:40–42, where judgment on the pagan "nations" will be based on their treatment of Jesus' disciples.

I think that such a view unduly limits and reduces the universality that is so patent in all the symbolic elements of the parable. Note this comment by Xavier Pikaza: "The underlying problem in the interpretation of our text here is its novelty vis-à-vis traditional language. Can we assume that its key words mean the same thing that they did in older Judaism? Or has the writer created a new meaning that fits in with the totality of Jesus' and the Church's message? Everything justifies the assumption that Matthew 25:31–46 is creating this new idiom, so that *ethnē* are simply 'human beings' and the *adelphoi* of Jesus are the neediest of them" (Pikaza 1981, 227).

16. And also the criterion for recognizing that "God spoke to Moses." In John's Gospel the solution of that problem is assumed and taken for granted by those who call themselves the disciples of Moses (see John 9:28–29).

17. This proves that, for Luke at least, sharing one's goods with the poor is viewed by Jesus as an indispensable expression of love for neighbor on the part of any rich person.

18. See Segundo 1975.

Chapter IX: The Demands of the Kingdom: Prophetism and Conscientization

1. The difficulty remains in Matthew, despite his alteration in the prophecy cited here by Jesus (Isa. 6:9–10), which attributes the intention of closing their eyes, so they will not see, to the people rather than to God. Nevertheless, in this version too, God resists their conversion by way of punishment. Luke suppresses the part of the prophecy dealing with conversion—the largest part—leaving only the intention of making blind and deaf those who hear the words.

2. One can only wonder whether those who insist that Jesus transcends all conflicts and teaches people to resolve them by pardon and reconciliation have really read the Gospels.

3. Changes in political structures are not effected the way individual transformations are. The prior structure must prove its inhumanity *in action* if the power to replace it with another is to arise. The politician knows this. The moralist, preoccupied with individual responsibility, does not. When guiding the destiny of Israel, Yahweh did not proceed any differently from a good politician. When he wants to replace Saul's monarchy with that of David, we are told: "The Spirit of the Lord departed from Saul, and *an evil spirit from God tormented him*" (1 Sam. 16:14; see verses 15, 16, 23). The euphemism is as obvious as is the political intention of Yahweh.

4. And "of Herod," adds Mark, though some manuscripts omit that or have "of the Herodians." This addition would situate the context in Galilee. Matthew's text, alluding to the leaven "of the Pharisees and Sadducees" (Matt 16:6), presupposes a Jerusalem context or an effort to bring together the outlooks that are radically opposed to Jesus. We know very little about the mentality of Herod or the Herodians (except for the conspiracy of the Pharisees with them, which is not really part of the image of the leaven). Certainly Jesus' preaching about the kingdom of God, with its revolutionary values, would hardly satisfy the expectations of the Herodians. In any case, Jesus reveals the "secrets of the kingdom" in direct opposition to the mentality of the Pharisees, and that is what interests us here.

5. Without using a political key, it is hard to imagine where this hatred of "the Christian" might come from. Jesus certainly was not hated by all, in numerical terms. He was hated by the representatives of that totality—the authorities. With the means at their disposal, they could bring the full weight of reprobation to bear on anyone who defended sinners and the poor with such arguments. And at least it would seem to be the weight of the whole society.

6. Other demands are consequences of these: general ones, such as taking up the cross (Matt. 10:38; 16:24 and par.), or particular ones, such as the concrete conditions for following Jesus (Luke 9:57–62). On one occasion Jesus summons both the disciples and the multitude to him. And it is interesting to note that his purpose is to explain the conditions of discipleship: "If any man would come after me . . ." (Mark 8:34 and par.). This is obviously not a *demand* imposed on the multitude. It is an invitation to those who might want to join the group of his disciples. Such people would have to deny themselves, take up their cross, and sacrifice their lives.

7. According to Mark, only one miracle by Jesus concerns someone who could not be called poor by gospel terms: the daughter of Jairus, "one of the rulers of the synagogue" (see Mark 5:22–24, 35–42).

8. That the miracles are a sign of the kingdom, not the kingdom itself, is clear from their limitations in space and time. But the word "sign," specific to John's Gospel, is weak. The miracles point up something that is not only symbolic but real: the presence of the *power* that the kingdom brings into history. That is why the Synoptics prefer to call them *dynameis* in Greek ("powers" or "forces") (see Matt. 12:28; Luke 11:20).

9. Referring to one and the same case, the Synoptics sometimes say a "sick" person, sometimes a "possessed" person, and sometimes a person "possessed by the devil." In Acts, Luke has Peter say that Jesus "went about doing good and healing all that were oppressed *by the devil*" (Acts 10:38).

10. Sight is an exception, perhaps. The blind are not called possessed. Matthew talks about a blind man "possessed by a demon," but he notes that he was "mute" (Matt. 12:22).

11. This current conception would be countered critically by the famous passage in

the Letter of James: "Let no one say when he is tempted, 'I am tempted by God'; for God cannot be tempted with evil and he himself tempts no one; but each person *is tempted when he is lured and enticed by his own desire*" (James 1:13–14).

12. It is of little interest to us here whether he was possessed by a legion of demons or one demon named "legion," or that, as a legendary result of this misunderstanding, the demons are sent into the swine and end up in the sea (Jeremias 1971, 86–87). If the term "legion" of demons had to be maintained, the quantity would be an indication of strong possession and would bring out even more the significant importance of the traits displayed by the man after his liberation.

13. That is how Luke understood it, and he was certainly correct. After this prayer, unique to the disciples of the Lord and centered around the petition "thy kingdom come" (Luke 11:2), there is a parable on the efficacy of prayer. An explanation of that efficacy follows, ending with the exclamation: "How much more will the heavenly Father give *the Holy Spirit* to those who ask him!" (Luke 11:13). We know that in the Bible the Spirit of Yahweh, or Holy Spirit, is the force that performs the great works of God. It is Luke who continues right here with the debate over whose power is behind the miracles of Jesus, that of God or Beelzebub. And Jesus concludes: "But if it is by *the finger of God* that I cast out demons, then *the kingdom of God* has come upon you" (Luke 11:20). In other words, the fundamental prayer has been heard. Matthew puts "Spirit of God" where Luke has "finger of God" (see Matt. 12:28).

14. Using the proverb cited by Jesus ("A prophet is not without honor except in his own country and in his own house"), Matthew apparently likens the Nazarenes' lack of faith to a lack of honor. It is also evident that in his redactional work Matthew changed Mark's impetuous remark ("could do no mighty work") to "did not do many mighty works." Hence there are grounds for hypothesizing that Mark did not intend to establish a causal link between lack of miracles and lack of faith.

15. Much the same occurs in the case of a possessed boy, where not his but his father's faith seems to be crucial. The narrative is difficult to interpret (see Mark 9:20–29). It seems to mix a miracle of Jesus with teachings about the infallibility of prayer to God (Mark 9:23, 29) and fasting. Note that in the Synoptics Jesus is not the object of religious prayer in the proper sense. He is asked to cure people as one might ask for a favor of anyone.

16. This is not to suggest that the coming of the kingdom is to take place only when this active awareness embraces all the poor. Using our political key once more, we can say that the change of structures may be imminent. But it will be all the more effective and fruitful, the more widespread is the conscious awareness of its values. That will make it less possible or probable that the new structures will make room for new ideological distortions. Speculating a bit, I might suggest that Christianity turned into an imperial religion too quickly for its full anti-ideological potential to take root and be understood.

17. That does not rule out the possibility that Jesus' awareness of his destiny and mission evolved along with his activity.

18. The placing of this parable a few verses after that of the sower suggests that the sowing has already been done. The "word" has been placed in the earth, like a seed. The central meaning of the parable is the inevitability of the outcome.

19. See Chapter X.

20. This, in fact, is the proper logical order in which I should have discussed the four groups of Jesus' polemical parables. Going back to them, readers can check this out for themselves. I chose the order I did for didactic reasons, based on our present

situation. I started off from the most superficial level (consequences) and ended up with the deepest level (premises).

21. Logically enough, it depends on whether one accepts most of the Synoptic material or rejects it as postpaschal interpretation. We know that Bultmann rejects the relevance of any quest for the historical Jesus (which he regards as impossible), and the use of a political key for a destiny that is thus bound to be absurd. These stances are closely bound up with his definition of the kingdom of God. But we have the right to ask (as any one of us does) whether this stance does not derive from his fear that the *soli Deo gloria* (the glory proper to God alone) would suffer too great a diminution if we allowed for any human cocausality (*synergism*), however secondary and feeble, in the building of the kingdom. It is a theme closely bound up with the Reformation.

Chapter X: The Arrival of the Kingdom

1. This raises the obligatory question that all christologies formulate in almost identical terms: "We are concerned with the question of the universal validity of this message. There is no doubt that Jesus erred when he announced that God's Lordship would begin in his own generation (Matt. 23:36; 16:28; Mark 13:30 and par.; see Matt. 10:23). The end of the world did not begin in Jesus' generation and also not in the generation of his disciples, the witnesses of his resurrection. Here we stand before the notorious problem of the delay of the Parousia . . ." (Pannenberg 1977, 226). "This immediate expectation creates a difficult and much-discussed problem. Was Jesus then wrong in his immediate expectations? If that were so, it would have far-reaching consequences both for his personal claim to authority and for the truth and validity claimed for his whole message" (Kasper 1976, 77–78).

These two examples suffice to show that even though the question is obligatory and universal, it is raised from differing presuppositions, and the answers offered are seen to have equally differing consequences, whether positive or negative.

2. We might also note that in Matthew the same announcement characterizes the start of the church. Jesus summons the Twelve and then sends them out to preach with these words: "And preach as you go, saying, 'The Kingdom of heaven is at hand' " (Matt. 10:7). It is tempting but pointless to ask if Jesus, or at least Matthew, thought that the nearness of the kingdom had increased between the first beginning (that of John the Baptist) and the third (the mission of the Twelve). We have no data whatsoever on the issue.

3. One might argue that if Jesus' preaching was favorable for the poor, it was equally inexorable for his adversaries (who were also the adversaries of the poor). In that case we would have to point out that the difference lies in the way they see the multitude (see Luke 3:7, 10, 12, 14, 15).

4. Why did Matthew put that expression on the lips of John the Baptist? It may have to do with the problem, recognized in Asia Minor, that the Baptist had his own followers and was not always associated with Jesus as his *precursor* (see Acts 19:3–4).

5. For some reason not easy to fathom, Paul does make the imminent universal judgment central in his interrupted address to the Athenians. Here the terms of his evangelization could be considered comparable to those of the Baptist, though they are in a different cultural key: "The times of ignorance God overlooked, but now he commands all men everywhere to repent, because he has fixed a day on which he will judge the world in righteousness . . ." (Acts 17:30–31). The theme of universal judg-

ment continues to be central in his Letter to the Romans much later, but now it is translated into an anthropological key instead of being proclaimed in apocalyptic terms. The Letters to the Thessalonians may bear witness to this evolution in his thinking.

6. Mark is more sober in his use of the term, for example, employing it only thirteen times. Except for two cases involving a similitude (parables), practically all the others allude to a dynamism—either that of the approaching kingdom or that of the human beings entering it.

7. We actually have an example of something like this in the way in which Mark cites one *logion* of Jesus: "Whoever does not *receive* [the kingdom comes] the kingdom of God like a child shall not *enter* [the kingdom is still, the human being moves] it" (Mark 10:15 and par.). It is more likely, however, that the image suggests that only some people will *reap the benefits* of the kingdom when it finally arrives: i.e., enter it.

8. I have already suggested that the gift of "the mysteries or secrets of the kingdom," which is reserved for the disciples, implies a change of people insofar as *responsibility* for the establishment of that kingdom is concerned. This is already made clear in the general observation that is included in the parable of the sower and that ends with "bear fruit" (Mark 4:20 and par.; see also Matt. 21:43). As if this were not enough, to this general observation Matthew adds the conclusion of the parable of *the talents* (see Matt. 13:12), which deals with the "usefulness" or worthlessness of the servants (Matt. 25:30) of the man who reaps where he did not sow (Matt. 25:24). But how could he do that if he did not share out responsibility and collaboration with respect to that kingdom? It is only in that sense that the kingdom is "given" (Luke 12:32) as an inheritance, and even transferred from one group of "sons" (Matt. 8:12) to others (see Matt. 13:38).

9. In this case Matthew has it that everything is to be left behind for Jesus' sake or name (Matt. 19:29), whereas Mark has "for my sake and for the gospel" (Mark 10:29). But Matthew agrees with Luke in the famous *logion* on those who have voluntarily made themselves eunuchs "for the sake of the kingdom of heaven" (Matt. 19:12).

10. To this set of images belong the examples in which Matthew tends to identify the kingdom with realities of this world—the church that will derive from Jesus, in particular, as opposed to the synagogue. The blind guides of the synagogue shut the doors of the kingdom to people instead of opening them (Matt. 23:13). The leaders of the church, by contrast, are the only ones who have truly been given "the keys of the kingdom of heaven" (Matt. 16:19).

11. J. Jeremias seems to be correct in saying that the characteristic of children that is crucial here for entering into the dynamics of the kingdom is their ability to say *Abba* (Daddy) to God (Jeremias 1971, 1:181). Of course that does not rule out a certain polemical thrust at the servile premises with which Jesus' adversaries interpret the word and, in particular, the law of God. But the teaching itself, even if framed in a political context, goes far beyond the key we applied to it.

12. Here we have Jesus' invitation not to counter evil with evil, to "turn the other cheek." The political tint is evident in the clear fact that here Jesus is attacking a materialistic interpretation of the law and calling for a creative law of the heart. But the invitation itself goes beyond that context and deserves to be examined *on its own territory*: i.e., as a human attitude that is gratuitous yet effective. On the one hand we must not turn the political key into an absurd form of reductionism. But neither

should we abandon it just because it does not fully explain all the elements in Jesus' life.

13. With this *logion* Matthew links another one, which he shares with Luke, but which Luke more logically places in another context: "For the Son of man is to come with his angels in the glory of his Father. . . . Truly, I say to you, there are some standing here who will not taste death before . . ." (Matt. 16:27; see Luke 9:26).

14. Or, in Matthew's words, "the sign of your coming *and of the end of the world*" (Matt. 24:3; Segundo text translated).

15. To *judge* (see Mark 13:27). We see that as the eschatological discourse proceeds, the resemblance to the Baptist (which had practically disappeared in the unfolding of Jesus' message and attitudes) is accentuated once again in a mysterious and illogical way. The illogicality, which makes the eschatological discourse look like an erratic block, though that does not entirely solve the problem, is noted in the following cursory observations by X. Léon-Dufour: "If the kingdom of God is at work since the arrival of Jesus and is growing and maturing step by step, then why talk about an end, a parousia? This extreme conclusion has been drawn by some recent interpreters, especially by English-speaking ones (C. H. Dodd, F. Glasson, J. A. T. Robinson). They say: if eschatology is 'realized,' then there is no reason to continue waiting for a parousia. Nevertheless even the parables make clear that in Jesus' thinking the inauguration and growth of God's kingdom do not in any way eliminate its future culmination. . . . Unlike apocalyptic visionaries, Jesus does not ordinarily fix a precise date for its arrival. . . . Some exegetes are not afraid to say that Jesus made a mistake in thus dating the end of the world during his own generation (T. W. Manson, O. Cullmann, W. G. Kümmel, G. Beasley-Murray). . . . Whatever may be the interpretation of the above cited passages (Matt. 10:23; 24:34; Mark 9:1), *it must not openly contradict the general sense of the majority of Jesus' sayings or his explicit statements*" (Léon-Dufour 1963, 392–93).

16. For example, this would seem to establish a logical connection between the first and second halves of the Our Father. The first half asks for the (proximate) coming of the kingdom; the second half asks for an abbreviation of the accompanying period of testing. Thus, "give us *today* our bread *for tomorrow*" (see Jeremias 1971, 1:201).

17. Remember that what I would call "Jesus' line" is made up at least as much by such prepaschal data as the *joy* which separates him from the Baptist and which brings down on him the accusation of being a glutton, drunkard, and friend of publicans and sinners.

18. Note in Acts, by Luke, very similar expressions in Peter's preaching in Jerusalem: "This Jesus God raised up. . . . Being therefore exalted at the right hand of God, and having received from the Father the promise of the Holy Spirit, he has poured out this which you see and hear" (Acts 2:32–33). Also in Stephen's preaching: "Behold, I see the heavens opened, and the Son of man standing at the right hand of God" (Acts 7:56). And in the narration of Jesus' ascension, when the disciples see Jesus amid the clouds and angels (Acts 1:9–10).

19. "The imminent expectation of the Kingdom of God, which determined the activity and the life of Jesus, is no longer a live option for us. . . . The two thousand years that lie between him and us make that impossible. . . . Thus we can no longer share Jesus' imminent expectation. We can, however, live and think in continuity with it and thus with Jesus' activity if we recognize Jesus' imminent expectation . . . as having been previously [Segundo text: provisionally] fulfilled in Jesus' own resurrection [and] . . . retain the expectation and hope for its universal consequence that has

not happened yet: namely: the universal resurrection of the dead as entrance into the Kingdom of God" (Pannenberg 1877, 242).

20. To be sure, there is no lack of hypotheses attempting to sidestep this "stone of scandal," but all they do is shift its weight from Jesus to his disciples, the community, or the evangelists. Let me try to sum them up in a logical way: (1) The historical Jesus structured his whole message in terms of an imminent and mistaken eschatological expectation. It was the mission of his community (consider Paul addressing the Thessalonians, or Luke in Acts) to rectify this course as a result of the delay of the parousia. (2) Jesus spoke only of the realization of the kingdom. His disciples mistakenly translated his message into the apocalyptic categories of the day. At the time they were writing, the evangelists could not yet know that Jesus' whole generation would die, thereby demonstrating the falsity of mingling essentially different futures. (3) This is similar to (4), with an addition. When the mistake began to be noticed, the evangelists faced a predicament. They were not firsthand witnesses but rather reporters of the catechesis of the various churches. They had venerable sources at hand, and they did not dare to alter them, even on this point. (5) Jesus must have dipped into the apocalyptic theme, even as he explored the theme of morality and others. He might well have accepted current ideas without noticing that they contradicted basic lines of his own message. So it was difficult for the evangelists to practice discernment in this respect. (6) Jesus pointed up different stages in the universal realization of the kingdom. Only the first of these, the universalization of the good news after the destruction of Jerusalem, was carried out. The evangelists did not sense this gradation and gave the note of imminence—the space of one generation—to the whole thing. The redaction of the Gospels, immediately after the destruction of Jerusalem, did not permit them even to rectify this course, as other christologies would.

21. One point is worth noting here. Even the most cautious Catholic exegetes, who are anxious to maintian the *inerrancy* of Scripture in its usual sense, and who talk about a confusion of different levels (some immediate, some remote) in the eschatological discourse, must concede that this confusion itself *is* an error, and that it leads readers into error. After this presumed mingling of levels in the discourse, and after the announcement of cosmic catastrophe specifically, the biblical text adds: "Truly, I say to you, this generation will not pass away before *all these things* take place" (Mark 13:30; Matt. 24:33–34; Luke 21:32). Something that can be evaded only by the scholarly exegetes' warning that there is a confusion here (which they know from the passage of time) is, materially speaking, an error.

22. As I indicated in the previous note, that still confronts the theologian with the equally weighty problem of the inerrancy of Scripture. Note this explanation by Walter Kasper: "The answer to this difficult question begins to appear when we remember a second characteristic of the biblical view of time and history. The tension between immediate expectation and the delay of the *parousia* is not just a New Testament problem, but prevades large sections of the Old Testament. This is connected with what Martin Buber called 'active history.' Buber said that history does not simply follow a plan, whether human or divine, but takes place in dialogue between God and men. God's promise opens up a new possibility for human beings, but the particular realization of the possibility depends on human decisions, on their faith or unbelief. God's Kingdom, in other words, does not bypass human faith, but comes where God is recognized in faith as Lord" (Kasper 1976, 78).

Pardon my irreverence but: If the Holy Spirit, who is not exclusively German, needs such an obscure explanation to make us understand the passage ("this generation will not pass away before all these things take place"), then I think the error is preferable. After all, an error can be detected and corrected with the passage of time.

23. Even a christology *from above* must watch out for the temptation to make Jesus' cognition a *mixture* of data deriving from his two natures. According to the councils of Ephesus and Chalcedon, those two natures operate *inconfuse*, i.e., without confusion or mixture (DS 111 and 148).

24. Because if Jesus did in fact foresee as imminent a cosmic catastrophe and the end of the world and history, and if he lived and acted on the basis of that foresight, then we must rectify everything we seem to have noticed in him in the previous pages. It is hardly possible that he would have devoted so much attention, or attributed such value, to historical mechanisms bound to disappear at any moment. Once again we would be confronted with an absurd destiny, a truly and intrinsically absurd destiny since in this case his death was not the result of a simple mistake. In short, the political key which we have been applying to his life and message, which he himself made us apply, would be invalidated by the radical ahistoricism of eschatological urgency. Léon-Dufour alludes to this in the passage cited in note 15, above, when he says of the eschatological discourse: "It must not openly contradict the general sense of the majority of Jesus' sayings or his explicit statements."

25. See Section III of the previous chapter for the theological suppositions underlying such a hypothesis.

Appendix I: The Resurrected Jesus

1. I hope this will prevent some theologians from being scandalized by the fact that I treat nothing less than the resurrection of Jesus in an appendix. If those theologians are of good faith, they will admit that I am going to deal with that topic and its decisive importance precisely where it plays a central role: i.e., in studying christologies such as that of Paul in Romans 1–8 (see Volume III). I append a treatment of Jesus' resurrection to this volume of the historical Jesus because, as we shall see, at first glance the evangelists do not seem to notice the radical difference between the narratives dealing with the activity of the prepaschal Jesus and those dealing with his activity *after* his death. Since they are our historical source, this fact calls for a historical explanation.

2. At first glance even Paul seems to do the same, inviting his readers to verify the fact of Jesus' resurrection in some sense (see 1 Cor. 15:5–8). It is true that he appeals to surviving *witnesses*. But we have every right to ask what sort of testimony those witnesses could provide. Pannenberg does not hesitate to say: "The historical question of the appearance of the resurrected Lord is concentrated *completely* in the Pauline report, 1 Cor. 15:1–11. The appearances reported in the Gospels, which are not mentioned by Paul, have *such a strongly legendary character* that one can scarcely find a historical kernel of their own in them" (Pannenberg 1977, 89; my italics). But what is more historical about a mere list of witnesses, unless it be mere sobriety? Even if we assume that this list contains everything historical we know about Jesus' resurrection, it is surprising to note Pannenberg's indifference to the gospel narratives as merely "legendary." If by that he means they are not trustworthy because they have been invented, we might ask why Mark or Luke (not to mention Matthew) did not take advantage of this opportunity to invent narratives that would corroborate Paul's list, which was undoubtedly known to them some years before they put together their Gospels. Moreover, a legend cannot simply be discarded as an invention. Even if it is

an invention, it has meaningful content that we must ascertain. That is what I will try to do in this appendix.

3. I made it clear that it was not my intention to explore the special christology of each of the Synoptics. I have looked in them for the most historically certain data about Jesus of Nazareth. Forced to choose between christologies, I prefer to move from the history of Jesus and an appendix on the historical experiences of his resurrection by his disciples to the christology of Paul in his Letter to the Romans (Volume III).

4. Pannenberg (1977, 100-105), for example, stresses the historical force of the argument from the empty tomb of Jesus. If the adversaries of Jesus and the proclamation of the risen Jesus by the disciples soon after the paschal events had an answer for this question, they would have pointed out where his real tomb was. But there is a wide gulf between the historical fact of a missing corpse and the theological, christological, and metahistorical fact of resurrection to a glorified life.

5. Even those who note the point do not seem to attribute any crucial significance to it. X. Léon-Dufour notes the identical *scheme* of the appearances: "initiative of the risen one, *slowness of the disciple in recognizing him*, speech of the risen one. This tries to get across the fact that it is the same Jesus of Nazareth they knew, although *he now lives in a condition different from his earlier one*" (Léon-Dufour 1963, 447).

Since Pannenberg discounts these narratives because of their "legendary" character, he is forced to argue from the opposite end. His argument is sound, but it has less historical grounding. His basis is the fact that Paul interprets Jesus' resurrection, not as an individual happening but as the start of the supreme eschatological happening: i.e., the resurrection of the dead. The risen Jesus differs from the prepaschal Jesus in that he now lives in a very different state: the *eschatological* state (Pannenberg 1977, 74-88).

6. One cannot evade the problem by saying that it is a matter of agnosticism rather than of strict negation. While that may be valid on the level of formal logic, it solves nothing on the existential level. It does not resolve the practical and ethical problems we are forced to formulate and somehow solve. It also signifies a no to a wager that could have been different and greater.

7. Recall the "invisible hand" of classic liberal capitalism, which somehow is supposed to reconcile complete competition in the marketplace with the satisfaction of everyone's basic needs. Or the implied invisible hand in Marx's state of perfect communism, which is supposed to reconcile the vocational work of each human being and the constant increase of spare time with ample provision for the basic necessities of society. See Volume I, Chapter X.

8. Paul seems to say the opposite (see 1 Cor. 15:12-19), but his argument is not only ambivalent but also more complex. It is aimed at people like the Sadducees, who have already said no in a general way to the transcendent datum of the resurrection *of the dead*, and who therefore say no in a priori terms to the resurrection of Jesus. It is the *general* no that Paul rightly regards as being opposed to *faith*, i.e., to the Christian values based on the transcendent datum that love is stronger than death. Paul sees death as the fruit of sin—that is to say, of egotism. See Volume III.

9. Hence the wrongheadedness of many exegetes (e.g., Pannenberg) in resorting to Paul (1 Cor. 15:5-8) for their discussion of the resurrection, not only because he has the older formulation of the event but also, and at bottom, because they think his formula is *more sober*. Exactly the opposite is the case. Paul's list makes one think of a historical sequence as verifiable as (e.g.) that relating to the death of Socrates. By

contrast the gospel accounts, with their odd literary genre, are much more reticent in identifying the facts narrated with any historical material.

10. In a world determined by science there may be nothing more obviously *mythical* than an office scientifically equipped to verify real miracles and distinguish them from false or dubious ones, such as we find in connection with Lourdes. But we see the initial signs of the same sort of thing, in a world without scientific instruments of verification, in the gospel accounts of the miracles (see, for example, Matt. 8:13; 14:20-21; 15:37-38).

11. In a different literary genre Paul does exactly the same thing when he "demythologizes" the "mythical" question of his addressees about the future body of the resurrected (see 1 Cor. 15:35f.).

12. That is why I have already insisted that the resurrection was not an indispensable prerequisite for *faith*, or even *religious* faith, in Jesus of Nazareth. It is not without reason that the Prologue of John's Gospel on the incarnate Word of God makes no mention of the resurrection. The fact of "having seen his glory" is situated by the evangelist in prepaschal episodes and reaches its culmination in the cross.

13. The fact that the faith of the disciples is clinched only with the paschal experiences is characterized as *unwarranted tardiness* in Luke's Gospel: "O foolish men, and *slow* of heart *to believe* all that the prophets have spoken!" (Luke 24:25).

14. We are faced here with an irremediable problem of language, of course, since the terms used ("inch by inch," "new datum," etc.) are already quantum expressions. The same would hold true for similar expressions that might be used.

15. No one would expect chemistry to unlock the secret of Mona Lisa's smile or mathematics to explain the laws of human language. But at the same time we all would admit that the laws of chemistry and mathematics continue to exercise their influence with respect to both.

16. Readers scandalized a priori may well wonder what they are to make of the results of this appendix on the "object of truth" of the resurrection. When I say that the resurrection is a datum of faith, not historically provable in the sense I use the word "history," I am saying that faith regards the resurrection as an *objective truth*. It is the truth proper to any transcendent datum, and I have just shown that the resurrection is such a datum. They will find the *objectivity* of the resurrection elaborated in christologies such as that of Paul (see Vol. III), where the resurrection as an objective datum occupies a central place.

Appendix II: More on the Political Key

1. I need not repeat that every effort at historical reconstruction implies some interpretation, some key, some meaning-world launched from the present into the past. On this whole subject see, for example, Hans Georg Gadamer (1975). When I refer here to "theological" or simply "postpaschal" interpretations, I am not suggesting that my reconstruction of the prepaschal Jesus so far is devoid of interpretation. It is all a matter of proportions. There are varying degrees and distances between the graphic nature of a photograph or film and theoretical speculation about a person.

2. As I said before, I am not suggesting that any one key can explain the whole life of a human person. In the case of Jesus, for example, we have religious and moral teachings that cannot be explained solely in a political key; such an explanation would be sheer reductionism.

3. Of course a (bad) christology from above—i.e., one based on Jesus' divinity—

does have a prefabricated answer for this question: God *uses* certain human beings so that God incarnate can give his life as a ransom. I am not rejecting the idea that the two intentions can dovetail. What I am rejecting is the use of the divine to minimize or displace historical causality (see note 1, Chap. V, above).

4. One cannot even use John 18:36 in support of this hypothesis: "My kingdom is not *of* this world." The preposition "of" is ambiguous, so that the phrase might mean that the kingdom does not "belong to this world" or that it does not have "its origin and source" from this world. Here the Latin Vulgate is faithful to the Greek text, and it makes absolutely clear that Jesus is referring to *the source* from which the power of the kingdom derives (see the rest of verse 36), not to *the plane* on which it is to be fleshed out in reality. The verse in John's Gospel could be used in conjunction with the next hypothesis I shall examine.

5. And they are mythical as well, since they envision a second parallel and determining causality in history alongside the simple human and historical causality we can concretely experience.

6. All this in the framework of a christology from below, of course. In a christology from above Jesus makes no mistake. Eschatology is already realized in the incarnation; his kingdom is the kingdom of truth, and his death is the ransom envisioned by God for the liberation of the many.

7. On this matter see my work, *The Liberation of Theology*, Chapter VI. The historical obliviousness of some lines of reasoning is absolutely incredible. Those who argue in terms of this crude either/or seem to forget that the very possibility of thinking and arguing freely was prepared and influenced, in the West at least, by Roman law. And Roman law was a structural change imposed by the political authorities without prior consent of the masses: i.e., without some prior conversion of their hearts. Not to mention the growing proportion of structural change over "conversion" as one delves deeper into the course of human, biological, and economic evolution!

8. See Volume I, Chapter X of this work. The use of the "death of ideologies" for conservative purposes is not as new as some people think. For a cynical formulation of it, note this remark by one of Balzac's characters: ". . . Pass me the asparagus. Because, in the last analysis, liberty engenders anarchy, anarchy leads to despotism, and despotism leads again to liberty. Millions of creatures have perished without being able to effect the triumph of any of these systems" (Balzac 1866b). The comment, "pass me the asparagus," is obviously a magnificent iconic expression of the speaker's adherence to the *status quo*.

9. Regarding the Beatitudes, A. Myre rightly maintains that they constitute a sort of missionary nomenclature: i.e., a list of those groups to whom the church, like Jesus before it, is sent to inform them that God does indeed love them (Myre 1977, 93). Contrary to what the sociopolitical structure might seem to suggest, they are God's favorites and he is preparing the best place for them in the structural transformation that his kingdom will effect. But we have every right to ask a question that Myre does not examine, since it lies outside his purposes. Did there exist a church that was actually shouldering that mission? And if our conclusion turned out to be no, where would that lead us logically?

10. The supposed universalism of Jesus is far from being a historical datum that can be fit in with the Synoptic data. Jesus' kindness in practice (not always in theory) toward some pagans that cross his path (see Mark 7:24–30 and par.), his recognition of their individual merits (see Matt. 8:10; Luke 7:9), and his conclusion that many of

them will sit down with Abraham, Isaac, and Jacob at the eschatological banquet (see Isa. 19:24): these are obvious exceptions rather than a fully worked out theory about the fate of pagans, much less about the fate of humanity as such.

11. I might add here that if Jesus had preached in a different context, he would have employed a different key, since the anti-ideological tools he used (e.g., his summons to an authentic understanding of Yahweh) had *power* only in that given context.

12. Recall how long Jesus took to educate the small group around him so that they might understand the essentials of his message, and with what limited success. We might ask ourselves what is undoubtedly being sacrificed by the first Christian community when it talks about *thousands* of people acquiring the faith, undergoing conversion, and joining the community on the basis of *one* session of preaching. And the question stands no matter how inflated the figures may be (see Acts 2:38, 41; 4:4; 5:14).

13. "Like him, but not in the same way. Because Jesus was *one* human being, whereas now it is a *community*" (Myre 1977, 88).

14. In his version Paul states that the only commitment he accepted and fulfilled was to "remember the poor" (Gal. 2:10). Most probably this is an allusion to the different needs of individual churches, especially to the poverty of the persecuted church in Jerusalem. But there is no reason to dissociate this problem from the one Jesus deals with in the Beatitudes, as my comments in this Appendix on the same theme in Acts have already suggested.

Works Cited

Ambrose, St. *In Psalmum CXVIII.*

Augustine, St. *In Ioannis Evangelium Tractatus.*

Balthasar, Hans Urs von. 1948. "Théologie et sainteté." *Dieu Vivant* 12.

———. 1957. *Teresa de Lisieux: Historia de una misión.* Sp. trans. Barcelona: Herder.

———. 1965. *La Gloire et la croix.* 2 vols. Fr. trans. Paris: Aubier.

Balzac, Honoré de. 1866a. *Histoire des Treize.* Paris: Houssiaux.

———. 1866b. *La Peau de chagrin.* Paris: Houssiaux.

Bateson, Gregory. 1972. *Steps to an Ecology of Mind.* New York: Ballantine Books.

Belo, Fernando. 1981. *A Materialist Reading of the Gospel of Mark.* Trans. Matthew J. O'Connell. Maryknoll, N.Y.: Orbis Books.

Boff, Leonardo. 1978. *Jesus Christ Liberator.* Trans. Patrick Hughes. Maryknoll, N.Y.: Orbis Books.

———. 1981. *Pasión de Cristo y sufrimiento humano.* Sp. trans. in *Jesucristo y la liberación del hombre.* Madrid: Cristiandad. Port. original: *Paixão de Cristo, paixão do mundo.* Petrópolis: Vozes, 1978.

Borrat, Hector. 1970. "El Cristo de la fe y los Cristos de América Latina: Para una cristología de la vanguardia." *Víspera* (Montevideo) 17:26–31.

Bultmann, Rudolf. 1951–55. *Theology of the New Testament.* 2 vols. Trans. Kendrick Grobel. New York: Scribner's.

Cazelles, H. 1971. "Bible et politique." *Recherches de Science Religieuse* 59, no. 4 (Oct.-Dec.).

Comblin, José. 1976. *Jesus of Nazareth: Meditations on His Humanity.* Trans. Carl Kabat. Maryknoll, N.Y.: Orbis Books.

Coppens, Joseph. 1954. "Les Origines du messianisme: Le dernier essai de synthèse historique." In *L'Attente du Messie.* Bruges: Desclee, 31–38.

Denzinger, Henricus, and Adolfus Schönmetzer (DS), eds. 1955. *El magisterio de la Iglesia.* Barcelona: Herder. Sp. ed. of *Enchiridion Symbolorum.* Freiburg im Breisgau: Herder, 1963.

Descamps, Albert. 1954. "Les Messianisme royal dans le Nouveau Testament." In *L'Attente du Messie.* Bruges: Desclee.

Dodd, C. H. 1961. *The Parables of the Kingdom.* Rev. ed. New York: Scribner's.

Dupont, Jacques. 1954. *Les Béatitudes: Le problème littéraire.* 3 vols. Bruges: Abbaye de Saint-André.

Duquoc, Christian. 1972. *Cristología: Ensayo dogmático sobre Jesús de Nazaret.* Vol. 1. Sp. trans. Salamanca: Sígueme.

Eagleson, John, and Philip Scharper, eds. 1979. *Puebla and Beyond: Documentation and Commentary.* Maryknoll, N.Y.: Orbis Books.

Ebeling, Gerhard. 1963. *Word and Faith.* Trans. James W. Leitch. Philadelphia: Fortress Press.

Gadamer, Hans Georg. 1975. *Truth and Method*. Eng. trans. New York: Seabury.

Gaudium et spes (GS). 1965. Pastoral Constitution on the Church in the Modern World. In *The Gospel of Peace and Justice*. Ed. Joseph Gremillion. Maryknoll, N.Y.: Orbis Books.

Gibellini, Rosino, ed. 1978. *Frontiers of Theology in Latin America*. Trans. John Drury. Maryknoll, N.Y.: Orbis Books.

Heidegger, Martin. 1962. *Being and Time*. Trans. John Macquarrie. New York: Harper and Row.

Jeremias, Joachim. 1963. *The Parables of Jesus*. Rev. ed. Trans. S. H. Hooke. New York: Scribner's.

———. 1966. *Rediscovering the Parables*. Abr. ed. of *The Parables of Jesus*. New York: Scribner's.

———. 1971. *New Testament Theology*. 2 vols. Trans. John Bowden. New York: Scribner's.

The Jerusalem Bible (JB). 1966. Garden City, N.Y.: Doubleday.

John Chrysostom. *In. Ep. I ad Tim.*

Kasper, Walter. 1976. *Jesus the Christ*. Trans. V. Green. New York: Paulist Press.

Küng, Hans. 1976. *On Being a Christian*. Trans. E. Quinn. Garden City, N.Y.: Doubleday.

Léon-Dufour, Xavier. 1963. *Les Évangiles et l'histoire de Jésus*. Paris: Seuil. Eng. trans., *The Gospels and the Jesus of History*. New York: Desclee, 1967.

———. 1978. "Jesus face à la mort menaçante." *Nouvelle Revue Théologique* 100, no. 6 (Nov.-Dec.):802.

Machoveč, Milan. 1976. *A Marxist Looks at Jesus*. Eng. trans. Philadelphia: Fortress Press.

Miranda, José Porfirio. 1974. *Marx and the Bible*. Trans. John Eagleson. Maryknoll, N.Y.: Orbis Books.

Moltmann, Jürgen. 1976. "Open Letter to José Míguez Bonino." *Christianity and Crisis* 29 (March).

Mowinckel, Sigmund. 1956. *He That Cometh*. Trans. G. W. Anderson. Nashville: Abingdon.

Myre, André. 1977. "Développement d'un instantané christologique: Le prophète eschatologique." In *Cri de Dieu*. Montreal: Paulinas, 75-104.

Niebuhr, Reinhold. 1964. *The Nature and Destiny of Man: A Christian Interpretation*. 2 vols. New York: Scribner's.

Ogden, Schubert. 1977. *The Reality of God*. New York: Harper and Row.

Pannenberg, Wolfhart. 1977. *Jesus, God and Man*. 2nd ed. Trans. L. Wilkins and D. Priebe. Philadelphia: Westminster Press.

Pawlikowski, John. 1977. *Social Ethics: Biblical and Theological Foundations*. Course given in Swaziland in August 1977. Publication under the auspices of the regional association of Catholic bishops in South Africa.

Pikaza, X. 1977. "Mateo 25, 31-46: Cristología y liberación." In *Jesucristo en la historia y en la fe*. Salamanca: Sígueme.

Proust, Marcel. 1970. *Swann's Way*. Trans. C. K. Scott Moncrieff. New York: Vintage Books.

Pseudo-Clementines. *Recognitiones*.

Rad, Gerhard von. 1962. *Old Testament Theology*. 2 vols. Trans. D. M. G. Stalker. New York: Harper and Row.

Rahner, Karl. 1961. "Current Problems in Christology." Chap. 5 in vol. 1 of *Theological Investigations*. Baltimore: Helicon Press.

Rahner, Karl, and Wilhelm Thüsing. 1975. *Cristología: Estudio teológico y exegético*. Sp. trans. Madrid: Cristiandad. Eng. trans., *A New Christology*. New York: Crossroad, 1980.

Segundo, Juan Luis. 1975. "Conversion y reconciliación en la teología de la liberación." *Perspectiva Teológica* 7:164–78. Abr. in *Selecciones de Teología* 15 (1976):263–75.

————. 1976a. *The Hidden Motives of Pastoral Action*. Trans. John Drury. Maryknoll, N.Y.: Orbis Books.

————. 1976b. *The Liberation of Theology*. Trans. John Drury. Maryknoll, N.Y.: Orbis Books.

————. *Faith and Ideologies*. Vol. 1 of *Jesus of Nazareth Yesterday and Today*. Trans. John Drury. Maryknoll, N.Y.: Orbis Books.

Sobrino, Jon. 1978. *Christology at the Crossroads: A Latin American Approach*. Trans. John Drury. Maryknoll, N.Y.: Orbis Books.

Tracy, David. 1975. *Blessed Rage for Order: The New Pluralism in Theology*. New York: Seabury.

Weiss, J. 1906. *Die Schriften des Neuen Testaments*. Vol. 1. Göttingen: Vandenhoeck and Ruprecht.

Zerwick, M. 1957. *Analysis philologica Novi Testamenti Graeci*. Rome: Pont. Inst. Bibl.

Index

Compiled by James Sullivan